Sacred Cyberspaces

Advancing Studies in Religion

SERIES EDITOR: SARAH WILKINS-LAFLAMME

Advancing Studies in Religion catalyzes and provokes original research in the study of religion with a critical edge. The series advances the study of religion in method and theory, textual interpretation, theological studies, and the understanding of lived religious experience. Rooted in the long and diverse traditions of the study of religion in Canada, the series demonstrates awareness of the complex genealogy of religion as a category and as a discipline. ASR welcomes submissions from authors researching religion in varied contexts and with diverse methodologies.

The series is sponsored by the Canadian Corporation for Studies in Religion whose constituent societies include the Canadian Society of Biblical Studies, Canadian Society for the Study of Religion, Canadian Society of Patristic Studies, Canadian Theological Society, Société canadienne de théologie, and Société québécoise pour l'étude de la religion.

Sacred Cyberspaces

Catholicism, New Media, and the Religious Experience

Oren Golan and Michele Martini

McGill-Queen's University Press
Montreal & Kingston • London • Chicago

ISBN 978-0-2280-1419-5 (cloth)
ISBN 978-0-2280-1420-1 (paper)
ISBN 978-0-2280-1518-5 (ePDF)
ISBN 978-0-2280-1519-2 (ePUB)

Legal deposit fourth quarter 2022
Bibliothèque nationale du Québec

Printed in Canada on acid-free paper that is 100% ancient
forest free (100% post-consumer recycled), processed
chlorine free

Library and Archives Canada Cataloguing in Publication

Title: Sacred cyberspaces : Catholicism, new media, and the
   religious experience / Oren Golan and Michele Martini.
Names: Golan, Oren, author. | Martini, Michele, author.
Series: Advancing studies in religion ; 13.
Description: Series statement: Advancing studies in
   religion ; 13 | Includes bibliographical references and
   index.
Identifiers: Canadiana (print) 20220260435 | Canadiana
   (ebook) 20220260516 | ISBN 9780228014195 (cloth) |
   ISBN 9780228014201 (paper) | ISBN 9780228015185
   (ePDF) | ISBN 9780228015192 (ePUB)
Subjects: LCSH: Cyberspace—Religious aspects—
   Christianity. | LCSH: Digital media—Religious
   aspects—Catholic Church. | LCSH: Communication—
   Religious aspects—Catholic Church. | LCSH: Experience
   (Religion)
Classification: LCC BR99.74 .G65 2022 | DDC 261.5/6—dc23

Set in 11/14 Adobe Caslon Pro with Plymouth Serial
Book design & typesetting by Garet Markvoort, zijn digital

Contents

Tables and Figures

Tables

Figures

Acknowledgments

Writing acknowledgments calls for a recounting of the history of the book and the odyssey it took in terms of the study, writing, and editing, as well as the biographies of its authors in their own journeys that converged to produce this manuscript, while spotlighting the silent or active supporting roles of others who generously contributed to its making.

I.   Exposition – Oren and Michele's Shared Journey

This book is the result of an eight-year journey. It was sparked through a substantial national Israeli grant that was awarded to a team of researchers from four academic institutions to study changes brought about by the information age. Specifically, the venture was titled LINKS – Learning in a Networked Society – and was part of the Israeli Centers of Research Excellence (I-CORE) initiative. Backed by its emergence, we were introduced through our shared acquaintance with Professor Tamar Katriel. At the time, Tamar was part of Michele's doctoral review committee at the University of Bologna. Michele was honing his expertise as a semiotician and had specifically been investigating activists' YouTube videos in Kosovo and Israel's tumultuous West Bank. Oren had already been involved in digital religious research after a postdoc at Northwestern University and the Center for Religion and Media at New York University. At that point, he was nested at the Faculty of Education at the University of Haifa in both the department of Leadership and Policy in Education and the department of Learning and Instructional Sciences. As our paths crossed, he invited Michele to join his emerging NetLab on media, religion, and community and become an active postdoc.

They say, "it takes a village," and, indeed, in this NetLab a cadre of advanced graduate students and postdoctoral experts were nurtured. A group that, to this day, is dedicated to online inquiry with special attention to digital religion. These bright members of the NetLab have gradually transformed themselves from curious students to colleagues in their own right, offering deep insight and repositories of knowledge that have informed and contributed in different ways to this book while creating a familial environment. Accordingly, we would like to firstly thank the late Yaakov Don. Yaakov's work focused on the legitimation of new media among the religious Zionist elite, a perspective that was later explored in the book at hand, albeit, among Catholic media activists and the Holy See. Yaakov was killed in a terrorist attack, and we wish to acknowledge his social and intellectual contribution to the group and to the early creative process of the study on which the book is centred. Further members of the research team include Nakhi Mishol-Shauli, a graduate student at the time who studied Jewish ultra-Orthodox WhatsApp groups and online journalists. Nakhi's advice has become an everyday source of support and creative fervour. Alongside Nakhi, we would like to acknowledge Eldar Fehl, who also studies the ultra-Orthodox community and whose sharp humour and acute intellect enriches the NetLab in so many ways. In addition, we thank Akiva Berger, who studies the authority of religious digital learning sites and responsa, a field which colours so much of believers' lived religion. Berger's deep knowledge of computer programming, as well as his religious studies background, continues to offer a rich source of knowledge and insight. In addition, we acknowledge Deby Babis, an exceptional ethnographer who became a postdoc in the NetLab and offered rich insight and support on the convergence between traditional ethnography and online visual communication analysis. Her work at the NetLab coincided with that of Noam Tirosh, an expert on collective memory and digital communications whose acumen enriched our knowledge of political apps and new media theory. Both Deby and Noam nowadays flourish as assistant professors in departments of sociology and communications, respectively, in Israel's academia. Further thanks are offered to Maya Magnat, a graduate student who studies YouTube influencers and has become one of the younger members in the team, as has Tomer Udi, who is currently involved in the study of Jewish identity on American campuses as they are forged through Instagram feeds. Adding to this there are several students who were not part of the NetLab but offer continuous support, such as the exceptional Yaara Peled, Ofir Sheffer, and Michael Sang. Through its evolution NetLab members met at scores of informal engagements, work sessions, and international conferences. These included LINKS meetings around the country, as well as NetLab members' joint travel to international congresses such as the Association of Internet Researchers (AOIR), the International Society for Media, Religion and Culture (ISMRC), the International Society for Science & Religion (ISSR), the American Educational Research Association (AERA), and the European Association of Social Anthropologists (EASA) in distant destinations such as Seoul, Boulder, Barcelona, Leuven-la-Neuve, Lausanne, and Toronto.

As the group's dynamics fluctuated and expanded over a plethora of topics, it offered ideas that inspired us in small conversations, lectures, shared silences, morning coffee at the faculty's cafeteria (thank you Julia), and ongoing WhatsApp exchanges. Through all of this, we continued the conversation on digital religion with a focus on Catholicism, the Holy Land, and digital mediascapes. At the heart of this group is Aref Badarne (aka *the Northerner*) who devoted hours to assist us in analyzing videos, discovering digital realms, and supporting our work in heart and mind. He personally witnessed the ebbs and flows that led to this book, to which he is bound by a vow of silence. To him, we owe our deepest thanks.

As the LINKS initiative ended (2019), the group continued to flourish and gained further support from other funding agencies. Oren received an Israel Science Foundation (ISF) grant to support this study (No. 624/17) and Michele received a generous postdoctoral grant from the European Union's Horizon 2020 Research and Innovation Programme (No. 837727) and was duly affiliated with the University of Cambridge. Through this generous grant, Michele was able to expand the study and spend a lengthy period conducting fieldwork in São Paulo, Brazil, at the heart of the Canção Nova movement. A movement that has been an important agent in the Catholic Church's digital outreach, particularly from the Holy Land. To the ISF and the Marie Skłodowska-Curie Foundation, we are deeply indebted, as well as to the University of Haifa and its research authority for supporting the publication of the book in its final stages.

We are also indebted to the formidable subjects we met in our research journey, a journey that took us to the Holy Land's sacred places of worship, including monasteries and newsrooms, shrines, and digital labs. They have been our guides in navigating these hybrid spaces in which religion resonates in a constant exchange between online and offline environments. Our gratitude goes to the friars of the Franciscan Custody of the Holy Land who have been protecting and keeping the sacred places of the Holy Land alive for more than 800 years. This research would not have been possible without their welcome and support. We also want to thank all the staff and members of the Christian Media Center, a pioneering multicultural and multilingual media venture, whose complexity and potential for innovation never ceased to surprise us. Among them, a special recognition goes to the Canção Nova community, both in Israel and in Brazil, whose devotion and ideas represent the backbone of this evangelical media project. Finally, these acknowledgments would not be complete without expressing our deepest appreciation to members of the Catholic community of the Holy Land and the Middle East who welcomed and supported our work and facilitated a network of personal contacts and interactions that made our study possible. This book may not make them famous, but we hope they like it should they choose to read it.

Special thanks to the excellent staff at McGill-Queen's University Press. To Kyla Madden and Kathleen Fraser who believed in the book from the start. To Shelagh Plunkett, who carefully read through the manuscript and identified the most detailed transgressions we made while skilfully and warmly helping to iron its creases. In Israel, we are deeply indebted to Avi Aronsky who carefully read through the manuscript, edited, and unravelled our often much too long sentences into accessible passages.

II.   Oren's Journey

In understanding my journey in and to this book, it is difficult to pinpoint the moments, stages, and people that supported its outcome. However, I refer to several milestones that shaped my intellectual growth and led me to much of the understandings that are overtly and covertly implanted in its pages. My pathway begins in my years of study at the department of sociology and anthropology at the Hebrew University. There I gained a love of sociological inquiry to a large extent from my late advisor, Professor Reuven Kahane whose macroscopic and comparative gaze, structural perspective, and innovation in processes of legitimation as well as informal theory, propelled my thirst for unveiling the underlying structures of digital worlds, the emergent cultures of the young and the religious. This curiosity was further kindled by my dear friend and colleague Nurit Stadler, an anthropologist of religion, whom I have known since her seminal work on the Opus Dei, and whose scholarship on saints, shrines, and fundamentalist publics I have closely followed over the years. Complementing her warm encouragement, I was inspired by Batia Siebzehner, a dear friend and an extremely acute sociologist of comparative religion, the enlightenment, and Catholicism, who has guided me into the rich worlds of religious scholarship and has always been there for me with questions and late-night discussions. Further, David Lehmann of Cambridge University, who collaborated with Batia in the past, has also been a true friend for me and the book project. His intellectual breadth and shared interest in comparative religion, the Holy Land, religiosity in Latin America, and ethnography have continued to illuminate my work as he is an exemplar and friendly source of learning and support.

Complementing my journey into religion were my mentors who helped me in my study of digital worlds, including the late Professor Brenda Danet, a pioneer and visionary of early internet research, and Carmel Vaisman, an internet scholar whom I have known since graduate school and who has accompanied me on my journey through digital research with fascinating discussions in Tel-Aviv, Jerusalem, and conferences that took place during our postdocs in the Midwest and at the Association of Internet Researchers. I wish to further acknowledge Ariel Klinger-Inbar, a friend since my youth, a tour guide to the Holy Land, and a student of its Christian history. His exuberant thirst for knowledge and mastery of its holy sites has enriched and inspired me. I further thank Jacob Hecht, a brilliant and independent internet scholar who advised me on my early steps in the field, and the marvelous Eyal Ben Ari, who also served as my PhD instructor and continues to advise and inspire my work, and, finally, from the Hebrew University, I wish to thank Ori Eyal for years of friendship and profound intellectual exchange.

It was in the spring of 2006 that I started a new phase in my intellectual journey as I expanded my scholarship from a primary focus on digital youth to that of digital religion. This shift occurred as I met Heidi Campbell. At the time, Heidi was on a visit to Israel and was seeking partnerships at the University of Haifa. Although I was not affiliated with Haifa at the time, I met with her and by 2008 we had begun a study of digital religion with a focus on the Jewish ultra-Orthodox community in Israel. This grew into a friendship and collegial relationship which led to a few publications in leading journals. Afterwards, I embarked on my postdoctoral years in New York and Chicagoland where I continued to pursue fieldwork and engage with scholars at conferences in Boulder, Colorado, New York, and beyond that fed my interest and further introduced me to the fields of knowledge surrounding digital religion. They include folks such as Lynn Shofield-Clark, Gregory Grieve, Stewart Hoover, Giulia Evolvi, Christopher Helland, Nabil Echchaibi, Tim Hutchings, and many wonderful others that I continue to meet and learn from in international meetings.

As I received my appointment at the University of Haifa, I was warmly received by colleagues in different disciplinary fields that through the years opened me to new perspectives and fields of knowledge that have inspired ideas in this book. Most notably is Sarit Barzilai, whose original ideas on post truths and personal epistemology are a source of inspiration; I am honoured to be her friend and colleague. Others I would like to mention are Clara Sabbagh, who has always offered her support and acumen; Lotem Perry-Hazan, who shares my curiosity for the study of religious groups and is a leading expert on law, education, and religion – together we currently lead a program on informal education that is supported by the Rothschild Foundation, and I continue to learn from her and enjoy her friendship; and Ayelet Baram-Tsabari of the Technion – the Israel Institute of Technology – whom I collaborate with in the study of science dissemination and education among the ultra-Orthodox. Ayelet and I also co-supervise a PhD student on digital religion, and I enjoy her comradery, curiosity, methodological rigor, and intellectual insights. Back in the University of Haifa, Dani Ben Zvi and Yael Kali are deeply thanked for their support. They have taught me so much on issues of education in the digital age, have accepted my sometimes unconventional fields in the learning sciences – with my emphasis on informal learning and religious media – and have warmly supported my journey at the university.

As aforementioned, in Haifa I met Michele Martini, the co-author of this book. A young scholar who has taught me so much on semiotics and visual culture and whose knowledge, curiosity, and youthful drive continue to feed my mind. I am deeply indebted to him for joining my journey and collaborating with me on this project. I continue to thank the brilliant Tamar Katriel for initiating our acquaintance.

Writing a book and managing an academic career burdens the soul and takes a toll on the body. I wish to extend my gratitude to people who have supported my physical journey: my calisthenics instructor Or Eicher and my former trainer Yuval Elroy have both added balance to my life, as has my gym friend Avi Chanes who adds humour and friendship to my workouts. Also adding balance, I wish to thank two of my closest friends: Yael Ron, a zealous defender of workers' rights who continuously advises and supports my work and daily life, and Michael Attali, a dear lifelong friend and an economist whose humour and astuteness continue to broaden my perspective.

For my part, I dedicate this book to the memory of my father Yoram (Goldwag) Golan, a survivor of the Holocaust horrors and a man of deep scholarly disposition, who encouraged my journey and opened me to different cultural nodes through family travels and his rich background in languages and cultures. My mother, Judith (Dita) Kolodny-Golan, who has always been supportive of my scholarly journey and offered strength and support through it all. I am indebted to my beloved sisters, Donna and Sharon – Donna, the eldest, who has always taught me self-discipline and perseverance which were deeply needed to author this manuscript, and Sharon, whose attention to symbolic culture and belief systems from East and West has taught me so much. Both their beloved support aids me in my daily life as do their wonderful spouses, Shlomo and Tal, and children, Adam, Rona,

Tia, Emma, and baby Ann. Finally, I mention Arnon Kolodny, who is a pilot, a business entrepreneur, and, most importantly, my beloved uncle. My journey starts with these kin and they inspire my wor(l)ds.

III.   Michele's Journey

Publishing a first monograph is an important milestone for an emerging scholar and, like all milestones, it marks the border between the path already walked and that which lies ahead, a route whose navigation requires a lot of experience and knowledge, by and large not your own. Indeed, in the course of my career I have had the honour to encounter and be guided by several mentors. They have shared with me their knowledge and experience but, perhaps most importantly, have shown me what it means to be an intellectual in these troubled times. For that reason I want to thank Professor Patizia Violi, who supervised my rather massive MA thesis and first saw in me the potential to pursue academic research as a vocation. My gratitude goes also to Professor Tarcisio Lancioni, who supervised my PhD dissertation and patiently hammered down its most convoluted theoretical claims. Few people, however, have left a mark on my life as has Professor Tamar Katriel, whose example has become for me a model of intellectual and moral integrity. To her, I also owe my encounter with Professor Oren Golan, who has been my mentor for several years and who taught me those skills and crafts that are essential for a scholar in today's academia. This book, which we co-authored, is first of all a proof of his success. Researching in the field of digital religion led us to meet many wonderful scholars such as Professor Valentina Napolitano, Dr Giulia Evolvi, and Dr Carlo Nardella, whose work continues to enrich our knowledge and ignite our curiosity. Among them, my gratitude goes especially to Professor David Lehmann, whose support has been crucial in enabling me to expand my research from the Middle East to Latin America, making it truly a global study, and to Professor Frank Usarski, who welcomed me at the Pontifical Catholic University of São Paulo. Finally, I want to express my deepest gratitude to Professor Susan L. Roberson, with whom I had the honour to work at the University of Cambridge. We live in a time of deep crisis, a time in which we doubt human societies will ever be able to build just and sustainable futures for themselves. In this unprecedented conjuncture, Professor Roberson gave me what I most needed: the conviction that our intellectual work does matter.

To conclude, I would like to thank my family, who have been by my side through this journey: Marco Martini, Daniela Malench, and Francesca Martini. They are the one community I can always come back to and have a good fight. My deepest gratitude goes also to my partner, Dr Larisa Olteanu, whose intellectual courage and curiosity is for me an endless source of inspiration and headaches.

Sacred Cyberspaces

Introduction

The Global Coronavirus outbreak of 2020 challenged the basic modes of human interaction and pushed many to seek technologies for learning, maintaining relationships, engaging in commerce and practising religion. While these online practices have certainly been brewing over the last two decades, the outbreak has stimulated a grand legitimation process that introduced these technologies to apprehensive and often reluctant publics. Thus, workers have been pushed towards homebound production. Teachers have been compelled to redesign their pedagogies to accommodate distant learning, city centre store owners resort to online delivery and believers affirm their faith as they turn to livestreaming of holy sites (i.e. St Peter's Square, Lourdes, or Nazareth). For example, on the Vatican News website, Fr Arthur Ntembula of Milan expressed an urgency for clerics to embrace cyberspace:

> One might say, "But I am not even on Facebook or Instagram or Twitter etc. … how will I do this cyberspace thing?" Well, the situation now requires that you consider joining the social media community or at least create content that those who are already connected to the virtual community can post on your behalf or on their platforms. If the Church must move together with the people, priests cannot sit back and only wait for people to come to the parish. We need to step up and go out to meet them wherever they are. If they are on Facebook, let us pitch the tent of our parish in that space and continue to reach out to them.[1]

For Catholic believers, particularly in gravely virus-struck Italy, the challenge to maintain faith and uphold religion's ceremonial and congregational facets requires social and, as it seems, communicative action. This statement addresses believers' predicament at hand, it further affirms legitimation to the use of online platforms and is underpinned by a growing appreciation of the internet and communicative tools. Tools that peak in times of social separation and may have long-term repercussions for lived religious praxis. While the long-term repercussions of the Coronavirus outbreak may presumably be of major concern for scholars in years to come, the pandemic has impacted the legitimation of new media for religious and, often reluctant, groups. For those who have been gradually embracing these tools, the global circumstance has furnished a *ventus propitius*. This is to say, (unintended) contingencies that propel the already growing use of new media for religious activities (e.g. learning, prayer, ceremony).

Given its quickened growth, the main objective of *Sacred Cyberspaces* is to reveal how long-standing conflicts over power, influence, and legitimacy within religious organizations are being waged in the digital sphere. Our point of departure is that the fledgling new media production enterprise within the Catholic world is part and parcel of a raging struggle between traditional and new sources of religious authority. Against this backdrop, the book will assay the tension that the internet – above all, the need to present institutional identities and reach audiences online – spawns within various faiths and denominations labouring to maintain established hierarchies and boundaries.

Upon launching this research project in 2014, we were fascinated by the evident growth in media production at venerable holy sites. A few years ago, at the Easter procession in Jerusalem, the research team observed a young Latin American priest entering the Church of the Holy Sepulchre while holding up his smartphone and soliloquizing into his Bluetooth headset. All of a sudden, the father turned to a team member and asked him to describe "for my community in Mexico, how it feels to be next to Jesus' grave on the day of the resurrection. We are livestreaming on Facebook." Throughout the conversation, "likes" and "hearts" were popping up on his screen.

This encounter sparked our curiosity. On future visits to sacred places, we took note of the uptick in media usage not only among visitors personally documenting their experience on their smartphones or tablets but professional media crews as well. The latter have increasingly become a familiar sight at pilgrimage venues. In light of their presence, the following questions beg asking: Who are these media operators? What are their goals and affiliation with the Church? And how does their work impact the religious observance and worldviews of believers?

While newfangled spirituality movements (e.g., neo-Paganists and New Age sects) have long availed themselves of new media to disseminate their beliefs, their well-established religious counterparts are steadily embracing these same tools. For instance, thousands of members of the Korean Pentecostal Yoido Full Gospel Church have integrated digital broadcasts into their devotional routine. Over the past ten years, *Visual T'filah* – a program that projects fitting imagery (e.g., art and photos) onto synagogue screens – has become a standard feature of Reform Jewry's prayer services in the US. This sort of media consumption is not limited to formal liturgical settings, has been popularized, and is increasingly played on the monitors at shops, hospitals, youth centres, and retirement homes as well as personal computers, tablets, and smartphones.

In response to the mounting integration of visual technologies and new media into faith-based practice the world over, *Sacred Cyberspaces* grapples with the following question: how do religious agents and institutions promote their "brand" and social programs via digital communications? The overriding purpose of this book is to shed light on the rise of online media feeds (videos, Instagram images, and livestreaming) in organized faith as well as the emerging role of the attendant webmasters.

Drawing on our research into the Church's key media operations, we assert that the Catholic new media structure has branched out into two distinct wings. While both of these online edifices are dedicated to the Latin rite, each one has specific aims, emphasizes different online activities, and possesses its own codes.[2]

The first branch includes websites of the Holy See that are formal in the sense that they abide by the Church's hierarchical authority, disseminate highly vetted information, and feature approved practices. Also falling under this rubric is the bevy of Vatican media arms that upload documents, statements, and news pieces on popular social platforms (i.e., Twitter, Facebook, and Instagram). Furthermore, the

Church runs applications and mobile platforms that are available on Google Play and the App Store. Put differently, there is a symbiosis between major companies and a bevy of Vatican-owned websites, digital media outlets, and mobile apps. As illustrated in chapter 1, among these products are Vatican.va, Vatican Media, and ClicktoPray. The sites are usually flagged under the Holy See's domain (.va). To reiterate, these ventures conform to the papacy's policies. Nevertheless, the creators are given autonomy to experiment with, say, design, content, and degree of user participation. Highly globalized, the websites are published in major languages (i.e., Italian, English, Spanish, French, German, and Portuguese), yet they do not cover every region throughout the Catholic world, lacking a presence in "smaller" tongues like Catalan or Welsh.

For believers, this cyber realm offers a direct link to the bishop of Rome, free of clerical mediation. Throughout the Church's history, such intercession fuelled discontent from both myriad protest movements associated with the Latin rite and heterodox movements. By means of these outlets, users can easily access a wide range of papal statements and documents, from airy Tweets to intricate encyclicals. A world of knowledge and apostolic recommendations on ethical and practical concerns are all but a few clicks away.

An unintended consequence of these establishment platforms is the tension in creating a top-down source of information that provides a direct link to the Holy See but eschews dialogue – contentious or otherwise – with the *hoi polloi*. Moreover, this branch of the Catholic webosphere offers tools for independent learning through which users can potentially challenge the authority of low-ranking ecclesiastics. This same type of empowerment also informs the webmasters managing these outlets. Similar to the plight of other knowledge workers (e.g., doctors and teachers), new media publics are exposed to information that might lead them to dispute established professional's opinion. By dint of this expansive access to esoteric information, webmasters are also likely to modify, re-examine, and seek further legitimation for their occupational practice and identity (Susskind and Susskind 2016). Owing to these developments, the role of the "first estate" is increasingly in flex, as believers are less reliant on the clergy's expertise.

The second wing of the Catholic internet is run by grassroots believers, namely subgroups associated with or that have an affinity for the Church. These factors use new media tools to develop communal settings that either mimic or are independent of offline settings. For instance, Catholics living in the same neighbourhood often establish a WhatsApp group. Likewise, Facebook pages are launched for co-religionists sharing an external interest (e.g., chats for fans of Christian rap music). These trends have also spawned more controversial alternative movements, such as Catholics for Choice and LGBT Catholics of San Diego. As discussed in chapter 1, these organizations furnish unencumbered platforms for authentic self-expression on heated issues. While the positions taken by these groups do not constitute a full break with the establishment, the members object to certain facets of the accepted creed. In addition, they offer devotees an alternative community, be it on a regional or supra-territorial basis. Anti-LGBTQ groups, such as the Italian Sentinelle in Piedi, make concerted efforts to provide an outlet for conservative views on their website and blogs. First and foremost, the movement's activists criticize what they view as the Holy See's ambivalent or lax approach to homosexuality (Evolvi 2017).

Ideologies aside, the strength of these movements lies in their flexibility and relevance. Like many informal education ventures (Hamadache 1991), they are responsive to the needs and moral sensibilities of their flock. Moreover, these sorts of outfits can readily adapt to contingencies, for there is no need to build heavy infrastructure for a brick-and-mortar parish. Responding to attitudinal and demographic shifts, their platforms enable activists who might not receive direct attention from the Holy See to cultivate a distinct niche within the greater Catholic community. At any rate, there is a dissonance in these groups between members detaching themselves from the faith of Rome's core institutions and nurturing a Catholic identity.

Another challenge that these movements face is their dependence on transnational platforms, such as Facebook or Instagram. While these corporations provide an inexpensive means for growing a network of devotees, the literature has recently identified a number of pitfalls in the use of such digital outlets (Vaidhyanathan 2018). To begin with, the outlets can be fleeting. A case in point is GeoCities, a popular web hosting service that Yahoo acquired and proceeded to shut down. Furthermore, megaplatforms are susceptible to external manipulation; the product can be unreliable; and users must contend with shifting policies. By relying on another entity's infrastructure, these groups also expose their publics to micro targeting of interested third parties and compulsory monitoring.

While these regional and/or minor groups are often short-lived, they can be replaced with relative ease. There are indeed a panoply of outfits catering to the many and manifold needs of the Catholic devotees. Whereas some consider these movements transgressional or dissident groups, others deem them to be a source of affinity that buoys the Latin rite. While maintaining the Church's boundaries, these outfits relax some of its taboos and expand its cultural frontiers. In *Sacred Cyberspaces*, we will home in on the establishment's new media ventures. Be that as it may, the grassroots counterparts also merit increased attention. More specifically, it is incumbent upon scholars to develop a research model that befits heterodox movements, faith-driven activism, and NGOs. While the two branches of the Catholic internet appear to be steadily drifting apart, it appears that the lines of dialogue between them are expanding. For the Holy See, this exchange is perhaps conducive to building trust, mobilizing social and monetary capital, and identifying issues that concern the flock. Correspondingly, this pipeline to the Vatican can legitimize and empower the communities. Although the rupture outlined herein may well persist, it is not impervious to informal negotiations.

Concentrating on institutional efforts to advance the Latin rite, *Sacred Cyberspaces* is divided into three primary sections. In the first (chapters 1 and 2), the stress is on "Digital Faith: Emergent Agents and Technologies for Devout Publics." Surveying the rise of ICTs (information and communication technologies) as acceptable, normative components of religious observance, we will contextualize various historic and theological facets of ecclesiastical approaches to media. By keying in on emergent professionals that design and disseminate these tools, this section also explores how faith-based movements are adapting to and incorporating new media into their rites (e.g., confession, mass, and baptism). The next strand (chapters 3 and 4), "Holy

Land YouTube Videos: The Visual Language of Religious Outreach," takes stock of institutional efforts to produce videos intended to help devotees formulate their beliefs. The third and final cluster (chapters 5 and 6), "Bolstering Religious Authority through Visual Means," delves into the building, re-affirmation, and wielding of religious authority in the digital sphere.

More specifically, in the first chapter, "Digital Religion and Global Publics," we survey the new field of digital religion and discuss how religious movements have historically responded to and often "tamed" technologies for the purpose of advancing their communal, ritual, and outreach goals. Against this backdrop, we examine the Catholic leadership's media policy and contemporary praxis. Above all, this chapter expounds on the Vatican's gradual integration of media technologies since the advent of cinema and radio, with a focus on its official websites, and mobile phone/tablet apps. All of which are designated for mid-level clergy and modern-day uses thereof in both monastic communities and by lay devotees. Platforms that are contrasted with grassroots Catholic groups that mobilize through social media.

Due to the growing importance of new media in the Church's relationship with its believers, the second chapter, "The Rise of the Religious Webmaster," examines the elevated standing of web operators in all that concerns religious education and change. With this in mind, we conducted fieldwork on the enterprise of these webmasters in both the US and Israel. The research design included interviews on webmasters' motivations, communication strategies, and theological outlook regarding media work. Far from being mere technical transmitters of the faith, these webmasters edit content, create images, vet information, serve as gatekeepers, and interact with believers on a daily basis. We inquired, how do religious professionals grasp their roles and standing vis-à-vis the community at large and, alternatively, the ecclesiastic authorities? With this question in mind, we surveyed and compared the interviews that were held with these webmasters and other clerics. Our findings demonstrate that the former perceive ICTs as a means of gaining exposure, legitimacy, and clout.

The third chapter, "Digital Gates to the Holy Land: Mediatizing the Religious Experience," elaborates on the above-mentioned video production of the Franciscan Order and the Canção Nova's webmasters in

Israel/Palestine. At present, these two Catholic organizations are collaborating on videos of faith that put an emphasis on the Holy Land. In the process, we uncover how long-standing conflicts within religious groups over status and legitimacy are being played out in the realm of new media production. We argue that this case study opens a window onto an intensifying struggle between traditional and new sources of religious authority. The nub of this chapter is our ethnographic field-work on video production. We draw insights from twenty-five comprehensive interviews with monastic webmasters on their efforts to improve the religious experience for both on-site pilgrims and remote viewers by documenting and re-enacting rituals performed at sacred places. Last, but not least, the chapter analyzes the end results of this new media partnership – the videos themselves.

In chapter four, titled "Networking the Sacred for Global Publics: New Media Strategies for a Re-enchanted World," we further our focus on holy sites and online pilgrimage. Over the past two decades, pilgrimage sites have been represented in the virtual sphere (e.g., Facebook and Second Life). Lately, this has taken the form of quasi-informal instructional videos that depict the place's religious significance. In addition, devotees are encouraged to become active supporters of the venue. This chapter will concentrate on online efforts by religious institutions to underscore their affiliation with prominent holy sites. By virtue of an in-depth analysis of sixty videos that Catholic monastic groups have produced on and in the Holy Land, we have elucidated the ways in which sacred places are represented online. In the process, the book contributes to the literature on the "re-enchantment of the Holy Land" through visual communications. All the more so, the Church is aspiring to varnish its credentials by, inter alia, filming rituals and pilgrim activities – both important annual events and routine daily practices – at such venues and by then disseminating this content via social networks.

Correspondingly, chapter 5 turns to explore the ways that the emergent format of religious livestreaming fortifies the meanings of religious sites by instilling a sense of authenticity through the arguably unexpected format of virtual engagement with the sacred. This ensues as major religions have turned to live-media streaming as a means to engage their devotees and reach out to new audiences. From the

Wailing Wall in Jerusalem to the Sanctuary of Our Lady of Lourdes, many religious websites are offering live coverage of select events and/or a continuous, twenty-four-hour live feed of holy sites. Given the innovative nature of religious livestreaming, chapter 5 identifies the key agents behind this phenomenon and documents its founders' original motivations. In addition, we share our insights from interviews conducted with livestreaming staff and examine clerical responses to this trend. Drawing on Walter Benjamin's concept of the aura, we formulate a theory on how religious livestreaming pushes holy sites back into the public spotlight and offers traditional denominations an avenue for global outreach. Additionally, we uncover how the webmasters' status is elevated within the religious hierarchy by micro-managing the lenses that frame livestreaming platforms.

Reverting to Catholic leadership, and in particular, Pope Francis's Instagram feed, chapter 6, "The Pope on Instagram: Managing Religious Authority and Globalized Charisma in the Digital Age," explores the way religious institutions run their social media outreach. The pontifical account, which has been active since March 2016, offers daily images of the pope fulfilling his duties: administering major Vatican ceremonies, visiting countries around the world, presiding over interfaith meetings, and the like. We have conducted an extensive survey of all the content that was posted on this feed during its initial eighteen months of activity (March 2016 to August 2017). Building on construal theory, this analysis explicates the struggle between organized religions for hearts in today's competitive devotional landscape. For instance, this chapter sheds light on informal outreach initiatives, the emergence of alternative sources of ecclesiastic authority and knowledge, and socio-religious transformation amid the exponential growth of new media.

Finally, in the concluding chapter, "Catholicism, Rupture, and Media Efforts," we take a bird's-eye view to explore Catholic mediatization. Accordingly, we discuss the Catholic Church's key impediments, recount its top-down initiatives as well as review Catholic believers' grassroots online expressions. Framing these changes through current scholarship on both anthropology and digital religion, this conclusive chapter canvasses ebbs and flows that the Church has withstood since the 1960s (in terms of religious proselytization, religious sites, authenticity, and leadership), and how it addresses responses that resonate in their media activity and is further progressed in contemporary Catholic (social) media.

For more than a decade, communication scholars have been considering the religious social shaping of technology as a perspective that counters notions of technological determinism. Accordingly, this line of research demonstrates how collectives have coloured technologies to fit their walk of life and contingent circumstances (Campbell 2010; Barzilai-Nahon and Barzilai 2005). In *Sacred Cyberspaces*, we follow this perspective while spotlighting the Catholic Church and its mediatized activities. We further inquire on the ways that ICTs impact religion and its institutional layout, transforming structures and leading to the emergence of new power brokers and collective worldview. Drawing on methodological tools that converge ethnographic inquiry with semiotic investigation, *Sacred Cyberspaces* aims to address key concerns that are threatening well-established religious leaders and show how they are addressed through communicative means. Means that, we contend, are underpinned in their deep structure (employing Levi-Strauss's [1974] terms) by the informal nature of modern new media platforms, to create alluring spaces for religious activity, consumption and participation.

Sacred Cyberspaces leans on a novel research methodology we developed which involved an ethnographic fieldwork of Catholic initiatives, a semiotic analysis of Catholic videos and images circulated on social media, and forty in-depth interviews with webmasters, media support staff, and stakeholders, including prelates. While the majority of our interviewees were stationed in the Holy Land, quite a few reside throughout the Catholic world, from Italy to Brazil: a macroscopic gaze that is merited due to the global and interconnected landscape of the religious market and its activity in the twentieth and twenty-first centuries.

Over the past half-century or so, there has been a massive wave of intra-Christian conversion. For instance, historical data suggest that until 1970, the Latin American population was at least 90 per cent Catholic. However, a 2014 Pew Research survey indicates that only 69 per cent of the 425 million adults across the region currently identify with the Holy See. What is more, two-thirds of the remaining Catholics have joined affiliated charismatic movements. During this fifty-year span, about 75 million Latin Americans have switched over to the competing Pentecostal movement. This sea change can largely be attributed to the development of communication technologies, as charismatic movements have vigorously incorporated these means – most notably, the production of religious videos (for television and, more recently, the internet) – into their outreach programs.

Sacred Cyberspaces draws the attention of policymakers to on-screen devotional activities. The study may help them design and implement visual communication strategies that influence the rapidly evolving socio-political and religious environment. As antagonistic contents continue to fuel inter-faith discord, scholars and policymakers are becoming ever more concerned with the online religious offerings of various groups. For this reason, this book may constitute a valuable resource for regional and international bodies endeavouring to promote mutual understanding in the digital sphere.

PART 1

Digital Faith: Emerging Agents and Technologies for Devout Publics

1   Digital Religion and Global Publics

1.1   Religion on the Electronic Frontier: Socially Structuring the Internet amid Hype and Apprehension

Religious movements have historically "tamed" technologies for the purpose of advancing their communal, ritual, and outreach goals. From integrating Church organs to augment the religious experience to Christian web filters that screen unwanted content. With this in mind, *Sacred Cyberspaces* takes stock of the dialectic relations between faith-based groups and cutting-edge technologies through the lens of Catholic media policy. This introductory chapter will expound on the Vatican's gradual integration of media technologies since the advent of cinema and radio. In addition, we delve into the emergence of religious smartphone applications (apps) in global faith-based communities, with a special emphasis on Catholic products that are developed by and for the Holy See.

The immense growth of online religion over the past few decades has come as a surprise to many observers. The link between tradition and the digital realm, which is strongly associated with profane learning and entertainment, may seem like an odd fit. Despite the reservations of some prominent clergy, though, the internet has flourished as a platform for devotional undertakings, even among conservative and fundamentalist groups, be they institutionalized or decentralized. Given the exponential growth of the web, the following question begs asking: Does the emergence of various online platforms, not least mobile devices, constitute a game changer in terms of socio-religious activity, or does the internet merely reproduce existing structures, theologies, and modes of devotee interaction? With this question in mind, *Sacred Cyberspaces* will turn the spotlight onto developments in Catholic (new) media, especially as they pertain to religious authority, praxis, and holy sites (chapter 5). For instance, we will explore the perspectives, affordances, and aspirations of stakeholders and key actors, such as webmasters, in this transformation (chapter 2 and 4). Another focus of this book is content posted on or via technological interfaces (e.g., videos, livestreaming, and Instagram posts) and the social objectives behind these productions.

To enhance our understanding of these phenomena, let us review the hype that has accompanied the internet's growth over the past few decades and identify the role of religion in this story. During these years, digital religion has evolved into a distinct field of inquiry. Notwithstanding its relevance to the study of lived faith, communication scholars – rather than religion specialists, theologians, semioticians, or sociologists of religion – have dominated this enterprise. The pioneers in this field (e.g., Heidi Campbell, Stewart Hoover, Mia Lövheim, Christopher Helland, Stephen O'Leary, Douglas Cowan, and Gregory Grieve) have assayed online manifestations of faith and their influence on authority, proselytization, community, and social norms.

Established in the late 1960s within the framework of a Pentagon-run project known as ARPANET (the Advanced Research Project Agency Network, Castells 2002), the internet seeped into the academy over the next two decades. Web use only began to catch on among the general public in the 1990s (Danet 2001), largely on account of visual-technological developments, foremost among them the launching of visual web browsers in 1993. These events gave rise to the field of internet studies, which tracks the ebb and flow of online culture. In the parallel sub-field of cyber studies, researchers exposed the deviant behaviours that turned up on the internet as well as its exploitation by terrorists (Weimann 2004) and criminal organizations. Scholars have discovered unintended consequences of new media that threaten the socio-political order (Vaidhyanathan 2018). Back in *Silicon Snake Oil* (1995), Stoll posits that the information highway was exacting a heavy toll on everyday life. With respect to faith, he averred that computers and the internet were spawning inauthentic experiences. "We don't need a computer," Stoll lamented, "to say a prayer" (1995, 10). Other scholars cautioned against the internet's addictive draw, particularly among youth (Young 2009), and its strain on educational achievement and the development of personal relations (Beniger 1987).

These dangers aside, the literature points to a utopian rhetoric that has accompanied the internet's rise (Fisher and Wright 2006). For many of its enthusiasts, the web represents a new electronic frontier on par with the nineteenth-century American ideal of manifest destiny or the space program in the 1960s. Moreover, the digital realm was billed as a new hub for culture. Beyond this romanticism, the technology seemed to address a host of twentieth-century socio-political ailments. The internet's exponents were confident that it would, say, boost democratic participation, cut into knowledge gaps hampering the third world, and expand global markets. UN programs to ramp up the number of internet service providers (ISP) in Africa and the idyllic optimism of prominent politicians, such as Al Gore, exemplify the high hopes that were placed on digital technologies.[1]

Beyond the hyperbole, the major milestones in the internet's evolution over the past twenty years have been the introduction of Web 2.0 (O'Reilly 2009) and the proliferation of mobile phones. Succinctly put, Web 2.0 was the phase at which users could share content and participate in enormous social networks like Facebook, Twitter, and Instagram (John 2017). Rather than the unidirectional flow of information that characterizes radio, television, and Web 1.0, there is now a multi-directional exchange. This turn of events has had a major bearing on personal lives and has galvanized political, social, and religious movements. The emergence of the smartphone can be viewed as a social revolution that turned the internet, especially Web 2.0, into a ubiquitous technology-of-the-self (Carolus et al. 2019). As the gaming and virtual reality industries, among others, released a bevy of improvements and new technologies (Boellstorff 2015) the distinct research fields of mobile phones, apps, the internet, and cyber studies united under the heading of "new media." Schejter and Tirosh (2016) consider this juncture to be the inflection point that gave rise to a new kind of mediated sociability offering an abundance of interactive, storable, mobile information that can be accessed and shared in numerous ways. The emergence of religious actors, stakeholders, and users who are embracing Web 2.0 have reshaped devotional experiences in the information age.

Innovations in media platforms and technology have certainly transformed the affordances at the disposal of religious users and webmasters. Elster (1989) points to both the opportunities available to and desires of social actors. Similarly, Lessig (2006, 121–5)[2] has demonstrated the importance of the internet's architecture to the agency of users, their social position, and communicative activities. With respect to faith-based groups, "taming technology" refers to a creative process in which existing products are modified or new ones are developed in an effort to tailor an innovation to a community's lifestyle and system of beliefs (Barzilai-Nahon and Barzilai 2005). Scholars have documented many examples of this phenomenon, such as Rashi's work (2013) on "kosher phones" – devices that block content and platforms that are deemed to be inappropriate for ultra-Orthodox Jews. In devising her methodological approach to online religion, Campbell (2017, 20–1) has referred to these modifications as "the social shaping of technology (RSST)."

A dichotomy between technological and cultural determinism has often been used to explain the connections between innovation and society. However, the level at which a technology is assimilated into a collective differs from group to group. While some societies acquiesce to technology, others fully embrace it. This distinction is salient among Jewish subgroups. Haredi communities have long shunned television, but they have gradually come around to radio, internet, and most recently WhatsApp chat groups (Mishol-Shauli and Golan 2019). Alternatively, modern-Orthodox create technologies that suit their devotional needs. This includes a bevy of tools for upholding Sabbath prohibitions against turning on electric devices, foremost among them automatized elevators and timers for lights, water boilers, and hot plates. Similarly, they have also patented technologies for enhancing rituals, like electric pumps for purifying the water in *mikvot* (ritual bath houses). As we shall see, Christian groups have primarily adopted and developed innovations that promote learning and outreach.

Notwithstanding the resistance to and/or apprehension from integrating technologies into religious practice, ever more devotees are willing to take advantage of these breakthroughs. A growing concern for such communities is finding the most suitable online venues for religious expression. Researchers have plumbed manifestations of these developments, the worldview behind their adoption, and their impact in terms of social mobilization. While some faith-based groups have emphasized this sort of digital activity as a supplement to religious learning and offline engagement, others have stressed the independent tracks that Web 2.0 has midwived, including online networks that accompany users throughout the hours of the day. With respect to the auxiliary approach, there are communities that only use these outlets to promote their offline frameworks. A case in point are neighbourhood churches that advertise weekly activities, like prayer services and marriage prep classes, on Twitter or Facebook. In contrast, there are practices that are mainly conducted online. According to Young (2013), movements like Wicca, Scientology, and the Flying Spaghetti Monster run the majority of their activities in the "third space."

Building on Oldenberg's scholarship, Hoover and Echchaibi (2014) define the "third space" as a "fluid, conceptual, and imagined location … (3) where new logics of religious identity, meaning, community, networks, and action can be explored and instantiated" (31). In our estimation, much of the success behind these digital expanses can be attributed to their informal nature. Oldenberg (1989) suggests eight defining characteristics of third spaces: they are neutral ground, social levellers, conversation is the main activity therein, the significance of "regulars," heightened accessibility, they maintain a low profile, a playful mood, and they provide a "home away from home." For brevity's sake, we will not get into each and every trait. However, the common denominator is that all of them help foster a sense of community that assembles in a liminal space, which overlaps with the individual user's other social frameworks.

The communal engagement that informs the third space is analogous to danah boyd's "networked publics" – a term that underscores the way in which groups navigate certain technological environments (Boyd 2010). In this respect, the digital realm offers new and/or marginalized groups ample space for theological debate, learning, and ritual activity. This sphere also elicits a sense of imagined belonging (Boyd 2010; Papacharissi 2015). Moreover, it restructures faith-based communities via socio-technological affordances. In sum, the digital realm can be viewed as both complementary to mainstream theological-cum-devotional praxis and a catalyst for independent frameworks, which may lead to disengagement, conversion, secularism, and other forms of religious deviance.

1.2 Learning the Faith: Online Religious Information, Sourcing and Self-Educating Communities

As part of the spike in internet use, many believers are availing themselves of this medium for religious information. Needless to say, there are many and manifold online sources that vary in their underlying, and often covert, motives, perspectives, standing, and communal affiliation. This abundance can bewilder individuals and lead to unrealistic expectations, and social anomie (Durkheim 1964), as information and know-how found in these sites can widely diverge from one another. Within the field of learning sciences, Barzilai, Tzadok, and Eshet-Alkalai (2015, 738) have recently delved into issues of sourcing for the purpose of determining how individuals construct knowledge – a topic of particular relevance to the information age. This process naturally involves epistemic and cognitive development. According to Barzilai, Tzadok, and Eshet-Alkalai, sourcing can be defined as the pursuit, evaluation, and employment of information outlets for the sake of validating and making sense of the world. For these researchers, this action is implicitly grounded on a scientific outlook that emphasizes critical and evidence-based reasoning. However, other factors, such as dogma, communal values, and adherence to ecclesiastics, may impact the manner in which devout users gauge information. As a result, webmasters are encouraged to create pedagogic designs that present their information as legitimate and trustworthy.

For devotional learners, in both formal institutions and other frameworks, online searches can potentially lead them to question their existing beliefs. This is evident in public controversies over, say, creationism, the legitimacy of the religious establishment, and vaccinations for children. These doubts are exacerbated by web-disseminated (mis)information that tends to be peddled by religiously inclined outfits and gains traction in communities predisposed to distrusting governmental and scientific authorities (e.g., fundamentalist enclaves and disadvantaged minorities). This is also linked to the democratization of information conundrum. As per Schejter and Baram-Tsabari (2019), the abundance of outlets is a "double edged sword" because the public occasionally struggles to distinguish fact from fiction, paving the way to uninformed decisions.

In our estimation, the primary objective of many religious websites is to serve as educational hubs. These platforms rest on two discernable forms of learning: unidirectional learning in a multi-faceted environment and self-educating communities. In the former, top-down teaching is conducted for the most part by representatives of the establishment who strive to pass on the organization's doctrine, ideals, and other types of information to participants. This strategy dovetails neatly with Web 1.0 formats. While this form of outreach might appear to be a direct form of indoctrination, it has revolved around soft forms of pedagogy since the early days of the internet's bulletin board systems (Zaleski 1997). Due to the legions of competing websites in the religious marketplace, the players have little choice but to treat the audience with kid gloves. Put differently, they cannot strong-arm the flock into compliance. In *Sacred Cyberspaces*, we will discuss various manifestations of this educational approach (i.e. videos, photographs, and livestreaming).

Another top-down initiative is responsa (Golan 2019). Also known as religious Q&A, this generally involves posing questions and answers on legal, theological, and personal matters to religious authorities by either their peers or laymen, who are occasionally anonymous. There is a strong legacy of responsa in the rabbinical literature. As opposed to codified law, this genre is usually arranged in a less formal and more eclectic manner. This format attests to the popular demand for expert advice. In many instances, the questions are actually broached by the experts themselves. The granting of such a forum to an individual can be seen as a form of socialization and a way of recognizing religious authority. For example, a prominent section of the catholic.com website is dedicated to "Catholic Answers" – a forum in which users engage an American priest by the name of Charles R. Grondin. By responding to online queries on theological matters, the father seeks to varnish his ministerial reputation.

To this end, Grondin is pictured donning his ecclesiastical raiment. Likewise, he avails himself of a Catholic rhetorical style mottled with Latin and esoteric terms, the language draws on the Church's

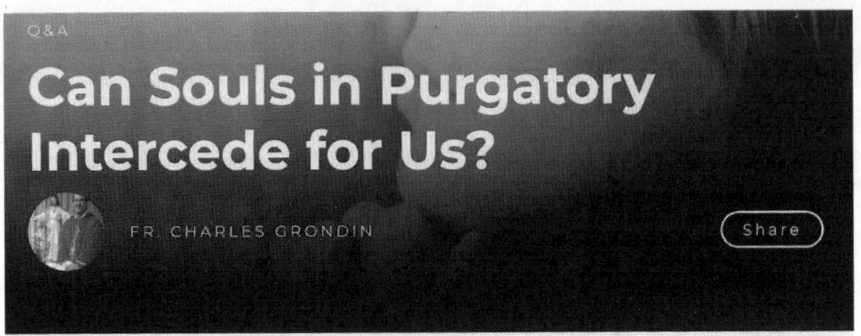

Question:

Can the souls in purgatory intercede for us?

Answer:

Whether or not the souls in purgatory can pray for us is an open theological question. The principle of *lex orandi, lex credendi* (the law of prayer is the law of belief) would seem to argue against it, since the liturgical prayers of the Church never ask the souls in purgatory to pray for us. However, prominent theologians throughout history have been on both sides of the question.

Figure 1.1 | Screenshot of the Q&A section "Catholic Answers" on www.catholic.com.

theological corpus. With respect to the actual content, this responsa offers some top-down information on transcendental issues that are meant to spark the participants' imaginations.

In contrast to this top-down pedagogic approach, online social networks (e.g. Facebook, Twitter, Instagram), forums, and designated webpages offer platforms for what Burbules (2006) refers to as self-educating communities. Falling under the category of Web 2.0, these frameworks are openly committed to sharing information, initiating newcomers, and extending their collective knowledge through joint problem solving, experimentation, and independent inquiry. When searching for outlets to quench their religious curiosity, many of these seekers turn to what James Surowiecki has dubbed the "wisdom of the crowds" (2005). A case in point is the comment sections of religious YouTube videos, which constitute an open forum for talking about spiritual and theological issues. In figure 1.2, a post has triggered a grassroots discussion between several users.

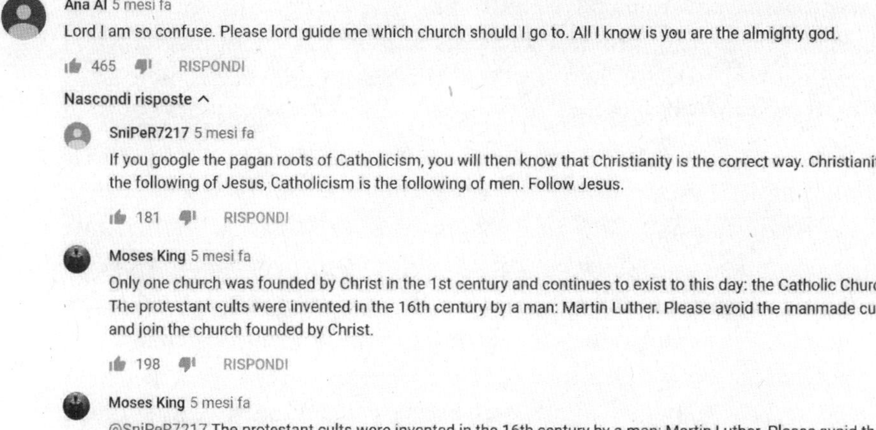

Figure 1.2 | Screenshot from the comment section of the YouTube video "Why Be Catholic and Not Just Christian" on the Ascension Presents channel.

This short YouTube discussion is a fine example of interdenominational convergence. In the opening post, an individual admits that he is confused and in need of guidance. Thereafter, participants raise arguments either in support of or opposition to the Catholic Church. The multiple "likes" each post has garnered bears witness to a wider audience. Apropos of a self-educating community, the respondents draw on personal and web-extracted information.

In light of the above, this forum fits under the rubric of informal or non-formal education. Probing deeper into learning beyond institutional settings (e.g. school and army) researchers have defined incidental education as knowledge that is bestowed without a conscious effort to promote learning from both instructor and beneficiary. Non-formal education occurs when either the benefactor or pupil has the intention of engaging in a learning process. Finally, informal education is where both sides consciously wish to do so (Hamadache 1991). The use of these terms has varied in the literature, as researchers even occasionally conflate their meanings (Bhola 1983; Rogers 2004). Nevertheless, this terminology contributes to our knowledge on educational initiatives that transcend the spatio-temporal confines of formal study (Silberman-Keller 2006).

Against this backdrop, digital religion practised by self-educating communities can be seen as a lifelong enterprise that includes formal, informal, and/or non-formal approaches to learning. Participants eschew standardized, regulated, and top-down methods in favour of more independent activity driven by a strong personal or collective interest. Accordingly, they engage in open-ended and perpetually unresolved learning, rather than focusing on a sealed corpus that is meant to be repeated. By dint of constant exegesis and improvisatorially contextualizing sources to everyday life, users and clergy make their own teachings relevant and comprehensible. Upon working on a sermon, for instance, priests consult their favourite websites or YouTube channels. In other words, they borrow from a constantly shifting corpus of knowledge that is readily accessible through solitary or group study sessions. By virtue of such learning, a marginalized community in, say, the Gaza Strip can find inspiration in the Christmas story or contextualize the yearly Assumption of Mary procession to modern day political events.

Forgoing the brick-and-mortar institutions of standard, face-to-face approaches to Catholic outreach, new media ventures run by informal subgroups and other non-government bodies targeting distinct religious communities have flourished over the past few decades. These organizations provide alternatives to the Church's mainstream, centralized, and monolithic voice on both Web 1.0 and Web 2.0 frameworks. For example, Catholics for Choice, an NGO raising the banner of women's health and reproductive rights, has maintained an active Facebook (facebook.com/pg/CatholicsforChoice) and Twitter presence (see figure 1.3) since 2008. Owning Our Faith, a grassroots Catholic-American LGBTQ organization, invites members of its community to share their life stories (facebook.com/pg/owningourfaithlgbt). The Vatican tends to steer a non-confrontational approach towards such flammable issues, and the groups themselves reciprocate with an ambivalent posture vis-à-vis the traditional authorities. Nevertheless, the stances that these organizations take render them counterpublics (Giorgi 2019). During the COVID-19 pandemic, Palmisano and Giorgi

Figure 1.3 | Twitter homepage of the Catholics for Choice movement.

(2021) observed how emergent minority factions within the Catholic Church have brought attention to doctrinal and governance issues. A case in point is Donne per la Chiesa – a group of Catholic monks and nuns striving to empower women by putting an end to their subordinate roles in ecclesiastic institutions. In sum, these opposition elements have built platforms on which like-minded users congregate, express themselves, and forge alternative ways to manifest their religious identity.

Scholars have demonstrated that the third sector is attentive to communal issues and responds well to flux (Zychlinski and York 2009). While LGBTQ Catholics certainly face doctrinal and ritual hardships, their cybernetic outreach fosters solidarity, particularly among far-flung constituents and members of small communities. These groups have also introduced viable replacements for mainstream Catholic conventions without jettisoning fundamental precepts of the Church. In a similar vein, their online associations build social capital in the form of access to practical advice, spiritual guidance, and social support.

For some conservative ecclesiastics and laypersons, these NGOs and their self-educating communities are "rogue groups" that threaten the integrity and ultimate authority of the Holy See from within. Our findings suggest that these frameworks paradoxically induce some users to bolster their commitment to Catholic teachings and identities. Wary that these organizations' influence will grow, the Church is investing in digital platforms that adhere to strict canonical teachings. Confronting the emergent alternatives to mainstream Catholicism, the Vatican and its allies are strengthening traditional values by ratcheting up their use of modern media.

1.3   Vatican Media Projects

Despite the centralized nature of the Catholic Church, there are beyond-the-scenes struggles for representation within the faith. These fights are not only being waged by various sub-movements and institutions but also by an assortment of grassroots initiatives. In addition, local parishes constitute the venue for quite a few of these jousts. Many of these opposition elements operate primarily in the cyber realm. To counter these developments, the Vatican has presided over a formidable initiative aimed at expanding its visibility on the internet. Above all, the Church is sponsoring digital outlets that raise the banner of mainstream Catholic doctrine.

To understand how the Holy See represents itself in the cyber realm, let us begin by surveying its historical approach to modern media. The establishment of the first Catholic organizations dedicated to this topic coincided with the rise, as well as and massive political exploitation, of cinema and radio. In 1928, the Church founded two bodies – the International Catholic Bureau for Broadcasting and the International Catholic Organization for Cinema and Audiovisual – with the express goal of advancing "the human and spiritual progress of professionals working in the cinema and audiovisuals and of the public of these media" (Union of International Associations website, accessed 29 July 2019). Eight years later, Pope Pius XI released an encyclical, *Vigilanti Cura*, that put his doctrinal imprimatur on both the production and consumption of movies. This communiqué attests to the Vatican's early enthusiasm towards the cinema and to its awareness of the big screen's far-reaching impact on public opinion. Consistent with earlier positions, the pontiff urged his fellow bishops to exercise "painstaking vigilance over the motion picture" while assuring them "that a great international force – the motion picture – shall be directed towards the noble end of promoting the highest ideals and the truest standards of life."

Following the Second World War, the Church continued to ratchet up its involvement with mass media. In 1948, Pius entrusted The Pontifical Commission for the Study and Ecclesiastical Evaluation of Films on Religious or Moral Subjects with assessing and instilling Catholic values in mass media productions. Renamed the Pontifical Commission for the Cinema, Radio and Television in 1954 and the Pontifical Commission for Social Communications a decade later, this body set Church policy on these matters until the outset of the digital age. The Second Vatican Council weighed in heavily on this discourse. The 1957 encyclical *Miranda Prorsus* (literally "the Magnificent Invention") defined mass media as "gifts of God," thereby encouraging Catholic representatives to personally avail themselves of these tools. With the pontifical decree *Inter Mirifica* on 4 December 1963, the Synod of Bishops officially recognized "its duty to treat ... the principal questions linked with the media of social communication." Moreover, this group undertook to "promote not only the eternal welfare of Christians, but also the progress of all mankind." To these ends, Pope Paul VI established World Communications Day in 1967. Marked by Catholic communities across the globe, this annual event has pushed the Church to regularly reflect on the opportunities and challenges that modern media pose to its institutions. The pope's annual remarks on World Communications Day are a principal source for ascertaining the Vatican's priorities and apprehensions in all that concerns the media landscape.

Since the 1970s, the Vatican has intensified its efforts in the competitive media market. Many religious media enterprises find their doctrinal-cum-theological roots in publications circulated by the Holy See during this period. *Communio et Progressio* (1971) is often cited as the papacy's initial attempt to lay down basic pastoral guidelines for the use of mass media. The positive attitude towards mass communications that was expressed in this papal instruction reverberated twenty years later in the digital utopianism of Silicon Valley. According to *Communio et Progressio*, the media is an integral part of God's design, as they unite "men in brotherhood and so help them to cooperate with His plan for their salvation." Besides illuminating the strategic value of information technologies, this communiqué set the tone for their expanded role in Catholic communities. Ushering in a new wave of evangelization, the apostolic exhortation *Evangelii Nuntiandi* of 1975 paved the way for new actors on the Catholic stage: individual devotees and organizations dedicated to conducting outreach via these means.

Over the last two decades, a swell of media-based evangelization projects has challenged traditional Catholic doctrine. The use of cybernetic tools, from social networks to official websites, requires professional know-how and detailed communication strategies. While improving and personalizing outreach, the web platforms' global scale exposes users to a host of different, and possibly conflicting, sources of information. The growing presence of Catholics in digital evangelization has raised questions of theological legitimacy and progressiveness. The launching of Twitter and Instagram accounts by Pope Benedict XVI and Pope Francis, respectively, have informally merged social media into the Catholic lifestyle. These particular feeds do not engage in theological discussion or seek to become a part of the devotee's everyday life. Nevertheless, they have evolved into channels for fervently communicating papal ideals and varnishing the Holy See's credentials (see chapter 6). Alongside these platforms, the Vatican runs a number of websites aimed at improving ties with the faithful.

1.3.1 *The Vatican State Website*[3]

Vaticanstate.va conforms to online self-representation practices of modern-day nation-states. Like its counterparts, this site possesses a symbolic, almost totemic quality. Moreover, it has been the target of cyberattacks, such as the one perpetrated in 2012 by Anonymous — a decentralized anarchist hacker movement. The smallest recognized state in the world, both in terms of population and area, the Vatican is an unusual entity. However, vaticanstate.va helps place it on an equal footing with other countries. To begin with, the city-state holds a top-level domain (.va). That is to say, it has a monopoly over a 2-letter URL suffix on the World Wide Web – a symbol of status reserved for individual countries, sovereign states, or autonomous territories. Above all, the website hammers home the point that the Vatican is not a satellite of Italy.

Although vaticanstate.va contains permanent information, it also has dynamic features that are in constant flux. On the one hand, it publicizes the opening hours of the local pharmacy, and on the other, it automatically updates photos furnished via a live camera system that offer users a glance at the city around the clock. As illustrated in chapter 5, there is also a livestream feed of its most famous sites.

Vaticanstate.va also constitutes a travel guide. From a design standpoint, users can access content without reloading the page. The menu invites tourists to browse information on the Vatican's museums and other iconic landmarks. These elements are juxtaposed with other types of content, such as news regarding the government's civic operations. In addition, regional activities are posted on the site. A case in point is information about the cycling routes that traverse the polity. Highlighting the website's local nature, this information appears in Italian even on the English version. Last but not least, Vatican City's religious significance permeates the entire website. For example, the section on the Vatican gardens notes that they were re-designed in accordance with the historic *Laudato Si'* encyclical of 2015 (Gori 2019). While vaticanstate.va is a place-centric outlet, the official website of the Holy See revolves around a particular figure.

Observing this website, we contend that it works on a dualistic format. One that involves contradictory orientations such as the sacred and the profane, the global and the local, and between its independence as a sovereign state versus that of its being part of an outreaching space that traverses geo-political boundaries and "belongs" to all Catholics. Mixed orientations that enable a sense of a vital state with governmental operations, and pragmatic activities, alongside its awe as the seat of holy activity and centre of the Catholic world.

1.3.2 *The Holy See Website*

The Holy See's website w2.vatican.va is an outlet for informing the public of the pope's current activities, public engagements, and verbal communications, all of which are presented within the historic context of this venerable institution. Upon entering the site, which is available in ten languages (including Latin), users have three principal sections to choose from: a textual repository of Francis I's communications, itineraries of his foreign trips, and medallions-cum-links with pictures of all the Church's pontiffs throughout its annals. All of these parts confirm and bolster Pope Francis's standing as the reigning successor of a celebrated dynasty.

The primary function of w2.vatican.va is to serve as a public archive for the vast majority of the Holy See's official documents (e.g., encyclicals and apostolic exhortations). In so doing, the site latently reaffirms the historical cachet of pontifical institutions. W2.vatican.va is intended to neither socially engage the public nor host theological debates. Instead, it constitutes a direct, unfiltered, and comprehensive source of Church doctrine. The site's design calls to mind an ancient stele bearing reverential inscriptions. This concept diverges from the basic idea that a website is inherently mutable. In this respect, the design is commensurate with the site's role as a dependable repository for official Catholic documents.

By hovering over a menu tab, users reveal a section titled "Abuse of Minors: The Church's Response." As opposed to the site's other parts, this one is somewhat hidden from plain view. The link offers the Church's defenders a trove of rhetorical and ethical arguments parrying the criticism levelled against the institution's handling of the sex-abuse scandal.[4]

These two websites portray the Vatican as a full-fledged state and the pope as the sole head of the entire Catholic world. In the process, they mark the Church's boundaries and underscore the authenticity of its trustees. Given these far-reaching objectives, vaticanstate.va and, all the more so, w2.vatican.va forego the internet-based-logic of highlighting the subject's popularity and catering to the masses. These findings supplement the literature on the capacity of faith-based organizations' websites to advance goals like fundraising and recruiting new members (Smith 2007). A repository of learning, w2.vatican.va conserves the Church's "great truths." Though open to one and all, it mainly serves the intellectual religious elite: clerics, theologians, and students. For instance, the elites can tap into historic pontifical teachings for the purpose of writing a sermon or essay and contemplating religious issues. The site also presents these holdings as embodiments of the faith. In effect, w2.vatican.va links between knowledge and power. While the information is accessible to both lay and clerical users, the content buttresses the authority of the Holy See *qua* the primary conveyor of the faith and the Bishop of Rome as its ultimate leader.

1.3.3 The Vatican News Website

Over the past decade, the website Vatican News (vaticannews.va) has emerged as the principal information outlet of the Holy See. Underscoring the Church's global mission, the site is currently published in thirty-three languages and purports to offer a "multilingual, multicultural, multichannel, multimedia and multidevice" experience. According to its statement of objectives, vaticannews.va is also devoted to "interpreting news and information in the light of the Gospel."[5]

The interface of vaticannews.va is reminiscent of several prominent online news outlets, foremost among them the BBC and *The New York Times* (Boczkowski 2010). According to Deuze (2003), online journalism is a distinct branch of the news industry. He posits that the digital arm is shaped by its unique technological characteristics, which have spurred on innovations in production, design, distribution, and consumption. Through its standardized language, vaticannews.va communicates adherence to journalism's code of ethics. These steps build trust and add legitimacy to the website's brand. Like many other religious media outlets, there is tension between the goals of conforming to the profession's standards and interpreting the news through a Catholic prism (Mishol-Shauli and Golan 2019). This balancing act is manifest in the selection and reportage of news items.

In all that concerns layout, the website's top-tier categories are Pope, Vatican, Church, and World. The default section, "Pope," is comprised of titled images that can be clicked for reports on papal visits, statements, and the like. This section is predicated on self-generated news reports from the Church's own news agency, which also furnishes content to external news outlets. Conversely, the "Vatican" and "Church" categories are fed by sources from both within the institution and outside news agencies. Lastly, the "World" section covers international issues that either relate directly to the bishop of Rome or pertain to some moral issue that is used to highlight Catholic values. A case in point is the article "Merkel visits Auschwitz amid rising anti-semitism" from December 2019. At any rate, the site's overriding goal is to engage Catholic believers from around the globe and link their religious activities (though not necessarily in a direct fashion) to the Holy See.

While this platform may not be the top choice for devotees wishing to engage with the Holy See, its appreciable impact and mutable content have made it an invaluable resource for the Church's top brass in all that concerns spreading orthodox ideas and addressing traditional, current, and recurrent issues. Therefore, ever more religious establishments are maintaining such outlets, to the point where they have indeed become supplements to and, in certain cases, surrogates for more traditional sources of religious information.

1.4   The Vatican and Smart Technologies

For more than a decade, there has been massive growth in the production, distribution, and quotidian use of mobile applications (apps; Fagerjord 2012). An app may be defined as a software program that is typically downloaded to a mobile device via an integrated, monopolistic outlet, like the Google Play store (Fagerjord 2015). The rise of smartphone communications has triggered a proliferation in apps. Human computer interaction (HCI) scholars have underscored the functionality of apps and have sought to pin down their technological affordances. Along with their unprecedented flexibility, efficiency, and connectivity, the fact that apps are tailored to user needs (Chang et al. 2013; Yan and Chen 2011) is responsible for their immense popularity. Not only have legions upon legions of people incorporated apps into their daily routine but they organize their lives around them, especially the data accessed through these products (Fagerjord 2012; Frizzo-Barker and Chow-White 2012). A demand that has swelled for user communication, entertainment, commerce, politics, and religion. The advent of mobile phones has revolutionized how people communicate and share information. In these fields, the cellphone has indeed become among the leading providers (LaFrance 2016). By entering the app market, religious agents endeavour to strengthen denominational affiliation, believer participation, and commitment to church policies.

In many respects, applications embody the new media's unique interactivity, mobility, abundance, and multifacetedness (Schejter and Tirosh 2016). As opposed to stationary internet-based activities like browsing and gaming, the inherent mobility of apps bridges the gap between cybernetic and offline realms. Exemplars of this phenomena are health and fitness apps (West et al. 2012) as well as GPS (Chang et al. 2013). While the assimilation of these products into everyday life is well documented, policymakers, political activists, and a mélange of devotional factors are increasingly aware of these tools' potential for mediating knowledge and advancing religious causes.

Some critics posit that apps by and large offer the same age-old devotional content in a new format (Ess 2004). In contrast, other scholars emphasize their unprecedented ability to enable devotees to run, "play" with, and in a sense control the text (Wagner 2013). An exemplar of this sort of product is scripture-related applications. As Hutchings (2014) illustrates, the YouVersion Bible app (downloaded more than 400 million times, according to the company's website) is designed to encourage devotees of all ages to study from the canon on a regular basis. A religious learning practice that is encouraged by virtue of facile access, planned routines, frequent prompts, rewards, and opportunities to enhance, personalize, and share their biblical experiences. Instead of merely reflecting traditional forms of knowledge dissemination, devotional apps offer believers a new way to acquire and share information, expose themselves to different perspectives, and generate content with others (see the ensuing chapter on religious agents). Propelled by a wide range of religious, financial, and other motives, the Church, interested parties, and tech-savvy individuals have developed many and manifold Catholic applications. For instance, one product, the Catholic App, helps users find and reach nearby Churches. In the following discussion, we will zero in on several apps that have been released by the Holy See.

1.5 The Pontifical App Landscape

The Holy See's apps are predicated on their users' imagined relation between the content and its source. More specifically, developers anticipate that as devotees-cum-learners evaluate the type (e.g., communal and denominational) and status of the acquired information, they will associate it with a particular source of knowledge. Only upon completing all these steps will the individual decide whether to trust the content.[6] To understand how the Vatican employs apps to further its spiritual and social goals,[7] we will turn our attention to a pair of Catholic apps.

1.5.1 Vatican.va

Vatican.va is part of an official line of applications that has been developed by and for the Holy See (see figure 1.4). Connected to the official website w2.vatican.va, the app touts itself as a repository of the "Papal Magisterium and the institutional information of the Apostolic See" (Google Play, accessed 17 December 2019). For the Church leadership, the development of this app has entailed a monumental effort to transfer its ideals, aesthetics, and creed to the digital realm. In order to generate an engaging and current user experience, Vatican.va adheres to the standardized interface aesthetics of apps including menus and clickable hypertexts. The app features an online crawl that leads to Pope Francis's Twitter account, a collection of his public statements (e.g., encyclicals, homilies, letters, and prayers), and a *virtual tour* of the Sistine Chapel and St Peter's Square.

By dint of this epistemic content, the app implicitly lauds the Vatican's significance. The multipronged interface leads users to different types of information: experience-based knowledge that is conveyed by means of a VR tour of holy sites; news pieces directed at literate publics on theological issues; updates on Pope Francis's agenda from his Twitter account; and a slide show of the pontiff in various encounters with followers or solitary acts of reflection (cf. his Instagram representation, a featured topic of chapter 6). In sum, the app informally disseminates religious knowledge. Vatican.va's affordances bear witness to its multiplexity, which Kahane (1997, 26–7) deems to be an informal trait. To wit, the application pitches a broad spectrum of activities that are presented as more or less equivalent in value. For this reason, the product appeals to myriad users with varying religio-cum-educational literacy levels, socio-economic backgrounds, ethnicities, and the like.

Similar to other religious apps, Vatican.va is designed to enhance the user's positive image of the Catholic Church. Moreover, this app can

Figure 1.4 |
Vatican.va homepage for
smartphone app.

also be seen as an epistemic means for fostering Catholic identity and bolstering the pope's standing as the ultimate religious authority. Vatican.va implicitly encourages believers to reflect on what Catholicism has to offer on a transnational level. This multilingual app mounts the pontiff's knowledge on the highest pedestal – veneration that is liable to turn away members of other streams or faiths. On the other hand, it enables Catholics from all across the globe to embrace their common identity. Similar to other pontifical websites and apps, Vatican.va does not welcome user comments. In so doing, the app underscores the non-negotiable superiority of the Holy See and its proclamations over the flock's opinions and attitudes.

1.5.2   Click to Pray: The Pope's Worldwide Prayer Network

Click to Pray is the official application of the pope's Worldwide Prayer Network (Apostleship of Prayer). According to its description on Google Play, the product is designed to "revolutionize praying." The app, along with its webpage and analogues on Twitter and Facebook, offers a row of socio-theological features that centre on prayer and other rituals. In many respects, Click to Pray inverts the Catholic liturgy. While eschewing brick-and-mortar houses of worship, it revisits several of the activities that are traditionally conducted in church. For brevity's sake, we will home in on the app's main components.

To begin with, Click to Pray reminds its users to pray three times a day: morning, evening, and night. Unlike the daily services in Islam and Judaism or the Catholic mass, these sessions are non-obligatory. The app's interface consists of five main menu categories: Prayer Campaigns; Pray with the Pope; Pray Every Day; Pray with The Network; and Donate. As may be inferred from this list, users are coaxed into praying with others, rather than in solitude. Moreover, they are encouraged to choose a specific holy text, with the assistance of a local parish and its clergy. Devotees are also invited to pray with the bishop of Rome himself and adopt his suggested object of prayer. For instance, the screenshot in figure 1.5 documents Francis's recommendation to pray for the "people who suffer from depression." The weekly pontiff-led service indeed attracts quite a following and is directed at major issues of the day.

Click to Pray is universalistic in the sense that its rhetoric is not geared towards any particular group but rather "every country." Likewise, the application addresses general problems, like the coronavirus. As stated in the developers' blurb on Google Play, the app invites believers to help the pope contend with "the challenges of humanity and [fulfill] the mission of the Church."[8] In so doing, Click to Pray offers a sanctioned global blueprint for rituals (one that merits a longitudinal socio-linguistic study of its own).

Another salient feature of Click to Pray is counters. For example, these meters tally the number of prayers amassed on the app *in toto*, per section, and per specific prayer, *inter alia*. This tool calls to mind displays of page visits to a website, unique views on YouTube, or "likes"

Figure 1.5 |
Click to Pray homepage
for smartphone app.

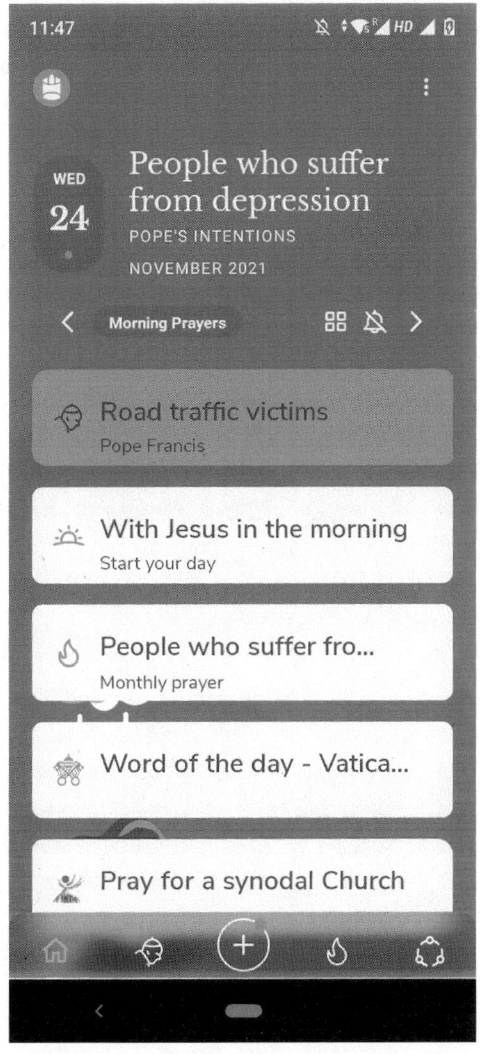

on Facebook and Instagram. The counter assigns symbolic value to
the online prayer, allowing users to gauge its popularity and signify
their own participation. In this sense, the index amplifies or constitutes a surrogate to communal prayer. While the Church deems performing mass on hallowed ground to be the most rewarding ceremony,
app-based prayers and their quantification offer an alternative ritual.
In fact, this papal app often endorses the latter as a more effective

spiritual means for approaching the divine and seeking transcendental intervention. The app indeed helps devotees *personalize their prayers* by sharing their objects of prayer with this community in the hopes that they will join in. For example, one user posted the following appeal on 23 December 2019: "Please may the relationship remain intact and the misunderstanding be positively resolved. and bless and keep the family together [*sic*]." By the time we came across this entreaty several hours after it was made public, ten users had added their own prayers. For instance, a user turned to God for help financing his son's studies.

These are all examples of a public yet individualized prayer that is conducted in a religious online forum, as opposed to a private or clergy-mediated appeal. By encouraging users to lead a service, this feature seems to cut the distance between lay believers and members of the cloth including, to some extent, the pope. In so doing, this online volitional community empowers the flock and transforms the dynamics of religious practice.

Conclusion: Catholicism beyond Catechism on Media Platforms

Investigating the Holy See's online operations, uncovers an underpinning tension that constitutes its deep structure. Much of what we know about this faith and the internet would suggest a lack of cohesion between the two. The resolutely conservative and orthodox aspects of the Catholic Church, which are grounded on age-old traditions, doctrine, and practices, stand in contrast to the young, dynamic, ephemeral, shifting, and occasionally frivolous elements of media production and consumption. However, the collaboration between the two has engendered new forms of learning, ways of praying, and globe-spanning interactions under the Vatican's purview.

In this introductory chapter, we shed light on the emergence and educational sway of Catholic new media platforms as informal avenues for socialization, communal solidarity, and global outreach. Unlike the Jesuit missionaries of yesteryear, who aspired to strengthen Christian belief through formal modes of teaching, Catholics are moving beyond the brick-and-mortar model toward mediated remote experiences. *Sacred Cyberspaces* analyzes this development through the prism of its agents' motivations, their strategic production of videos, creation of apps, and posting of images on social media, and livestreams from holy places. In so doing, we will demonstrate how new media have revitalized and re-affirmed the meaning of Catholic symbols, ideas, and precepts amid substantial setbacks for the Church, not least its plummeting attendance in Western Europe, scandals that have decimated parishioner trust, and a mass exodus in Latin America to other denominations (Lehmann 2013; Jörg et al. 2016). The book will take stock of numerous media ventures that, in aggregate, comprise the Holy See's pathway towards invigorating the Church and regaining the esprit that at this time is nearly the sole preserve of charismatic movements and televangelists.

While the embracement of new media is likely to benefit the Catholic establishment, it is also likely to trigger some unintended consequences with respect to the secular–profane divide and the borders between authentic, replicated, and superficial devotional experiences. In addition, this turn of events has unexpectedly given rise to new, increasingly formidable players on the Catholic stage.

2 The Rise of the Religious Webmaster: A Comparative Perspective

2.1 Introduction

The proliferation of new media has transformed the way religious information is disseminated. While established forms of knowledge socialization certainly persist, digital outlets offer believers instant access to a panoply of devotional content in either web or app formats. This includes religious Wiki pages, blogs, online Q&A, social media forums, and more. In effect, these frameworks are increasingly becoming popular sources of devotional learning and venues for socio-religious interaction. While these platforms tend to be anonymously run, legions of users consider them authoritative sources on matters of faith and ritual. For less established religions (e.g., Wicca, neo-Paganism, and Flying Spaghetti Monster), these platforms often serve as a hub for interactions, such as the exchange of information, a secondary authority, and a key tool for publicly representing the movement. All in all, these developments have significantly increased the sway of webmasters.

Against this backdrop, the present chapter explores the agency of ofttimes invisible content providers, editors, designers, and creators that stand behind religious new media. These faith-oriented professionals attempt to strike a balance between technological issues and religious principles. A comparative look at these factors illuminates Catholic efforts – both mainstream and oppositional – to embrace digital tools. This state of affairs leads us to the following question: How has the rise of new media technologies influenced the occupational standing of the religious webmaster? The answer to this question not only promises to enhance our understanding of these agents but also of the changes – doctrinal and otherwise – to religion in the opening decades of the third millennium.

During times of social and technological flux, the viability of numerous jobs comes under fire. Threatened by anomie, professionals undertake to consolidate their occupational tenets, praxis, and legitimacy. Nowadays, webmasters are securing a foothold in the religious world. Over the pages to come, we will unfurl the life histories of three webmasters in an effort to comprehend who are filling these important positions and how their activity is being institutionalized into a full-fledged profession.

Our case studies open a window onto how the beliefs and subjectivity of webmasters (or appmasters, as the case may be) come to expression in their social and communicative enterprise. By assaying the narratives and identifying themes that webmasters – many of whom are relatively young – relate to their missions, we hope to comprehend this innovation-driven experimentation with religiosity (on the social conditions for innovation, see Eyal 2009). Scholars have already delved into the early phases of the cyber realm. Though the internet is now at a fairly advanced stage in its development, the same cannot be said for its role as a catalyst of religious socialization. Webmasters are extemporaneously introduced or introduce themselves into their jobs. In our estimation, this constitutes a passing phase. Over the next few decades, institutionalized tracks will emerge for the qualification and job placement of religious webmasters. Against this backdrop, the present chapter is a time capsule of sorts, documenting the trailblazing spirit of webmasters and their professional outlooks. We also hope to chronicle the grassroots emergence of these specialists, which stands in contrast to the top-down genesis of the internet (Danet 2001, 43).

With these objectives in mind, the ensuing discussion will place the spotlight on three case studies. Rather than measuring the size of the religious webmasters' "guild" or the scope of its activities, we will expose the qualitative aspects of this vocation. Drawing on numerous data sets, the research team has interviewed scores of website personnel in different fields (political, social, and religious). Our focus is on contrasting and comparing three webmasters who operate in disparate structural frameworks, all in the service of the Jewish or Christian faith. To this end, we will analyze empirical data from interviews with a Catholic webmaster in the Holy Land and two Jewish appmasters in the United States. More specifically, the chapter revolves around three new media ventures, each of which offers a different type of service (ritualistic, recreational, and educational-missionary) at disparate scales (large, small, and middling audiences). Likewise, these entrepreneurs come from different backgrounds in all that concerns technological and religious schooling as well as institutional affiliation. As such, each case represents a different profile with contrasting variables that are germane to assessing online religion.

2.2   Occupations, Professionalization and the Internet

Building on the rich literature concerning the division of labour, researchers in the sociology of professions field have long been interested in how occupations claim the status of professions and the disputes along the road to such recognition (Harper and Lawson 2003). As we shall see, occupations can be classified into groups according to the degree of monopolization over knowledge, codes of conduct (ethics), and their members' independence in the workplace.

The most distinguished professions (e.g., medicine and engineering) are informed by esoteric knowledge and complex skills, relative autonomy vis-à-vis clientele and employers, and adherence to an elaborate set of ethical-normative professional guidelines. Owing to these moral standards, these disciplines profess to serve loftier goals than mere economic self-interest (Wallace and Abbott 1990, 2). The professions are organized around systems of peerage that self-regulate members and socialize novices. Moreover, these frameworks ensure that only members can practise the vocation.

According to Etzioni (1969), these characteristics are weaker in semi-professions. Teachers, social workers, and nurses have been labelled under this heading because they depend on scientific and esoteric knowledge to a lesser degree than the above-mentioned disciplines. Furthermore, the training of practitioners in these less prestigious fields is shorter, and member conduct is generally regulated by employers, not colleagues. Professionals tend to come from upper-class backgrounds, whereas semi-professionals are often from lower

SES sectors. Lastly, marginalized groups typically work in non-professionalized jobs (e.g., on assembly lines, as strippers, and as custodians) that require no formal training, are monitored by supervisors, and lack well-developed codes of conduct (cf. Harper and Lawson collection 2003).

According to a handful of scholars, these three occupational rungs underpin the social order and are a principal component of occupational and individual identity (Becker, 1956; Harper and Lawson 2003, xiii). This identification process apparently starts during the workers' training period and continues as they strive for social acceptance and prestige. Simply put, occupational identity stands at the confluence of "who we are," "what we do" (Nelson and Irwin 2014), and what distinguishes so-called professionals from the rest (Singer 2015). Little has been written, though, about the identity of religious webmasters.

Studies on job identity have discussed how lower-status workers elevate their vocational identities, both in their own mind and the view of others. For example, Lee-Treweek (2003) shows the extent to which nurses have redefined their roles. More specifically, members of this "semi-profession" directly contravene general notions of nursing as a benevolent vocation by only performing those tasks that, in their opinion, suit or enhance their occupational identity. In other words, workers are endeavouring to gradually boost their social standing and the public image of their field. By dint of these efforts, it appears that some jobs are assuming responsibilities from more prestigious occupations. For instance, social workers and nurses might handle a few tasks that were once the sole preserve of psychologists and doctors, respectively. The jobs themselves have evolved to incorporate and accentuate some practices while masking and phasing out others. It stands to reason that technological and social developments will radically transform some vocations, render others obsolete, and create a host of new jobs. Travel agents, say, are facing stiff competition from direct-purchase options, whereas demand for web designers is booming. On the other hand, technology-driven changes in the spread of information are prompting an end to field-specific librarians, as the entire profession is shifting to internet resource guidance (cf. Nelson and Irwin 2014).

In both incremental and far-reaching changes, workers are modifying their job descriptions in the hopes of elevating their professional status. Labourers in marginalized occupations lack robust collegial systems and primarily lean on unspoken personal knowledge, rather than the arcane, formal variety. As a result, they put a premium on symbolic image building. Moreover, the duties of these workers are usually negotiated on the fly with their employers and are not bound by ethical guidelines. For example, barbers mainly hone their skills on the job and by serving as apprentices, as opposed to accredited training programs. Sela-Sheffy and Shlesinger (2008) deem translation to be a marginal occupation. Drawing heavily on Bourdieu, they accentuate the skills and symbolic capital that translators value and cultivate. To clearly distinguish elite literary translators, say, from their ordinary "commercial" counterparts, the formers adopt the identity of "artist" or "professional." As opposed to nursing with its stress on different tiers within the occupation itself, translators highlight their broad range of knowledge. However, this emphasis on personal traits and virtuosity (e.g., talent and creativity) is said to hinder the institutionalization of knowledge and the building of an effective guild.

The literature expects the proliferation of online knowledge to transform the status and social roles of professions. In Susskind and Susskind's estimation (2015), the rise of cyber outlets is whittling away at the monopoly of different vocations as exclusive gatekeepers of specialized information. The experience of physicians, attorneys, teachers, tax advisors, and architects, *inter alia*, bears witness to the erosion of professions in the digital age. With respect to social status, new media have apparently become a powerful agent for change in many, though not all, occupations. Given the desire to preserve their own social rank, the medical profession is distinguishing between offline and online consultations. Furthermore, physicians are liable to develop contempt for online information (see Mostaghimi and Crotty 2011). A few semi-professional occupations have undergone a metamorphosis. For instance, information providers, like online journalists, have shifted their ethical focus from transparency to accuracy (Singer 2015). In so doing, these practitioners have bolstered their relevance and standing as providers of a meaningful social service, especially in comparison to newspaper reporters.

Over the past four decades, the webmaster has steadily emerged as a new player on the vocational stage. As per the above-cited studies on occupations and professionalization, the webmaster's role, the field's institutionalization, and its struggle for legitimacy are still works in progress. For example, webmasters are still negotiating with the establishment over the purview of their vocation, against the backdrop of unfettered technological innovation.

2.3   The Agency of Webmasters

Webmasters can be seen as the human engine behind cybernetic platforms. While their role may have changed over the last forty years, the basic foundations of this occupation remain in place. Moreover, their sway as information brokers has only risen. In their pithy account of the webmaster's functions, Spainhour and Eckstean (2003) file this job under the heading of content provider. They also note that online platforms stand out for their reliance on texts that need to be updated on a regular basis (see Eshet-Alkalai 2004). Among the functions assigned to webmasters are content providers that write and edit HTML texts, image and interface designers, programmers that are comfortable using state-of-the-art software and programming languages (e.g., Java), and administrators charged with maintaining servers around the clock. In short, webmasters produce new content, safeguard sensitive information, and orchestrate the entire cybernetic process.

These clearly delineated activities notwithstanding, webmasters' socio-cultural functions are often vague. Are they behind-the-scenes technicians who simply facilitate web activity or major players that serve as innovators, entrepreneurs, and gatekeepers of information? A host of studies concentrate on the final outcomes of webmasters' enterprise, such as webpages and online games, or user activity – forum threads, postings, and the like – that they have laid the groundwork for. That said, relatively few scholars have addressed the background, gospel, and comportment of these same workers, especially in religious frameworks. Our findings demonstrate that webmasters serve in the following capacities:

Producers. Webmasters are prime catalysts of user text production. In many instances, they are also the primary writers themselves. An illustrative example is the role of blogger.

Gatekeepers that monitor, vet, and lubricate the flow of
information.

Institutional Agents. Quite a few webmasters represent a large
body, such as government ministries, third sector NGOs, and
religious movements.

As technicians, webmasters ensure the smooth functioning
of information outlets, primarily in terms of software
management and, to a lesser extent, hardware operation.

This list attests to the fact that webmasters are increasingly serving as
cultural agents and wear a number of different occupational hats. Most
researchers stress their gatekeeping duties (Beard and Olsen 1999),
namely as active yet anonymous information brokers that evaluate and
select images, comments, and other media content. Although companies scrutinize the hiring of their gatekeepers (e.g., newspaper editors or
marketing strategists) and lay down institutional guidelines for their
conduct, Shoemaker and Vos (2009) note that it is the employees who
ultimately make the influential day-to-day decisions. A skilled information gatekeeper is capable of representing the organization's values,
while creatively adapting its identity to various developments. In mass
media organizations, Berkowitz (1990) and McNelly (1959) claim,
gatekeeping is not a personalized task but a collective effort. Often-
times, this process constitutes an informal renegotiation of an organization's value system and discourse. Not surprisingly, gatekeepers have
a marked impact on their company's identity. Encouraging further research on this topic, McNelly considers gatekeeping an inter-subjective
and potentially creative undertaking that sits at the intersection of different levels of decision-making autonomy. In the cyber realm, there
are myriad opportunities for anonymous and non-supervised forms of
gatekeeping. Therefore, webmasters frequently wield quite a bit of discretion and are seemingly less answerable for their deeds than conven-
tional gatekeepers. The launching of new empirical studies promises
to shed further light on the modes of information brokerage that are
emerging from organizational power relations.

Shaw (1998) explored webmasters' decision making through the lens
of their views on privacy. Although this power ultimately rests with
the webmaster, his or her decision is swayed by what can be termed

an ethical "negotiative process of communication" involving various players both within and outside (e.g., web users) the organization. Moreover, these specialists take into account their perceived relationship with the targeted collective or group. Although Shaw underscores the webmasters' internal processes, he also stakes stock of information flows in which gatekeepers defend the users' key interests. While this description accentuates the more functional and perhaps technical aspects of a webmaster's job, it also includes pushing an agenda as well as the creation and management of content.

The webmaster's role should be understood in light of the new professional conventions that are taking shape amid the far-reaching changes presently roiling the job market. According to Susskind and Susskind (2015), a handful of occupations appear to be in decline (e.g., travel agents), and others (doctors, teachers, and engineers, *inter alia*) are renegotiating their positions. Some fields are completely altering their occupational practices. For example, librarians are transforming themselves into information experts. Reviewing articles in the popular and trade literature from a socio-historical perspective, Beard and Olsen (1999) break down the webmaster's responsibilities and daily activities. Between the early 1970s and early 1980s, they claim, webmasters served primarily as "screen editors" – video-screen text specialists that combined a working knowledge of contemporaneous journalistic standards with a familiarity of databases, computer technology, and graphics. These skills enabled them to file topical information into digital databases. Besides serving as so-called "videotex system operators (vso)," the early webmaster's job description included the responsibilities of primary publishers of banking information, breaking news, developments in marketing, and the like (Aumente 1987, 15). Technological advances transformed the job specifications of this emergent profession. More specifically, webmasters expanded into other fields of knowledge and know-how: content selection, graphic design, information gathering, providing updates, and the management of limited organizational resources under executive and media-related pressures.

In the hopes of elucidating the professional identities and activities of Catholic webmasters, we will compare the latter to their peers in other faith-based groups. The credal and functional peculiarities of any religious collective is liable to hinder the profiling of specific webmasters. Due to a larger set of classifying principles and contexts that have yet to be explored, these oddities can potentially cloud a researcher's impressions of a new media professional's operations. In any event, a comparison is bound to help us assess the Catholic new media professionals' vision and endeavours as well as their social representation in the Church's mediascape. As such, a plethora of case studies ranging from Catholic subjects to those from other denominations and faiths is likely to explicate the motivations, goals, and viewpoints that animate the webmasters under review.

By dint of a generalizing life-stories approach and identical guidelines for all questions, we endeavoured to elucidate new media professionals' functions and social standing. This effort required a sizable comparative framework to investigate the "lived (digital) religion" of various communities. Given the limited scope of this book, we sufficed with Catholic and Jewish subjects. While the former open a window onto the contemporary enterprise of webmasters (a topic expanded on in later chapters), our fieldwork on Jewish appmasters exposed the dynamic process of creating surrogate forms of devotional praxis.

From the standpoint of dogma, Jewish tradition centres on religious practice (Cohen, Siegel, and Rozin 2003). Alongside *halakha* (Jewish law), praxis has long served as the ballast for Jews' lifestyle and observance. These activities run the gamut from minute personal blessings to large-scale communal rituals. For the most part, this legacy is anchored in material culture, is geographically bounded, and set to an annual cycle. All of these factors shape religio-ritualistic behaviours. These attributes of the Jewish heritage stand in stark contrast to the ephemeral, non-materialistic, and deterritorialized lineaments of digital media. While subject to unflagging objections within the ultra-Orthodox Jewish community, the emergence of the cyber realm has spurred on a flurry of new activities and has even left its mark on traditional praxis. For example, digital tools have seeped into Jewish praxis, setting the stage for online prayer, learning, and rituals as well as videos, games, apps, and digital simulations, *inter alia*, that facilitate religious observance. Against this backdrop, scholars have explored user conduct and the efforts of new media developers and webmasters to adapt offline conventions to the cyber world. These sorts of modifications are abundant and rather extreme in the Jewish webosphere, to the point of exemplifying the characteristics of webmaster activities. In turn, we undertook to establish those attributes that pertain to the identity, objectives, and motives behind the online activities of religious, as opposed to profane, new media professionals. These steps promise to illumine the role of the Catholic agents and the possible tracks that pave the future of their vocation.

2.4   Streamlining Rituals through Commercial Apps: Religious Purity and Smart Technologies

2.4.1   *Ta'hara, Religious Mediation, and IT*

Whereas some observant webmasters preside over information outlets or develop tools for religious learning, some concentrate on ritualistic elements. Within the latter category are websites and apps that support, monitor, or facilitate the performance of a rite. One example of support is the provision of instructions or explanations for ritualistic procedures, such as the information provided by the Buddhist Walking Meditation app (see Wagner and Accardo 2015, 144). User monitoring or watching of ceremonies is enabled via livestreaming or uploading videos (see chapter 5 herein). Lastly, rites are being facilitated by initiatives that are entirely online, like the Anglican Cathedral on the cyber video game Second Life (Hutchings 2017), the performance of various Wicca customs (Radde-Antweiler 2006), and a "portable" Buddhist altar (Wagner and Accardo 2015).

While previous studies (Campbell 2005; Wagner 2012) have discussed the online/offline dimensions of rituals, the literature has yet to weigh in on the doubts that are being raised as to the legitimacy of the cyber variety. Our first case study illustrates how an app can improve a ritual, or the performances thereof, by helping users approach what Otto dubbed the transcendental "numinous" (1916 [1958]). This example revolves around an app that was developed for the rite of *ta'hara* (carnal purity).

Before we expand on this app, let us survey the rules of *ta'hara* and many of the developments in this field. A *mikveh* is a bath in which Jews immerse themselves to restore a state of corporeal purity. While ultra-Orthodox men seldom go to *mikvehs*, their female counterparts

Figure 2.1 | Thread exploring the question of algorithmic indication of female eligibility for mikvah immersion – Forum on Parenting and Family, Kipa, 2014.

generally visit this institution on a monthly basis, following menstruation. Contact with menstrual blood is deemed to be contaminating. In order to resume marital relations after such a discharge, an observant woman must perform ablutions in a ritual bath. Figuring out exactly when to perform this dictate is a complicated step that often involves advice from experts, traditionally a rabbi's wife (*rebitzen*) or, for the past few decades, *yoatzot* (female *halakhic* advisors). Not-for-profit organizations, such as Nishmat, offer this service online (http://www.yoatzot.org/home). Though even observant women are ambivalent about this halakha (Hartman and Marmon 2004), several apps have recently been developed to facilitate its observance. We found six products of this sort on Play and Apple's App Store.

In the parenting and family forum of Kipa, a popular Israeli website for modern Orthodox Jews, a user posted an opinion in the summer of 2014 on whether a lay Jew can resolve a *halakhic* matter via an app without the intercession of a flesh-and-blood rabbi (see figure 2.1).

It appears that these "purity apps" are capable of algorithmically determining the user's status along the menstruation cycle in the absence of a physical check-up with a rabbi. At face value, determining a woman's menstruation cycle is no more complicated than, say, an automatic driving system identifying traffic signs. In fact, it is reasonable to assume that such algorithms are more reliable than a human expert. However, as the commenter noted, if the rabbi has "the assistance of the heavens" (*siyata di-shmaya*) and the algorithm doesn't, "we are liable" to find ourselves "standing before a broken water trough" if we rely solely on an app. While quite a few of the participants in the Kipa thread shared this view, most of them emphasized the strength of technological-cum-communicative means vis-à-vis human authority figures.

While popular attitudes toward cybernetic *ta'hara* products are beyond the scope of this book, our discussions with informants revealed an on-going debate over this issue within the Israeli and American modern-Orthodox community. Many observant Jews photograph women's undergarments and forward them to *yoatzot* for the sake of determining ablution eligibility. Furthermore, technologies are used to ensure that *mikveh* water simulates its natural properties in accordance to the precept of *mayim ḥayim* ("living water"). Likewise, YouTube ads and websites (e.g., https://bit.ly/2M44G9l) highlight advances that have improved the amenities at *mikveh* facilities (heating the rooms and baths) and streamlined the purification process itself.

In sum, the Jewish community has endeavoured to improve this sensitive rite via WhatsApp communications, websites, and algorithmic apps. Moreover, we have discerned four areas in which the related practices have been modernized: feminization, professionalization, cybernetization, and scientification. With respect to the first, there is an uptick in the participation of women in all that concerns the supervision, preparations for, and execution of this rite. A case in point is the rise of *yoatzot* as accepted religious authorities. The emergence of these female advisers also signifies the "professionalization" of *ta'hara*. More specifically, there is a division of labour between these consultations and the rabbis, as the former are viewed as specialists in obscure fields of knowledge. In addition, the *yoatzot*'s input complements the role of the *mikveh* attendant (*balanit*). The "cybernetization" of this rite involves the use of tools to pare down human intervention and maximize the woman's comfort and privacy. Lastly, "scientification" refers to the introduction or machine use and scientific-cum-rational principles (in the Weberian sense of the word) as opposed to traditional modes of observance.

2.4.2 The MikvahCalendar App

As noted, the *ta'hara* (purity) rite is being modernized through the development of computer programs and smartphone apps that are designed to help users perform the attendant steps. Smart technologies often involve a process of functional hybridization in which an IT feature (usually a communicative one) merges with a social, educational, and/or entertainment activity. With respect to devotional apps, the convergence of technology and the sublime fuels tensions over the legitimacy of facilitating a rite with IT. To grasp this synthesis between tradition and cutting-edge technologies, we have delved into the process of creating and running a *ta'hara* app by examining a product of this sort that was developed by a religious-cum-commercial app entrepreneur by the name of Rachel. This application features a high level of customization for a handful of Jewish practices and the individual user's biological clock. In addition, the product offers direct engagement with religious experts.

In our interview with Rachel, she discussed her Jewish background and technological proclivities:

I grew up in North Carolina, where my family wasn't religious; but we became more religious through Chabad [a Jewish ultra-Orthodox group that is heavily involved in outreach]. There was no actual Orthodox *shul* (synagogue) [where we lived]. So after a few months, my parents found [the local chapter of] Chabad … [which] had a little *shul* in their garage. We still drove to *shul* and didn't keep kosher or anything, but that is where they got to meet people. It [i.e., our home] was actually [located in] the heart of the Bible Belt – North Carolina. There are churches everywhere, and there weren't that many Jews. And when I was about seven, my parents were very worried [about my upbringing] and didn't know what it even meant to be Jewish.

Figure 2.2 |
The MikvahCalendar.com
app.

As a child, then, Rachel's family was not overly religious. Notwithstanding the miniscule Jewish population in their area, her parents displayed an affinity for Jewishness. The family's isolation may have heightened Rachel's appreciation for workarounds that accommodate believers who are detached from co-religionists. Alongside a growing interest in Judaism, Rachel displayed a talent for computing:

> I went to a college prep school, where I was always very good
> at math and science. I actually went to Carnegie Mellon for a
> science camp in the summer. And that is maybe why I started
> [down] the track of computer science. I first started working
> on this [purity app] with someone that I went to MIT with …

[W]e first started with a website, and we had that going for four years. At the beginning of 2012, we came out with the app. First, we came out with the mobile site, then we came out with the apps.

Rachel continued to develop the product:

I was speaking to some people who had become newly observant, and they mentioned [that] "I wish there was some sort of computer program that you can just type in my date and I'd have everything calculated for me." And I'm like "This is such a smart idea." I also thought of my mother a lot because my mother had become religious later in life. And she did not know a lot about how to calculate things; there wasn't anyone [to guide her along]; she never really took classes, and she is not so computer literate either. So my goal was … for newly observants [*sic*] to be able to very easily click their dates and times and everything would be automatic for them … They would be able to [perform the relevant commandments] without any instructions, without being computer literate.

As a "newly observant" Jew, Rachel comprehended the benefits of a program or app that is simple to use and easily accessible to co-religionists interested in maintaining a religious lifestyle. In her view, an app can offset a hole in Toranic knowledge and guidance. This situation tends to characterize isolated devotees that maintain an ongoing, if sporadic, engagement with a faith-based community and have limited access to formal religious education.

2.4.3 *MikvahCalendar's Affordances and Sources of Legitimacy*

In Rachel's estimation, MikvahCalendar is a highly accessible and affordable product designed for practising Jewish women:

The app is free, and then what happens is, after, like, you use the app … or the website for 2 months … a subscription [kicks in, and] you can continue to get the reminder [about your menstrual cycle], the Email the Rabbi feature, and everything that we offer … [for] only $18 a year, which is cheaper than a paper calendar that people used to buy to keep track of everything themselves. So they get text reminders all over the world, and they get their emails, they even get an ovulation reminder, which a lot of people find very helpful … There are even some people that are not even Jewish, but they asked us if they could use the program because we are so specific. I guess more than most other companies, we keep track of these cycles most specifically [i.e., precisely]. They find it very helpful to take [their accumulated information] to the doctors. [If] … you press an email icon from the App or the Website, […] you can get … your entire history by email. You can also print your entire history of when your periods started, when it happens, the interval between them, like when you had your pregnancy. Every single thing will be in [our report].

In the preceding excerpt, Rachel enumerated MikvahCalendar's features. The product draws its legitimacy from authoritative religious, scientific, and lifestyle sources. In terms of observance, the app possesses various functions that help customers adhere to halakha. Scientifically speaking, MikvahCalendar keeps track of menstrual cycles and pregnancies. Rachel even told us that non-Jewish users have signed up primarily on account of these reports. From a lifestyle perspective, online and mobile activities are pillars of the daily modern existence. App use, creating personalized databases, retrieving information, and sharing this data (with doctors and the like) are all part and parcel of the individual routine in the cyber age. Rachel integrates these lifestyle issues into her account, contrasting the MikvahCalendar experience to that of an outdated "paper calendar."

Expanding on the app's religious legitimation, Rachel shared positive responses to the app from experts in the field:

I mean we get feedback from rabbis and *rebetzins* [the said clergymen's wives] all the time saying that they recommend it [i.e., MikvahCalendar] to their whole communities. I don't know, but I see *rebetzins* that do recommend us, and there are people now that are asking me to come and give talks about it. I've gone like [to communities all] around Florida … [W]hen they get their *mikvah* classes, […] I come; everybody gets blown away [by] what you can get so easily.

Besides the above-mentioned *yoatzot*, rabbis' wives (*rebetzins*) traditionally counsel women on female issues. Drawing from the cachet of their husbands, the *rebetzins'* advice also bolsters the rabbinate's influence. Rachel says that MikvahCalendar has impressed both experts and laywomen alike.

The appmaster also claims that the information provided by her product is superior to that of established figures. Some women who avail themselves of long-standing means to estimate the date of their next period have been well off the mark:

We even had an email from someone who was like, I'm not going to mention any specifics, but … she was an expert in *ta'harat ha-mishpacha* [family purity laws], like these people that other people call … And she thought that we had calculated something wrong. So I got really scared when I saw this one. Like most of all, I was scared of her because she is such an expert. So [I looked into the matter] … and it was … a very obscure halakha. When I told her, she was like "Oh My Gosh, I forgot about that."

Rachel stresses how MikvahCalendar enables users to uphold the laws of purity with as much, if not greater, precision than traditional means. The app's mechanical and pre-programmed functions indeed seem to be an improvement over time-tested human methods. In one incident, her product even took into consideration an arcane law that one of the traditional mavens overlooked.

To conclude, MikvahCalendar combines venerable ideals and practices with a modern ethos. Building on respected sources, the app is viewed as a reliable secondary authority that both complements and competes with the knowledge and leadership of halakha experts. Rachel offers a pathway to piety by helping Jewish women fulfill a key monthly rite using a comprehensive set of tools and services. In this respect, MikvahCalendar diverges sharply from our next case study.

2.5   iShofar: Mimicking Religious Praxis via Recreational Apps

Whereas some religious apps and websites focus on core devotional activities (e.g., prayer, meditation, and canonical studies), iShofar ludically mimics a cherished ritual. On the Jewish New Year and the Day of Atonement, Jews the world over sound the shofar – a liturgical instrument comprised of a hollowed out ram's horn. The iShofar app is mainly downloaded and used in the run-up to these holidays, which fall out in the late summer or early fall.

This mobile app, which some of our interviewees described as a "novelty," simulates the blowing and customary peals of the shofar. The Cambridge online dictionary provides three definitions of novelty: "the quality of being new and unusual," "something that has not been experienced before and so is interesting," and "a cheap unusual object such as a small toy, often given as a present." iShofar indeed contains elements of all three definitions. For pious Jews, using this sort of cyber gizmo is by no means intended to replace any traditional customs. At any rate, iShofar's appeal perhaps rests in its whimsical novelty: an unfamiliar experience that mimics a well-known practice. Like the majority of apps, this product is free of charge and readily accessible. Similar to other smart technologies, iShofar is an amalgam of carefree and educational activities.

Over the past two decades, the app's creator, Scott (a pseudonym), has been developing mobile operating systems at one of the leading web service providers – a company that is regarded as a pioneer of the internet. For Scott, iShofar is a hobby. To understand the social circumstances that led him to enter the Jewish app market, we will reflect on the innovator's personal upbringing, education, and professional background.

Raised in the greater San Francisco area, Scott told us about his childhood in a Jewish Conservative environment. From nursery to the end of high school, he studied Judaism in informal and extracurricular frameworks. Thereafter, Scott was active in Hillel – a nation-wide Jewish student organization – throughout college and visited Israel within the framework of Birthright (a program aimed at strengthening the bond of young Jewish Americans with Israel). As is the case for many progressive Jews in the United States, he is enmeshed in a negotiative liminal state between the rigors of *halakha* and a modern-liberal

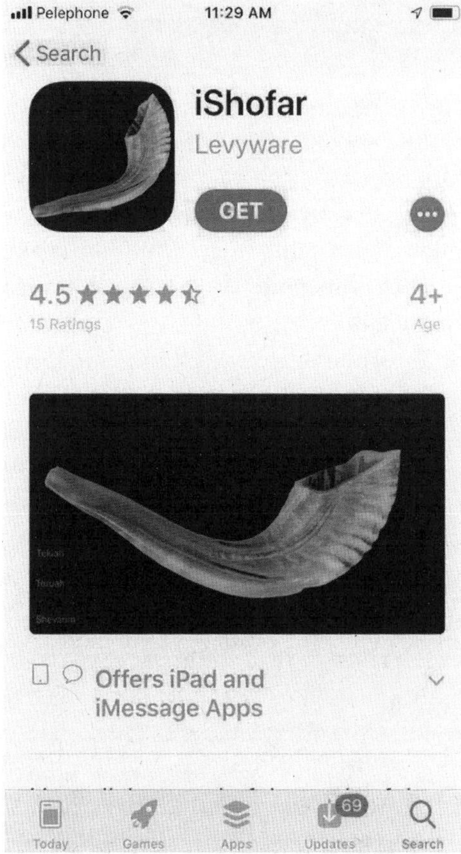

Figure 2.3 | iShofar presentation on the App Store.

outlook. For instance, Scott does not always abide by the laws of Kashrut but is keenly aware of his dietary infractions. Moreover, his family has experienced intermarriage – a situation that challenges his Jewish identity. Scott also has few Jewish friends that he is in regular contact with. In retrospect, all these factors have apparently inspired him to find outlooks for his deep-rooted yet teetering Jewish sensibilities.

From a professional standpoint, Scott's profile renders him a typical denizen of the Silicon Valley. Recounting his career path, the appmaster fondly remembers instances from his young adulthood back in the 1990s where he remodelled existing products to fit his entertainment and cultural tastes. In the following excerpt, Scott describes his early fascination with technology:

I was always trying to push technology to the limit. I guess one good example is when, not too long after high school, I built this mp3 device in my car because it's so cumbersome to bring CDs into the car. They get scratched up, and it's impossible to change them unless you have a CD changer. So, I took several computer scraps, attached an old Pentium motherboard to a 4-gigabyte hard drive, loaded all my mp3s, and stuffed it under my car seat. You would step into this junky car and see all of this futuristic equipment.

This ethos of improvisation is reminiscent of the stories of early high-tech entrepreneurs or the hacker-cyberpunk culture, which is captured in David Kaplan's *The Silicon Boys* (2000) and a number of popular films (e.g., *The Social Network*, 2010 or *Jobs*, 2013). All these works depict major Silicon Valley figures as youth who were fascinated with technology and driven to break the mould. This narrative stands in contrast to present-day career paths in which employees gradually climb their way up the rigid corporate ladder. Be that as it may, Scott's career is not entirely a tale of socialization. Upon graduating from the computer studies program of a respectable university, he studied Mandarin and took classes in China. At that point, he entered the corporate world of high tech. His profile on LinkedIn includes the following statement: "I have always had a passion for mobile devices and love to observe how people use them in their daily lives for entertainment, productivity, and social networking. No matter where I am or what I'm doing, trying to change how mobile devices can improve, not hinder, our daily lives is always on my mind." Though one goal of LinkedIn profiles is to attract corporate headhunters, this proclamation reinforces his zeal for advancing IT as well as the correlation he draws between technology and the public good.

When the first iPhone was released, Scott was working on PC platforms. Soon after, he was offered a job developing applications for the emergent app store platform. Scott reluctantly agreed to take the plunge and ended up having a successful career in this cutting-edge field.

Given his passion for technology and religious background, Scott's interest in developing a Jewish app should come as no surprise. While Wagner (2013) demonstrates that religious apps are increasingly facili-

Figure 2.4 (*above*) |
Activation instructions for the iShofar app.

Figure 2.5 (*left*) |
App credits: publishing personal acknowledgments.

tating the construction of user identity, our subjected manifested his own "authentic" self through the creation of iShofar:

> I think people get some kind of Jewish feeling from the app because the Shofar is definitely hard to play. I think it was for Hannukah, when I was younger, I told my parents that it would be fun to have one, so they gave me a shofar. And after that, every year for the high holidays I would play it at our synagogue. I was the one to blow the shofar, and my first app was the shofar-app. I was trying to look for something to develop, but I didn't want to develop anything that was too complex; I just wanted to get one thing out the door, get the feel for the whole workflow from development to publishing the app. And we were coming close to the High Holidays. I got the idea from an app that had been really popular called Ocarina. You can find it in the App Store. It's pretty amazing; it's an instrument app; it really captures the essence.

Scott discusses his rewarding experience of blowing the Shofar before the congregation on the High Holidays, which may be compared to his subsequent yearning to display his technological skills by creating the app under review. The power of this tool, the developer claims, is its ability to give those who have not mastered the Shofar a feel for this liturgical instrument. Not only does iShofar recreate the sound, he argues, but more importantly captures "its essence." As in the Ocarina app, the user plays the virtual instrument through bodily engagement (pressing keys or blowing). By means of simulation, users experience the corporeal sensation of playing a real instrument.

2.6   Conclusions on iShofar and Its Appmaster

Reflecting on Scott's experience with the development of iShofar, much of his venture can be interpreted as a technological-cum-entrepreneurial response to the macroscopic conundrum of American Jewry. More specifically, the literature often describes this community as grappling with significant cultural, social, and institutional tensions. Intermarriage, the waning influence of venerable Jewish institutions, the sagging affiliation of young adults, and the increased emphasis of millennials on the quest for meaning and purpose at the expense of primordial bonds – all these developments point to far-reaching changes in American Jewish life. In an effort to buck these trends, the community has turned to formal schooling and informal extracurricular activities. Within these frameworks, American Jewish leaders have also endeavoured to strengthen young members' bonds with the State of Israel as a spiritual or national centre (Cohen 2014; Waxman 2010; Cohen and Kelman 2010). While the impetus behind iShofar derives from its founder's nostalgia for and affinity towards Judaism, his daily life somewhat distances him from these sentiments. Scott's ritualistic app can be seen in the light of this growing concern among both Jewish intellectuals and leaders. In other chapters, we have dissected religious outreach campaigns that revolve around videos, livestreaming, Instagram, and other new media platforms. Scott also endeavours, at least in part, to address the problem of communal disengagement.

Whereas religious institutions tend to address these sorts of challenges by formal pedagogical steps that demand an intellectual or ritualistic exertion out of devotees, Scott has devised a more experiential, playful approach involving meagre user engagement. The notion of blowing into an iPhone to emit a liturgical peal regularly induces a chuckle out of users. YouTube commercials and internet memes also utilize playfulness as a means of disseminating political, economic, or social ideas (Shifman 2014; Danet 2001). The integration of humour into religious apps may be unconventional, but the frisson triggered by this light touch attests to the socialization prowess that undergirds the iShofar enterprise.

Scott clearly fuses his Jewishness with his identity as a skilled programmer. Beyond the app's patently Jewish subject matter, he takes pride in its development and regularly tracks its download count. His stated target audience is comprised of young progressive Jews – a loosely networked group to which he himself belongs. While Scott is a professional software developer, his religious app endeavour is but a hobby (*not* only a pastime). Though clearly an expert in IT, our subject's religious devotion is somewhat lax. By virtue of his programming skills, Scott has found a way to participate in the Jewish world despite his limited core knowledge about the faith and its institutions.

iShofar hardly constitutes a breakthrough from either a technological or devotional standpoint (cf. other digital routes to professionalism; Golan and Babis, 2019). Hence, the app does not command any "hard" authority. This novelty item merely offers a soft approach to bolstering Jewish identity.

2.7   Proselytization through Webmastery

2.7.1   *Augmenting Traditional Modes of Outreach*

Religious webmasters are highly invested in proselytization. On the one hand, they wish to shore up their co-religionists' devotion. On the other, they encourage people from outside the denomination or faith to learn about their belief system, with the ultimate goal of securing their conversion. While scholars have already noted the emergence of the religious webmaster (see the case of Chabad, Golan 2013), Catholicism has only recently begun to evangelize online.

In this section, we will place the spotlight on the Christian Media Center (CMC). Comprised of members of the Franciscan Order and the Canção Nova community, the mandate of this organization is to advance the Catholic interpretation of the Holy Land. As discussed in chapter 3, the CMC is videoing and livestreaming events from various canonical sites in Israel/Palestine. To understand the motivation behind this venture, we will home in on the case of Father Carlos (pseudonym). An ordained priest in his early thirties from Pernambuco, Brazil, Carlos now resides in the Holy Land and is a member of the CMC team. In our conversations with this missionary, Father Carlos revealed his circuitous journey to the priesthood:

> I found our community [the Canção Nova] through my friends. I was returning to the Church because when I was a child, I had been … [a member of a Catholic parish], but after … many things happened, and I was far from God and also far from the Church and … the most important things for life. So, through this group and these friends, I found [the Catholic faith] again with the Canção Nova community. After one year and a half, I discovered also my vocation: that God has chosen me to be a

priest. This is a vocation; we say this in our community: a vocation is like a map. Where do you want to go? If I don't know how to go there, I need a map. If we can use another word, in our days, we would use the word GPS [he laughs]. A GPS, when you need to go somewhere.

Like Rachel and Scott, Father Carlos describes a religiously ambiguous childhood. During his early years, he intermittently drew closer and disengaged from the community, observance, and possibly even belief in God. However, Carlos came full circle, as he now embraces a monastic lifestyle. Drawing on the technological metaphor of GPS, his sacerdotal role clearly orients his pious route.

Father Carlos then expounds on the link between technology and Canção Nova's objectives:

Our founder [Monsignor Jonas Abib] thought of a community like this, like the Church. Because in the Church you have everything. You have priests, you have sisters, nuns, you have families, you have also single people. You have also celibate [members], you have every kind of people. What is the mission of Canção Nova? The mission of Canção Nova is to show the face of Jesus and the new life that he brought. This is our mission. The way – any person could do this – might be different, but every one of us has the same mission. For example, Gabriele [pseudonym] is an expert in internet and computers. He helps us in doing this work, he is helping us to show this face of Jesus to the world. If I have some problems with my computer, for example, and I can't evangelize through Facebook, YouTube … He helps me; he is doing the mission with me.

For our subject, Canção Nova's mission is strongly tied to its members' shared sense of purpose as well as their utilization of social media in an effort to replicate and disseminate "the face of Jesus." Put differently, devotional content is spread to believers and interested parties via social networks. New media allows the mission to transcend the physical confines of the parish. A sign of the times, Father Carlos asserts that social networks are of utmost relevance to his outreach program:

The first thing, if you think a little bit [of] what [it] means to have today, for example, the Bible in our hands. It means that those people, the Apostles, for example, and the others who were with them, they thought [of] a way to register the things, to copy them, and to make the things they lived with Jesus arrive, reach other people. At that time, they didn't have the internet or television or … radio, for example, but they had the papers, writing the things, making copies; and they used their technology – the technology of that age – to spread the Gospel. Day by day, year by year, century by century, this message arrived. And now it is here. Today the Holy Spirit, the Church, they continue using the technologies. They continue using the ways to make this connection with the people, no matter if they are near, from the same place, but the message could arrive to them in any place. Saying things through this microphone [he points at a microphone for recording the voice-overs] and showing something through the camera – the good things of life – is a grace for me, is something which makes me happy, especially because I am making other people happy. And today, this opportunity through the media … internet, television, radio, or other things to make the Gospel arrive to the people and make them happy is, for me, special because … what is the Gospel? The Gospel is that thing you have the right to receive. So, through this way – the media – we can say to everyone: "You can take it; this is for you."

As per Father Carlos's outlook, technologies come and go, but their legitimate function as outlets for spreading the faith has been a constant throughout the annals of the Church. This idea validates the Canção Nova's media campaigns and its webmasters, who the priest believes are essentially following in the Apostles' footsteps. Moreover, Carlos champions the idea that the scriptures are not the sole preserve of the religious elite but also belong to the population at large. For this reason, his movement's webmasters provide the masses access to these texts.

Father Carlos further elaborates on his religio-educational work with the public:

Many many people in our world unfortunately cannot come here [to the Holy Land]. Many many things can block them, but with this evangelization we can make them arrive here. This is really beautiful, this power of the mass media: make you arrive in a place where you couldn't arrive. So, for example, people in Brazil, USA, Italia … they go into the Church [of the Holy Sepulchre], they go into the [Milk] Grotto, the cave [and other sacred venues]. Many times in my comments I tell them: "Now, let's go in this procession and … pray inside the cave where Mary received the announcement from the angel Gabriel." I am putting the people with them, with the priests, with the seminarists, with the procession. And also during the communion, when people are receiving Jesus in the sacred communion, I used to say: "With the feet of your heart, go into this procession and receive the communion from the priest and say your Amen." Of course, it is a spiritual experience: not here, I am not touching the priest or the altar, no, but through the mass media we can share, we can promote this experience to them.

Father Carlos roughly equates the online experience to that of boots-on-the-ground pilgrims. In so doing, he underscores his own role as an agent charged with streaming ceremonies performed at a holy venue to online audiences. By interspersing voice-overs, Carlos involves remote viewers in the proceedings. In other words, online believers are invited to join on-site attendees at sacred events as they unfold.

The Brazilian missionary also places the religious webmasters' enterprise in a larger context:

What is history? History is not just something that happened, but also something that is happening. When I arrived in our community, Canção Nova, I read a book about our history. When I finished that book, I thought "Ok, now I know what is Canção Nova because here I have read all the history." But after, when I arrived here, in the Holy Land, I discovered that I was wrong. I hadn't read our history because our history is continuing in my life. With my life, God is also writing our history. Today, for example, doing this kind of things, we are building the history. And of course, I believe that in the future people will say: "Ah, we began like this" or "They began through the internet or television."

In this passage, Father Carlos describes himself as a pioneering innovator. Additionally, the clergyman identifies the present era as one of change, in which it is incumbent upon the webmasters to facilitate this transition to a new chapter in the history of the Catholic Church. In fact, he envisions a time when people will look back at Canção Nova's media campaign as an endeavour that ushered in a new wave of spirituality.

To conclude, the Christian Media Center's work demonstrates how the agency of religious webmasters comes to expression in, among other things, outreach missions. While proselytization is a shared goal of all Christian clergy, Father Carlos has devised his own strategy in which live voice-over commentary of streamed rites delivers information to and links remote publics with canonical sites. This outreach is integrated into a community effort that is steered by an institutional arm. Whereas the sermons of televangelists are meant to spark reform and/or reinterpret basic Christian tenets, the videos under review (livestreamed and otherwise) have no intention of breaking the mould. Under the Vatican's guidance and in accordance with its teachings, the CMC's webmasters undertake to promote the Church's established worldview.

2.7.2 Discussion and Conclusion

The focal point of this chapter has been the agency of webmasters and how they view their religio-occupational activities in light of their personal backgrounds. More specifically, we have explicated the new media's impact on the vocational role of religious webmasters. By dint of our fieldwork and after pondering the enterprise of these specialists, the research team ascertained several key functions and characteristics of this multi-faced vocation. Religious function is essentially the proclaimed purpose of these websites or apps. However, and again, this function is obscured by the wide range of interests and aims – both transparent and otherwise – that inform the webmaster field. For

Table 2.1 | Religious webmasters by function, institutional affiliation level, and knowledge base

	Function	Target Audience	Religious Authority	Institutional Affiliation Level	Webmaster Background
iShofar	Recreational	Small scale	Independent	– –	Professional
MikvahCalendar	Ritualistic	Meso scale	Semi-independent	–	Religious/professional
CMC Web Streaming	Educational	Large scale	Dependent	+	Religious

instance, the MikvahCalendar is a for-profit venture that adheres to a comprehensive economic model. Nevertheless, the app's developer expressly stated that it was designed to streamline a Jewish rite that has a major bearing on an observant couple's life.

Target audience. This category measures the scale of the webmaster's targeted or imagined audience. Alongside the number of potential users (be it in the thousands or millions), the index also measures the depth of an app's usage and its geographical (local to international) scope.

Religious authority pertains to the webmaster's relation to canonical sources (scriptural or otherwise) and clerical leaders. Our point of departure is that a stronger affinity with the establishment is likely to shore up a webmaster's reputation and his or her products, but hinder autonomy, novelty, and charismatic appeal.

Institutional level alludes to the organization, such as the Catholic Church or a think tank, that "owns" the website or app and sets the ground rules for the webmaster. Alternatively, the platform can be a bottom-up, individually driven venture.

Background refers to the connection between the webmaster's endeavours and his or her ken of knowledge, especially in IT and religious studies.

These categories help us grasp how webmasters run their operation. While having ample access to technological resources, the parameters of their enterprise is far from straightforward. Unlike other widespread platforms for religious communication (e.g., sermons or books), websites and apps are relatively new. As a result, their particular formats and conventions have yet to be fully explicated. Our findings demonstrate that new media are not necessarily inimical to organized religion. While each of the five categories is independent, together they demarcate the borders of the various online faith-based products. Not only are they defined in relation to the greater online market but correspond with the hierarchical relations, theological underpinnings, economic management, community engagement, and ritual praxis of the religious sector.

Religious webmasters' broad purview attests to their multi-faceted professional standing, as they concomitantly engage in the online market, the hi-tech community, and religious organizations. The onset of the digital era has paved the way for the new societal position of webmaster, which entails innate tensions and contradictions. In the light of the above, a webmaster's core set of practices and occupational status fill a liminal role.

2.8 Occupational Identity: Webmasters as Liminal Factors

There is a growing demand for webmasters across a wide range of sectors: government agencies, NGOs, corporations, news outlets, the leisure market (e.g., gaming outlets, personal blogs, and fan clubs), and the religious world, *inter alia*. Our findings corroborate earlier scholarship highlighting the liminality, or occupational ambiguity, of the webmaster position. Taking a page from Victor Turner's terminology, these specialists operate "between and betwixt" more established social roles. In other words, webmasters are involved in many and manifold tasks and occasionally possess contradictory impulses stemming from the dissonance between their formal training and informal learning, between the old and the new, and between their official standing within the organization and their emergent position as webmasters. A case in point is library webmasters. Since the 1990s, Kneip (2007) observes, mid-sized libraries have gradually turned their websites into important portals for academics and students. As the popularity of these sites grew, computer-savvy individuals from among the library's existing staff were often appointed webmasters, and they steadily assumed the requisite duties for this new role. Kneip indicates that the webmasters majored in a bevy of different undergraduate fields. Whereas most of these workers have a social sciences background, a minority completed degrees in the information sciences. To meet the institution's online goals, these webmasters acquired the skills they deemed to be necessary by undergoing a process of self-socialization. Given their lack of standardized training, webmasters often rely on pre-existing skills, sensibilities, personal characteristics, and attitudes (Beard and Olsen 1999). This is heavily reflected in the outlets they preside over, both in terms of gatekeeping and design. Often lacking advanced know-how and guidance in either website development or journalism, these employees face heavy workloads and often have a great deal of autonomy. In consequence, they lean on peer advice and independently devise gatekeeping routines.

This brings us back to the concept of liminality. The juggling of multiple roles enables the webmaster to tether different fields together. Likewise, his or her position at the confluence of multiple social functions animates many facets of the webmaster praxis and vocational orientation.

Scholars have long noted that rapid change imperils the durability of social roles. As a result, it behooves institutions of higher education, the state, and parents to socialize youth to be occupationally nimble (Shner 2012; Salomon 2000; Kahane 1997). All children should be exposed to technology, for this cultivates "marketable skills." The webmaster appears to be an informal vocation that draws upon multiple fields of knowledge. As a result, webmasters have outmanoeuvred elites and guild leaders occupying formidable positions that have historically leaned on professional training.

Drawing from our interviews, five elements can be said to define the religious webmaster: loosely institutionalized roles, vague occupational guidelines, access to knowledge, and a fledgling ethical code.

2.8.1 Loosely Institutionalized Roles

Since many religious apps and digital outlets are the product of *ad hoc* entrepreneurship, the overall levels of institutionalization are rather low. For instance, there is little staff work, organizational affiliations, hierarchical structures, and professional ties. This has no bearing on the function or aims of these pursuits, and it certainly does not imply an absence of organizational work, standardization, or positions that mirror and support the webmaster's duties. In contrast to bureaucrats or members of a formal religious organization, the comportment of webmasters is akin to that of volunteers at a philanthropic body or the fan clubs of sports teams.

With respect to our case studies, iShofar epitomizes the independently developed app that is devoid of institutional ties. The application conforms to the protocols and ethical guidelines of both Apple and Android, but its level of institutionalization pales in comparison to our other subjects. Owing to its *halakhic* nature, Rachel's for-profit Mikvah-Calendar app seeks out the approval of and works with rabbinical elements. Unlike iShofar, this company employs several workers and is more involved in the Jewish community. That said, MikvahCalendar competes with religious institutions that have wielded power for centuries (i.e., the rabbinate and with up-and-coming authorities, like rabbis' wives and specialized counselors (*yoatzot*). As a result, the app has earned some autonomy and functions as a quasi-institutionalized secondary form of authority on matters of female purity. In the case of the Christian Media Center's streaming operation, the degree of institutionalization is rather high, as the venture is deeply entrenched in the Canção Nova and the Franciscan Order, both of which have close ties with the Holy See. Moreover, the CMC constitutes a mid-sized organization with offices, an appreciable budget, and an ample staff (cf. Chabad.org; see, e.g., Golan 2013). Nonetheless, the centre offers a modicum of freedom to its employees, whose input is valued.

In sum, religious webmasters establish or work in loose or flexible institutional environments. This arrangement well suits the rapid technological changes underway and the internet's protean nature.

2.8.2 Semi-Professionalism: Opaque Ethical Guidelines

Researchers in the sociology of professions field have classified occupations according to their degree of knowledge monopolization, practitioner independence, and codes of conduct (ethics). The most distinguished professions (e.g., medicine and engineering) centre around esoteric knowledge and advanced skills. Relatively speaking, members of these fields enjoy a great deal of autonomy vis-à-vis their clients and employers. What is more, they are expected to adhere to an elaborate set of normative guidelines and profess to serve higher goals than mere economic self-interest (Wallace and Abbott 1990, 2). Professional associations self-govern these fields, socialize novices, and protect their members' exclusive rights to engage in these lines of work. Some vocations, like education, social work, and nursing, are considered semi-professions (Etzioni 1969), whereas assembly line workers, strippers, and custodians, to name but a few, are deemed to have occupations (Harper and Lawson 2003).

In the case of webmasters, the absence of institutionalization, training programs, ethical norms, and a well-established body of knowledge hinders the field's standing. That said, efforts are continuously being made to fill these gaps and bolster this up-and-coming profession.

2.8.3 Knowledge Holders

As noted, professions are characterized by closely held knowledge that is specific to the field. This information, which constitutes a formidable barrier of entry to the profession, can be divided into two types: *knowledge exploitation* and *knowledge exploration*. The former includes activities that draw on specific knowledge and competencies, whereas exploration refers to the pursuit of new sources of information and proficiencies (Keller and Weibler 2015).

All three of the webmasters under review – Scott, Rachel, and Carlos – lean on their religious background, technological knowledge, and media skills. Each of them unfurled personal strategies for disseminating their gospel. In our estimation, webmasters are involved in knowledge exploration, but questions of developing this resource and epistemology warrant further attention. Our case studies' main impetus (and source of legitimation) is apparently knowledge exploitation. However, they are constantly looking for new ways to engage with believers, the community, and the transcendental. This involves devising a religious practice that puts an emphasis on transcendental rewards or cultivating new means of engagement with the numinous.

For example, Father Carlos livestreams holy sites, creates pilgrimage videos, and covers the activities of high-ranking clergy. Through trial and error, webmasters assess the popularity of their work while promoting it. In other words, they develop novel approaches to sparking user interest, circulating information, and fulfilling the devotional objectives of both the individual and community at large.

2.8.4 Peer networks

A defining element of professions is collegial frameworks, which serve as, among other things, advisory and trustee boards charged with upholding the field's norms. Doctors, for example, work in different organizational settings (e.g., hospitals, schools, the military), but their main point of vocational reference is the peer network, be it a guild, a professional society, or an educational institution. With respect to religious associations, they are usually organized by some sort of network or hierarchical body. For computer experts, online colleagues serve as a major source of information, alongside their co-workers in the office. The association of religious webmasters tends to be limited, as many of them work in atomized and decentralized environments (as is the case for Scott of iShofar). Be that as it may, our findings show that these specialists are often inspired by the output of their peers and incorporate the online "templates" of the latter into their own projects. For instance, a colleague may emulate the user-interface of another's website (also known as institutional isomorphism; DiMaggio and Powell 1983). These paradigms influence the logic, the affordances, and ultimately the clout of religious websites. Much like teachers whose peer networks are divided between content and pedagogical groupings, webmasters associate themselves with both the topic of their platform, such as a medieval art site, and the field of IT in general. It appears that this duality is impeding the field's development into a semi-profession.

2.8.5 Ethical Code Construction

Professionals' commitment to clients and society at large is underwritten by ethical codes (Krogt 2007). Establishing professional values and standards – not least a body of rules – is deemed to be in the public's best interests (Crompton 1990). Apart from dictating vocational etiquette (Fournier 1999), these codes improve the aptitude of the profession's members (Evetts 2003; 2011; Freidson 1994; Sullivan 2000).

As far as can be seen, ethics derive from religion. This background is amplified in all that concerns devotional enterprise. Accordingly, the moral codes of the webmasters in question stem from both a religio-ethical impetus and a commitment to the occupation's *modus operandi* – two inclinations that may prompt contradictory actions. The first is predicated on a more traditional set of rules, which are consonant with the sensibilities of a faith-based community. On the other hand, the professional standards derive from a liberal approach whereby the internet is, to borrow Rhingold's turn of phrase (2000), an "electronic frontier." Moreover, this outlook is of a piece with the hackers' libertarian views regarding open access to information and democratic activism. Of course, the proponents of these causes are wary of government involvement (Coleman 2012; Ludlow 1996). The tension between these perspectives is manifest in the various decisions taken by webmasters. Scott and Rachel have created religious apps that do not necessarily correspond with the mores of the Jewish establishment, whereas Father Carlos underscores his firm commitment to mainstream Catholic doctrine. These divergent approaches are indicative of the discretion wielded by webmasters in their liminal capacities. By virtue of this power, they are gradually becoming agents of religious transformation.

This dissonance certainly warrants further investigation. At this point, we can establish some basic tenets of the webmaster vocation. Google's well-documented golden rule of "Don't be evil" applies to the entire field of IT. Conversely, some mores are tailored specifically for webmasters, and, all the more so, the religious subgroup. Within this general category are directives for protecting user anonymity. Moreover, webmasters are urged to completely refrain from all forms of public disparagement and to eschew rejecting other denominations and faiths. At one and the same time, the webmaster's own outreach activities and religious praxis are encouraged. While the webmaster code of etiquette is not etched in stone, its reach is growing in both theory and practice.

Scholars have long reflected on the different characteristics of professions and semi-professions, highlighting the autonomy, power, and social standing of fields in each category (Etzioni 1969; Suryamani 1989). Formal knowledge undergirds professional training and accreditation. Practical and tacit knowledge is also formally shared at workplaces on a daily basis. That said, this chapter has focused on a new class of professionals that has arisen from the encounter between the fast-expanding digital world and traditional religious groups. At present, hardly any ordination programs teach communications. However, this subject is making inroads in various other faith-based institutions, like the Canção Nova and Orthodox film schools in Israel (Jacobson 2004). For the most part, though, seminaries are reluctant to fully introduce new media courses into their curriculum, perhaps on account of its modernist connotations.

There are two emergent paradigms of the religious webmaster: the entrepreneurial loner and the institutional player. Both models have their own approaches to knowledge sourcing, networking, and external motivation.

The entrepreneurial loner is active in religious and/or technological circles of knowledge but independently launches a unique venture. Alongside religious schooling, these players usually have formal training in, above all, computer software, graphics, and the like. Much of their knowledge, though, is the product of self-socialization and self-educating communities (Burbules 2006). Two of our case studies, Scott and Rachel, fit this bill.

Institutional players are involved in entrepreneurial media ventures of sizable faith-based organizations aimed at fulfilling religious, communal, and/or ecclesiastical objectives. In pursuit of these goals, the institutions divide the labour between different wings. As in the case of Father Carlos, staff members are wont to share information and lend a hand in their particular field of expertise. While these endeavours are certainly driven by religious motivations, pecuniary considerations are occasionally part of the mix as well. A case in point is businesses that develop religious apps and software.

Over the course of this chapter, we explored the ascent of religious webmasters through the prism of three case studies. As we have seen, this vocation is fast becoming a key factor in the daily operations of both venerable and emerging faith-based movements. Looking ahead, webmasters' knowledge construction, training, ethics, occupational identity, and approaches to theology, as well as impediments to the field's professionalization, all merit the close attention of scholars.

PART 2

Holy Land YouTube Videos: The Visual Language of Religious Outreach

3 Digital Gates to the Holy Land: Mediatizing the Religious Experience

The rise of online videos, especially the viral popularity of such offerings on social platforms like YouTube, is dramatically reshaping power relations in economic, political, educational, and other spheres of life. A development that challenges established authorities. From online sermons to ISIS beheadings, faith-based movements are also embracing new media with the objective of communicating religious, political, and cultural ideas. Despite their widespread use and profound impact, online videos have yet to attract considerable scholarly interest, particularly for sociologists of religion.

Traditional inclinations aside, religious movements have taken notice of the potential to reach vast, far-flung audiences and "consecrate" virtual spaces through online videos. For example, the internet offers monks who are widely seen as detached from the "real" world an opportunity to engage society without leaving the cloister (Jonveaux 2014). At the same time, the digital realm allows believers to transcend geographical-cum-economic limitations and experience sacred places and related events from afar. With this in mind, the present chapter scrutinizes the emergence of religious videos. To this end, we will grapple with the following question: How do faith-based movements and their representatives, foremost among them webmasters, perceive their video production enterprises?

Organized religion in the West is threatened by secularization, steep declines in church affiliation (Stolz 2010; McMullin 2013), denominational conversion, and apostasy (Pew Research 2014; Lehmann 2013; Chesnut 2009). The adoption of ICTs and media strategies by ecclesiastical institutions is tied to these rapid shifts in faith-based identity. That is to say, religious organizations are availing themselves of these tools to sustain and promote their worldview and rite amid a struggle for exposure, legitimacy, and traction with competing groups.

Against this backdrop, we contend that the emergence of Catholic video production showcasing the Holy Land reflects the expanding collaboration between traditional and new sources of authority in the information age. Correspondingly, the internet is stirring up tensions within various faith-based institutions that are looking to balance these online efforts aimed at promoting their unique identities with the desire to maintain a traditional lifestyle. In the process, religious webmasters and their ecclesiastical supporters must legitimize the use of ICTs within their communities.

As surveyed earlier, the Canção Nova and the Franciscan Custody have launched a joint enterprise to produce digital content in Israel/Palestine. The basic premise of this chapter is that the players behind this enterprise deem videos an effective medium for leveraging what Walter Benjamin dubbed the aura of holy sites with the objective of engaging and promoting solidarity among fellow Catholics (see chapter 5). For this reason, we will also assay the emergence of religious leaders and entrepreneurs who are seeking to optimize traditional modes of proselytization via new media innovations.

3.1 The Mediatization of Faith-Based Organizations and the Rise of Online Religious Video

In light of the fact that cultural, political, and religious ties are increasingly conducted on digital frameworks, Lövheim (2017) views mediatization to be an important catalyst of social transformation. Other scholars have delved into the way faith-based institutions have adopted a media logic (Golan and Martini 2019; Hutchings 2011; Rinallo et al. 2016). Moreover, they are taking stock of the influence of cybernetic information flows on religion. For instance, values and ideals, such as transcendental beliefs, are being transmitted via blogs (Lövheim 2012), communal texting (Mishol-Shauli and Golan 2019), games (Zeiler 2014), and videos.

As depicted in the literature, religious videos are a popular means for proselytization and building community. Rosenthal (2007) has explored the twentieth-century outreach juggernaut of televangelism.

Thomas and Lee (2012) underscore the negotiation process between viewers and televangelist. The consumption of religious content no longer necessitates an affiliation with traditional institutions and leaders. From the comfort of their desktop, millions of believers tune in to charismatic speakers, like the renowned televangelist Joel Osteen.

As part of the general convergence of media (Jenkins 2006), this type of content is spreading to mass video platforms. Martini (2013, 2015) has documented the unprecedented manner in which YouTube, Vimeo, and other video-sharing websites have become engines for community building and knowledge transfer. What is more, this content is strengthening the bonds between existing community members (Burgess and Green 2009; Lange 2014; Orgad 2012). Shifting gears, Shouse and Fraley (2010) have analyzed a music video that uses blasphemous humour for the sake of lambasting the rhetoric of televangelists. Their findings dovetail neatly with the more general criticism of religion in American popular culture, especially among millennials. In fact, videos and websites devoted to resisting authority of all sort lean, in part, on humour. At any rate, a few scholars have examined how religious conflicts are waged and political perspectives disseminated on these platforms (El Marzouki 2013 and 2015; Van Zoonen, Vis and Mihelj, 2010). In discussions on "video battlegrounds," they highlight the ability of new media to bolster political and religio-communal affiliation.

The literature abounds in works on the televangelism and online videos of up-and-coming charismatic groups, such as Pentecostal movements in Brazil and Africa (Haynes 2013). Conversely, the response to these campaigns of more established, rival institutions has largely been ignored. To fill this vacuum, we will take stock of Catholic production and online distribution of Holy Land videos.

3.2   The Origins of Video Usage in the Catholic Church

Notwithstanding its conservative inclinations, the Catholic Church has gradually integrated digital media into its outreach strategies. Ortiz (2003, 182) dates this strategy to the first half of the twentieth century. In 1928, the Church founded the International Catholic Organization for Cinema and the International Catholic Association for Radio and Television. This was followed by the promulgation of the *Vigilanti Cura* encyclical of 1936, which discussed the potential of the cinema for spreading the faith. Twelve years later, the Vatican established The Pontifical Commission for Social Communications to address concerns about the effects of new audiovisual technologies on religious education (Campbell 2010, 36).

At mid-century, the Church began using visual media to train priests and socialize youth. A milestone in this process was *Miranda Prorsus*. Published in 1957, the encyclical deems media as "gifts of God" for affecting salvation.[1] Paul VI's *Evangelii Nuntiandi* of 1975 further sanctioned the deployment of media for evangelical purposes. These pontifical declarations gave rise to numerous initiatives over the years, such as *Radio Maria*, an international radio station, and the Catholic TV Network in the United States. Since 1967, popes have discussed the rationale behind this policy on World Communication Day. In May of 2013, Benedict XVI stated that[2]

> In social networks, believers show their authenticity by sharing the profound source of their hope and joy: faith in the merciful and loving God revealed in Christ Jesus. This sharing consists not only in the explicit expression of their faith, but also in their witness, in the way in which they communicate "choices, preferences and judgements that are fully consistent with the Gospel, even when it is not spoken of specifically." (Benedict 2011)

Heidi Campbell and Alessandra Vitullo (2019) elaborate on papal attempts to clarify the steps the Holy See has taken to legitimize media usage. They highlight the evolution of this top-down process since the convocation of the 1948 Pontifical Commission for Educational and Religious Films. Moreover, the two scholars discuss World Communication Day, on which Church leaders publicly voiced their thoughts on this matter from 1967. In Campbell and Vitullo's estimation, the Vatican's sanctioning of media laid the groundwork for "the texting pope" (John Paul II), "the tweeting pope" (Benedict XVI), and "the selfie pope" (Francis).

While some religious groups object to online media and consider the internet a theatre of sin and profligacy (Golan and Campbell 2015), the Catholic top brass deems it a suitable platform for disseminating the Church's messages. Pious use of online media is similarly encouraged, for it allows believers to tap into the gospel on a daily basis and places religion at the forefront of the public sphere (also see Cassanova 2008).

There is also a great deal of scholarship on the digital behaviour of Catholic users and producers. In their seminal publication on internet use in monastic communities, Cantoni and Zyga (2007) focus on issues that pertain to gender and monastic structure. They also map out the employment of ICTs throughout the Church. Overall, the study points to a growth in internet usage. These findings are consonant with those from Jonveaux's study on monastic Facebook activity (2014). In any event, there are considerable disparities between various monastic groups, especially female orders. These differences may stem from the unique nature of each monastery's connection with the outside world. While some communities maintain a website and/or provide all members with email accounts, others refrain from digital engagement as part of their withdrawal from modern life.

Noomen, Aupers, and Houtman (2011) compare webmasters of faith (i.e., Catholics, Protestants, and Spiritualists) employed at religiously oriented media outlets in Holland. The study reveals the tensions that the threat of secularization poses to these workers, which they believe is connected to the proliferation of internet use. In particular, Catholics in this field struggle with the occasional dissonance between adhering to Roman orthodoxy and the webmaster profession's ideology of fostering dialogue and diversity. Moreover, Noomen et al. explain how Catholic media producers take into account their viewers' sensibilities. That said, the researchers eschewed an analysis of the content itself as well as the objectives and nature of the Church's international outreach campaigns.

3.3 Pilgrimage, Media Entrepreneurship and the Holy Land

Pilgrimage is a significant part of the Catholic tradition for both lay and ecclesiastic devotees alike. Ethnographers and social scientists are wont to frame pilgrimage as a rite of passage that elicits liminal transformations in the believer's inner state and public standing (Badone

2004; Coleman and Eade 2004). These boots-on-the-ground journeys often involve a pursuit of the transcendental and/or a quest for physical-cum-spiritual healing.

The Holy Land has always been a major focal point of the Catholic rite. Although Christian pilgrimage to the region can be traced to the fourth century, the number of visitors has always varied from period to period (Coleman and Elsner 1995). Several researchers draw a correlation between the present upturn in pilgrimage and the advent of global tourism (Badone 2004; Coleman and Eade 2004).

Pilgrimage is by and large a corporeal undertaking, and the rising trend of faith-based institutions seeking to transfer this experience to the cyber realm goes against the grain of deep-seated assumptions regarding Church tradition and ecclesiastical authority. Several distinct lines of research are evident in the literature on the mediatization of religion. Schwartz (2010) has investigated the upswing in devotees posting family videos of religious occasions (e.g., Confirmations and Bar Mitzvah celebrations). Another prevalent topic is the mass outreach of charismatic televangelists like Jerry Falwell (Rosenthal 2007; Thomas and Lee 2012). Furthermore, some researchers (e.g., Grieve 2015; Falcone 2015) have delved into rituals that are performed online through videos and games (e.g., Second Life) as part of a group's effort to mediatize a religious experience. Given their loss of access to holy sites, the Tibetan Buddhist diaspora has embraced this approach (Helland 2015).

These inquiries have enhanced our understanding of the forms and functions of religious videos, but key aspects of this genre demand a closer look. In the pages ahead, we will fill this void through the lens of digital pilgrimage. The allure of this practice is analogous to the age-old fascination with icons and their presumed affinity to the transcendental. Digital pilgrimages are usually spearheaded by newfangled media authorities who negotiate with established clerical figures over the ground rules of this enterprise. Sacred Catholic places have long been under the conspicuous purview of the Church and are a major source of this institution's legitimacy. In the information age, online access to these sites is liable to jeopardize the Church's standing. Clergy-run digital pilgrimages, though, appear to be strengthening the institution's time-tested means for wielding authority. Besides its traditional face-to-face mode of interaction with the public, the Catholic leadership now influences believers in a less formal and more remote fashion.

With the rise of new media, affordable production and distribution methods have generated an increase in content featuring prominent Christian themes and venues. For what is now eight centuries, the Franciscan order has been the official custodian of the Church's Holy Land sites. In January 2008, the Episcopal Conference of the Holy Land duly mandated the Franciscan Media Center with the task of utilizing ICTs to produce and distribute content about these sacred places. To this end, the Franciscan Custody forged a partnership, the Christian Media Center, with Canção Nova.

A direct outcome of the encyclical *Evangelii Nuntiandi*, Canção Nova is a Catholic monastic community as well as a charismatic, vigorous, and media-savvy evangelical movement, which was founded in 1978. Its exponential growth is by and large a Catholic response to the Pentecostal revival sweeping through Brazil (Lehmann 2013). Like many other faith-based movements, the advent of the Canção Nova was accompanied by a founding narrative.[3] In early 1978, so the story goes, a youth group convened in the east Brazilian town of Areias for a "Seminar on the Spirit." At this gathering, Father Jonas Abib called upon the attendees to fully commit themselves to a mission of God. "Moved by an incredible force," twelve volunteers embraced this cause. In so doing, a charismatic network was born whose main objective is to proselytize far and wide by dint of modern communication tools (Abreu 2009). Canção Nova is thus advancing a "reverse transnationalism" whereby religious ideals that were developed in South America are being disseminated throughout Europe (Oro 2019). In the hopes of countering the decline of Western Christianity, this movement is following in the footsteps of Pentecostal and other charismatic groups, which have flourished over the past three decades in South America and Africa. More specifically, they are planning to re-evangelize the very continent whose emissaries brought the faith to their own shores centuries earlier (Maritz 2017; Währisch-Oblau 2009). This process not only calls for the dispatch of non-Western missionaries to the Occident but an inversion of both social positions (bottom-up evangelization) and the direction of religious colonization (Freston 2010).

In recent years, the Vatican has assigned an evangelical ministry to Canção Nova and has officially recognized it as an Association of the Faithful. Riding the wave of the Catholic charismatic renewal, the group has expanded the reach of its media activities within a few decades to the European Union (e.g., Portugal, Italy, Greece, France, and Cyprus) and beyond (Israel, India, the United States, and Paraguay, among other countries). By 2016, Canção Nova's main endeavour has indeed become media productions and distributing videos on its proprietary moderated platforms (rather than Vimeo or YouTube). The present chapter explores the motivating factors behind this substantial enterprise.

3.4   Occupational Motivations of Religious Webmasters

Subsuming a plethora of converging digital means (Jenkins 2006), video production is a growing field in religious outreach (Rosenthal 2007; Thomas and Lee 2012). To grasp the worldviews and particular opinions of webmasters regarding their enterprise, we designed a mixed-method study that consists, above all, of gleaning ethnographic data from participant observations and interviews, an in-depth look at digital footprints, and a comparative analysis.

(1) Participant Observations and Comprehensive Interviews. The research team attended services in various Holy Land monasteries and prominent sites that are informed by brisk video production activity, such as the Church of the Nativity (Bethlehem), the Church of the Holy Sepulchre (Jerusalem), the Basilica of the Annunciation (Nazareth), and the Cenacle (Jerusalem). As part of the field observations, we interacted with members of the Franciscan Custody and Canção Nova, especially production staff. What is more, comprehensive interviews were held on topical issues with twenty-five Canção Nova volunteers, monks, and clergy serving as webmasters for the Christian Media Center (CMC, see also chapters 4 and 5 for more on this organization). In terms of sampling, the interviews were obtained through a snowball referral approach whereby recommendations from one interlocutor secured the trust of the local charismatic community as well as access to Franciscan leaders and key CMC personnel.

Table 3.1 | Research objectives and corresponding interview questions

Research Interest	Topical Open-Ended Question(s)
Perception and legitimization of videos as an outreach tool	How does the visual character of new media fit your evangelical goals?
Religious motivations and perceived audiences	Does the global nature of new media suit your mission? And is it indeed a "global" mission?
Video producers' outlook on the benefits of their media endeavours	What are the main services you provide? And how do they advance your objectives?
The webmasters' perception that videos can encourage offline religious acts	Does online exposure to religious rituals enhance their importance? And if so, why?
Taboos, boundaries, and presumed affordances of religious videos	Are there religious limitations on filming rituals and holy sites? And if so, why?
Experience and perceived impact of religious principles and movements	Can an online video convey holiness? And if so, how?
Authority and standing of pilgrimage-based religious movements	Do you know any other faith-based groups that are making videos of the Holy Land?
Perceived status-cum-legitimacy of video work	In the long run, can videos be integrated into the accepted Christian tradition?

As enumerated in table 3.1, the interview questions addressed our research goals.

(2) Exploring Digital Footprints. While preparing for and conducting the ethnographic fieldwork, we parsed an assortment of Franciscan and Canção Nova productions (see chapter 4). The videos were garnered from several websites, like the Franciscan Media Center (fmcterrasanta.org), the Terra Sancta Blog (terrasanctablog.org), and TV Canção Nova's Facebook Page (facebook.com/tvcancaonova). Familiarity with this material came in handy during the interview sessions and shed light on our subjects' media productions and goals.

(3) Categorization, Coding, and Comparative Analysis. Field notes, videos, and interview transcripts were compared for the sake of discerning how webmasters grasp their media activities. The interviews were coded thematically using the Dedoose mixed-method analysis software. The codes – foremost among them pilgrimage, authority, religion, outreach, and community – were selected on the basis of the key topics that surfaced during our fieldwork.

3.5   Global-Scale Evangelization via New Media

The CMC's webmasters deploy video imagery for the purpose of re-establishing the Holy Land as a Christian centre of worship. Moreover, the videos help the Franciscan order and the Canção Nova redefine and bolster their position in the Catholic world. The webmasters pointed to five aims that underpin their video production enterprise:

> Digitally mediating the holy sites in an effort to become arbiters of place and religious narrative.
>
> Creating bonds between Holy Land communities and believers around the world. Ratcheting up the visibility and extolling the role of Christian communities in the Holy Land to co-religionists abroad.
>
> Cultivating agency. Validating the webmasters' role as digital carriers of the faith, while empowering users to proselytize via new media outlets.
>
> Offering and framing media experiences as a surrogate to boots-on-the-ground pilgrimage.

3.5.1   Mediation of Holy Sites

This goal focuses on the way monastic agents narrate holy sites. Franciscans deem the advancement of pilgrimage to the Holy Land, along with other sacred places (e.g., Assisi, Lourdes, and the Sanctuary of Greccio) to be an essential part of their mission. Among the Custody's means for pursuing this objective is the publication of official communications regarding the Holy Land, such as this excerpt from the group's official webpage:

The friars have not only been the "guardians" of the stones and of those places in order to preserve their value, but their mission has also been to make them living stones, so that they speak to the heart and to the mind of all those who set off on a pilgrimage in the Holy Land, to be able to see the "simple stones" as "beloved stones" through their faith. (Custodia Terrae Sanctae 2011)

Along with the primary responsibility of safeguarding the holy sites, this passage highlights the Custody's goal of facilitating the arrival of pilgrims, educating them, and personally mediating their religious experiences throughout their stay. To this end, Franciscans organize and give tours at the holy sites. Furthermore, they serve as webmasters for the CMC. In so doing, the Custody offers both actual and virtual pilgrimages to global audiences.

Jamal, a Palestinian Catholic, is an editor and graphic designer who has been involved in CMC's religious video and television productions for several years. He emphasizes the significance of facilitating visual access to the Holy Land for Christians abroad: "It is a way for people who cannot come here at least to see … the Holy Land, even from far away, even from the TV. It is beautiful to imagine the places where Jesus was praying" (interview, 18 November 2015). Jamal is referring to the wherewithal of new media to stimulate a viewer's religious imagination. By presenting inspirational sites and scenes, the CMC helps believers envision major scriptural events.

The outreach potential of media tools was a recurring theme in our interview sessions. Victória, an experienced digital manager who previously worked at the headquarters of Canção Nova TV in Sao Paulo, is among the mover-shakers at the Christian Media Center. She discusses the value of mediatizing sacred places:

So we know that these things [i.e., biblical events] happened in history, but for those who believe and have had this experience with Jesus, this experience with God, this person [*sic*] doesn't care that 2,000 years have passed. No. What matters … is that everything took place here [in the Holy Land]. And I think this is what people want to see in the work we do, in the broadcasts,

in the masses. When we broadcast a mass in one of the sanctuaries, this is what matters to people: that it happened here. It
is for these people that I would like to revive all these things.
(interview, 18 November 2015, translated from Portuguese)

By facilitating online pilgrimages, Victória hopes to create a dualistic sacred experience that connects the imagined past to present-day
cybernetic activities.[4]

In the estimation of these webmasters, then, the Catholic creed is
perpetuated by their mediation of holy sites and related experiences.
The videos are evidently meant to spark the believer's religious imagination by featuring places of canonical significance. Employing
a dualistic approach, webmasters actualize this (imagined) past and
showcase present events to create a meaningful experience.

3.5.2 Building Bonds between Holy Land Communities and Christians around the World

As per this objective, the webmasters under review see themselves as
advocates of local communities before what Benedict Anderson (1991)
may have seen as an "imagined" global audience of Christians. Imad, a
Catholic Arab working for CMC's Arabic media division, expands on
the goals of this enterprise:

This is our mission: to encourage people from outside to visit
the Holy Land, to be in contact with the communities here,
different communities. And these videos we prepare can actually
play a very good role, especially because they are … in … six
languages including Arabic, English, Spanish, French, [and]
Portuguese. (interview, 11 September 2015)

According to Imad, the digital content is a vehicle for spurring on
a diverse array of Christians to embark on a pilgrimage to the Holy
Land. Moreover, he calls for pan-Catholic solidarity and undertakes to
foster reciprocity between the local Arab-Catholic communities and
their co-religionists abroad.

Other webmasters and stakeholders also discussed the goal of representing the local community. For example, Youssef, a key local figure in the Maronite Church[5] and a religious media entrepreneur, elaborated on the significance of a living Christian presence in the area:

> We don't want the Holy Land to be perceived as a "museum." The presence of the local Christian community … is an added value to what the Holy Land already is. It is really important to spread awareness about the local community … People support it because they appreciate the work and the meaning of this presence. Of course, this also depends on the community itself, on how its [members] perceive their own value. (interview, 11 September 2015, translated from Italian)

In sum, Youssef touts the contribution of such media ventures to building "awareness" for the Holy Land's native Christians.

Reflecting on the centre's aims and organizational structure, Father Paolo, a top official of the Franciscan Custody and a major supporter of the CMC, explains the significance of the local populace and its bond with co-religionists around the globe:

> We have two teams, an international and a local (Arab) one … They communicate in two different ways to two different target [audience]s. We realized that the local community doesn't know anything about the Holy Land, their patrimony, and history … We [i.e., foreign clergy stationed in Israel/Palestine and local Christians] tend to form many little ghettos, one next to the other. (personal interview, 28 December 2015, translated from Italian)

Paolo highlights the educational objectives of the centre. In his estimation, the local communities, including the Franciscans, are all isolated in their own "little ghettos." That said, he hopes that the CMC's Arab content will drum up solidarity between all Christians dwelling in the Holy Land. The friar argues, perhaps ironically, that his Arab co-religionists are less mindful as to the importance of the area's sacred places. Through digital content, he aims to educate them and cultivate a local identity that embraces the Franciscan principle of custodianship.

While on the topic, it is worth mentioning the plight of Arab Christians in Israel/Palestine. Due to a surfeit of regional tensions, the local population has decreased severalfold in recent decades to 175,000 (CBS 2018) in Israel and approximately 49,000 in the West Bank, Gaza, and East Jerusalem (Kaartveit 2013). Against this backdrop, Paolo is seeking to educate, unify, and empower this at-risk community by accentuating their sacred role within the greater Christian world.

In this context, digital pilgrimage constitutes a means for reflecting on the identity, boundaries, and the very essence of the Catholic community. CMC webmasters emphasize that they are striving to relieve the hardships of the local community by bringing them to the attention of a global audience. Along the way, they hope to foster a pan-Christian identity that revolves around a shared affinity towards the Holy Land.

3.5.3 Cultivating Agents

By showcasing the religious centrality of the Holy Land on social networks, the CMC's webmasters aspire to cultivate transcendent experiences. In so doing, they assume the role of digital pilgrimage guides and experts on Christian lore. Additionally, the webmasters train viewers to evangelize on their own. Quite a few of the Canção Nova members that we spoke to recalled an epiphany that spurred them on to a life of proselytization. Through new media, they hope to replicate this experience for others.

The webmasters validate their role as the Church's agents by shifting the spotlight from religious erudition (i.e., scriptural learning) and practice onto religious experience, which they facilitate by either corporeal or online pilgrimage. For instance, a monastic webmaster from Brazil remarks that "In our community [i.e., Canção Nova], we learn, we evangelize as we are evangelized ourselves. So we come to the Holy Land to be evangelized. And once evangelized, evangelize" (personal interview, 18 November 2015). This interviewee highlights the learning process and personal transformation that proselytizers must undergo before reaching out to others. Adriano, a Canção Nova seminarian who also works at the centre, expands on this notion:

> [Pilgrimage] allows people to … experience Jesus – an experience you can see, an experience you can watch … You can come here, to the Holy Land, and you can see Jesus. You can see Jesus in the Eucharist, see Jesus in the Gospel, see Jesus in many things … Because that experience changed my life, I am in love. I want everybody to have the same experience I did. The evangelization was born from the Resurrection of Jesus. When Jesus was resurrected, he said: "Go and bring this news to my brothers in the Galilee, and there you will see me." Jesus said to the Apostles: "Go around the world and teach my gospel to the people. You cannot evangelize in the absence of an experience with Jesus; you cannot talk about Jesus, if you don't know Him; you cannot talk to Him, if you haven't had this deep experience with Him. This is evangelization: first I have an experience with Him, then I bring this experience to others. (interview, 1 October 2015, translated from Italian)

Adriano portrays the journey he went through to become an evangelist. The webmaster describes the prerequisites for achieving this pious state, namely different levels of experience with God. For instance, he says, "You can't evangelize in the absence of an experience with Jesus." As a result of this sort of encounter, "I am in love." These sorts of experiences can be induced by traditional ceremonies (e.g., the Eucharist sacrament), by reflecting on the scripture, engaging with Holy Land sites, and having video-mediated sensory experiences with the Lord. By drawing a correlation between the resurrection and global evangelization, Adriano adds a theological dimension to outreach work and his role as a religious webmaster. Put differently, the apostolic mission is fulfilled via online activities.

This same undertaking is bolstered by creating networks of outreach agents. In other words, webmasters pass on their evangelical skills to recent veterans of the "Holy Land experience," both boots-on-the-ground and virtual pilgrimage alike. According to Luiz, a CMC content manager from Brazil, when pilgrims come to Jerusalem and meet our reporters [and] editors, sometimes in the Old City [offices] or in the Sanctuaries, they always say "Ah, I saw that program; I watch it every week. I could watch that documentary." Even the materials we post on [the] internet, using social media, the [content attracts] "likes" and then people sharing it [advance the mission] … [T]he important thing is, what we produce. We don't produce only to ourselves. So if you receive it, share it. Add the link.… This is what we are doing, we are advising others to use such tools, to share, spread the content. This is the goal. Nothing should stay. It is to be spread [*sic*]. (interview, 18 November 2015)

Luiz depicts his CMC co-workers' encounters with pilgrims. At these meetings, the latter validate the webmasters' activities and take it upon themselves to share Holy Land content on their own social networks. Put differently, the visitors are empowered to assume some of the functions that historically belong to traditional evangelists (i.e., priests and monks).

Webmasters endeavour to amplify their impact by providing users with the tools and transcendent experiences they need to carry out the apostolic mission. The process of qualifying such agents – transforming the lay believer into an evangelist – involves myriad religious activities, such as a spiritual experience within the framework of a pilgrimage. On the basis of our interviews, it appears that this experience can be induced via digital means (e.g., watching videos). That said, the highest levels of piety are attributed to those who have actually set foot in the holy sites. Nevertheless, pilgrims and clergy attempt to burnish their credentials in the digital sphere.

3.5.4 Cybernetic Experiences as a Surrogate to Pilgrimage

This goal attests to the perceived aptitude of new media professionals to replace the boots-on-the-ground pilgrimage with an accessible, remote alternative. While the physical excursion is still the optimal and most intense experience, digital varieties constitute legitimate surrogates. These ideas came up time and again in our interview sessions.

Felipe, a Canção Nova member who works as a video editor and audiovisual technician at the centre, described his vocation thus:

> This is our work: to bring the land of Jesus all over the world. We want all people to know about this place, even without coming here. This is our objective. Because … we live here, we know how important these places are, how they talk to us. Paul VI said that the Holy Land is the Fifth Gospel: there are four written Gospels and the land. The cities talk, the buildings talk, the Grotto of the Annunciation talks, the Grotto of the Nativity talks, the Holy Sepulchre, the Lake of Tiberias talk. A person who comes here experiences this beauty. Our task is to bring the land of Jesus to those who might never come. (interview, 6 January 2016, translated from Italian)

Felipe underscores the religious potency of the Holy Land by citing Paul VI and stringing together a row of metaphors (e.g., "the buildings talk"). By bringing these sites to devotees who are spread across the planet and unable to embark on a corporeal pilgrimage, webmasters attempt to guide them to a state of transcendence.

A handful of our interviewees spoke highly of Catholics who visit holy places and then share their experience on social media. According to Victória, the aforementioned CMC manager.

> The dream of our [movement's] founder [i.e., Jonas Abib] is for all Christians to have the opportunity to one day visit the Holy Land. But we know that there are people who won't have this opportunity, this possibility. So we try to the best of our ability to bring the [land] to the people so they can have this experience, for it is different … to read about it in the Bible and try to imagine where and how this place was. And then you have the chance to see it. Wow, it was there, in that place; it probably happened there. It helps the person, I guess, to better root their faith, to strengthen their faith, what they believe in, their experience of God. (interview, 18 November 2015, translated from Portuguese)

Victória defines this goal as introducing the sacred experience of pilgrimage to the digital world. Devotees who are unable to physically access holy sites can approximate a pilgrimage through the mediation of the Canção Nova's videos. This content, in her estimation, arouses devotees' biblical imagination by means of contemporary visuals ("to imagine … how this place was"). The act of watching a video, Victória asserts, ultimately reinforces the believer's faith in God.

In summation, webmasters produce videos and livestreams for the purpose of disseminating holiness throughout the globe, strengthening the church's digital footprint, expanding the impact of sacred places, and enabling individuals to perform religious acts on their own (rather than collectively) whenever and wherever they please via the internet. Whereas the boots-on-the-ground pilgrimage has maintained its primacy as a catalyst of religious experiences and approaching what Rudolf Otto (1958) termed the "numinous," we contend that the digital variety is an effective, if somewhat less intensive, surrogate.

3.6   Discussion and Conclusion

Pilgrimage revolves around humanity's aspiration to approach the divine. According to Mircea Eliade, pilgrimage sites are predicated on the archetype of a sacred centre demarcated from its "profane" surroundings. At these venues, believers can presumably "hold communion with the sacredness" (Eliade 1958, 368). Though devoid of territoriality, digital spaces offer surrogate access to the holy site. Over the course of this chapter, we have discussed the institutional and personal aims behind faith-based web productions. By delving into the media enterprise of monastic groups in the Holy Land, this study illuminates webmasters' efforts to mediatize pilgrimage and sacred places. Besides widening the Church's selection of religious offerings, this phenomenon affirms the rising status of these monastic professionals throughout the Catholic world. In interviews on media consumption, video production, and, above all, pilgrimage experiences, the webmasters articulated the tensions between the physical holy site, which is widely perceived as authentic, and its media stand-ins. The holiness that emanates from the narrated figure of Jesus and the Holy Family has long been transferred to the ground on which these protagonists had presumably trodden. In other words, a sacred landscape has been embedded into Israel/Palestine's geography. Hence, the attendant religious experience is conceived as an order of proximity in relation to the sacred core. That is to say, the holiness permeates associated elements, including representations thereof in artwork (e.g., icons), on videos, and other cybernetic outlets (e.g., websites and digital games).

The emergence of online religious content presents new opportunities for mass cultural transmission. Our analysis of the interviews with webmasters sheds light on the strategies that they adopt in constructing these faith-based outlets as well as the meaning believers are encouraged to glean from its content (see the discussions in the ensuing chapters). As some of our interlocutors emphasized, pilgrimage is still the most profound Christian experience. However, video-mediated access to the holy sites is formidable as well, thereby suggesting a hierarchy of religious propinquity.

Our findings point to a realignment of the social structure around the sacred and its manifestations. This includes not only the holy places themselves but a mélange of digital actors, stakeholders, brokers, and devotees. To some extent, the reproductive nature of video content diminishes its impact vis-à-vis the "original" place and attendant rituals. The webmasters attempt to reprise an "aura of authenticity" (Benjamin 1928) by invoking a proximity to the sacred. Although videos do not afford the same experience as, say, the pilgrimages themselves, the former are quite capable of simulating an encounter with the divine. Put differently, the digital realm is an outlet where clergy disseminate their ideals to far-flung audiences. The videos constitute an authoritative, if "soft" or informal, guide to achieving religious piety. Over the course of our fieldwork, we unearthed a social hierarchy connecting believers to the sacred. At the nub of this system are holy sites and traditional clergy; webmasters serve as up-and-coming intermediaries, while internet users inhabit the lowest rung. To wit, a budding relationship between sacred places and online believers is mediated by elements filling the top and secondary tiers of this pecking order. While the present study centres on webmasters, the literature would benefit from a disquisition on the audiences of this visual content.

Though their sway also derives from physical venues, webmasters stress the advantages of videos. From an educational standpoint, these tools narrate sacred meanings by audiovisual means (objectives 1 and 4). Moreover, they validate local communities in Israel/Palestine by emphasizing their role in the pan-Christian consciousness (objective 2). By dint of their special media properties, the videos also help webmasters train lay believers to partake in the evangelization process (objective 3). As discussed in the next chapter, these goals are mainly pursued during the production stages. Just as traditional pilgrimage involves priests and other guides linking a canonical narrative to a particular venue, the online variety rests on similar contributions in the virtual arena. Taking advantage of their content's audiovisual nature, webmasters pair images of holy sites with the biblical text in the hopes of stimulating a religious experience that approaches the traditional, boots-on-the-ground pilgrimage.

4 Networking the Sacred for Global Publics: New Media Strategies for a Re-enchanted World

Over the past few decades, audiovisual communications have become a major platform for disseminating religious content. The proliferation of smart devices and broadband connections, for example, has spurred on the mass production and consumption of online videos. As part of this trend, videos uploaded by religious institutions onto social platforms, like YouTube and Vimeo, are reshaping the discourse and collective imagination of believers.

From online sermons to livestreamed ceremonies, a wide array of movements, including fundamentalist groups, are increasingly turning to online videos as a means for espousing religious, political, and cultural worldviews. Even conservative faith-based institutions, such as the Catholic Church, have taken notice of the potential of this "genre" for reaching vast, far-flung audiences and sanctifying virtual expanses. Notwithstanding its profound impact on social collectives, religious or otherwise, this phenomenon has garnered sparse attention in the literature. A handful of digital religion scholars have indeed examined the substantial increase in religious content available online in, say, chatrooms, Q&A response websites, and games (Helland 2005; Wagner 2012; Grieve 2015; Tsuria 2016), namely alternative forms of devotional expression that have taken root online in what has been deemed a "third space" (Hoover and Echchaibi 2014). That said, the literature has largely overlooked the grounded aspects of this phenomenon. Against the backdrop of the ongoing struggle for "souls" in the religion market, the populace's ever more fluid approach towards religious affiliation, and mounting conversion rates (Pew Research Center 2014), the objective of this chapter is to demonstrate how clerical factors are using the digital realm to interest the public in traditional faith. More specifically, we will delve into internet-based outreach programs that revolve around venerated brick-and-mortar sites. Owing to the cachet of traditional sacred places, in this chapter we inquire how webmasters of major religious organizations are endeavouring to bolster the legitimacy and centrality of such venues, along with their own institutions, via online videos.

To be more precise, this chapter focuses on Catholic initiatives to mediatize holy places in Israel/Palestine via online videos. As discussed below, these media practices are becoming a legitimate form of knowledge transfer within the religious public. By analyzing visual and textual representations of sacred landscapes, we hope to elucidate the contemporary Christian discourse on biblical landscapes. Our findings indicate that some of these videos explicitly refer to contemporary faith-centred news in the Middle East, peppering their accounts with image-based allegorical interpretations, metaphorical comparisons, and biblical allusions. In broaching this topic, we are filling *lacunae* in the research on contemporary pilgrimage, the venerable tradition of Holy Land homiletic rhetoric, and the Western Catholic perception of "self" vis-à-vis the "other."

4.1 Proselytizing on the Internet: Possibilities and Challenges of New Media Environments

Over the last two decades, there has been a notable uptick in organized religion's efforts to reach a transnational public via websites, Instagram accounts, and web 2.0 exchanges on Twitter, Facebook, and sundry other public forums. Before the onset of the digital era, the outreach campaigns of religious figures centred on radio programming (Lehmann and Siebzehner 2006), cassette distribution (Hirschkind 2006), and televangelism (Rosenthal 2007). As per the literature, these efforts were often aimed at subverting the competition, such as grassroots organizations and up-and-coming stars – religious agents that also availed themselves of these same tools.

Countless small, remote, and/or marginalized religious groups have turned to the internet for the purpose of expanding their flock. For instance, Wicca, Satanism, and Sufi groups have developed proselytist websites (Piraino 2016; Cowan 2007; Petersen 2005). Well organized and/or major religious groups, which tend to have ample budgets, have stepped up their online activities. The literature has already surveyed these organizations' textual websites. For instance, Chabad's media outlets are designed to both strengthen religious boundaries from within and reach out to Jews living outside the movement's enclaves (Golan 2013). Scientology also invests heavily in online representation with the objective of countering the movement's negative image in the press as well as sharing its ideals (Westbrook 2018; Halupka 2017). Likewise, the Holy See has sanctioned and encouraged the use of media as educational platforms from as far back as the 1920s (Lynch 2018; Campbell 2010; Ortiz 2003).

More recently, the Church has adopted new media tools for the sake of improving its outreach. Even the pope has taken to social networks like Twitter in the hopes of burnishing his leadership credentials and opening new channels of communication with the masses (Lynch 2018; Narbona 2016). Similar to other public figures, this online presence enables Pope Francis to connect directly with followers, while circumventing clerical or press intermediaries that are liable to filter or adapt his message to their own particular leanings. On the other side of the equation, these channels allow networked publics to build remote yet direct and personal relationships with celebrities. Through visual means, both sides have apparently forged experiential leader–acolyte bonds. These ties are becoming more relevant as politicians and other stars, like Donald Trump and Cristiano Ronaldo, increasingly express themselves on Facebook, Instagram, and other social platforms (Russmann and Svensson 2017). In this respect, digital posting not only serves as a gateway to political figures or institutions but as way to evince leadership.

While researchers have expanded on these interactions in politics and entertainment, surprisingly little attention has been directed at religious activity. Studies have already exposed the motivations behind the online presence of faith-based organizations, but their self-presentation and meaning-making processes merit a closer look, especially as online communications shift from more textual to image- and video-heavy content. An exception to this rule is our disquisition on Pope Francis's Instagram feed, accounted for in this volume, which explicates the visual markers that are used to enhance the Holy See's charismatic appeal (Weber 1978).

In sum, the literature has documented the efforts of religious institutions to legitimize and appropriate the internet in pursuit of outreach goals within the framework of their ongoing struggle for prominence within a competitive global religious market. As they build an online presence and try to create a riveting textual, audio, and visual experience for users, these groups often lean on their prior body of work in the fields of radio programming, cassette/CD distribution, and televangelism.

4.2   Narration of the Holy Land and its Holy Sites

Sacred places can be viewed as expanses that are imbued with meaning by a certain group(s) and thus viewed as endowed with a metaphysical presence. The magnitude of such sites is the outgrowth of ideas, rituals, and a belief system. In consequence, these venues bolster Catholic identity and denominational boundaries.

Following in Emile Durkheim footsteps, Maurice Halbwachs's *La topographie legendaire des evangiles en terre sainte* (1992) assays the spatial infrastructure of the New Testament (1992) by exploring the role of pilgrims, crusaders, and others over the centuries in the building and transformation of the Holy Land's topography. In shaping this landscape, he posits, "It was important that the believers be confident they were seeing and touching the very places where the facts subsequently transformed into dogma ... [I]f a truth is to be settled in the memory of a group it needs to be presented in the concrete form of an event, of a personality, or of a locality" (200). As opposed to the work of a museum curator or archeologist, Halbwachs claims, revering a site does not involve rediscovering some long lost past. Instead, he links site veneration to collective memory, identifying the former as an essential meaning-making process that helps crystallize a group's worldview.

Over the past two millennia, religious figures have indeed occupied themselves with the Holy Land's veneration and devotional portrayal (Ron 2009; Wilkin 1992). Throughout these years, the Judeo-Christian imagination has been continuously sparked by, *inter alia*, Church frescos, icons, homilies, reenactments of canonical events, and popular (*vulgare*) theatrical expression. This reverence has long been an impetus behind personal pilgrimage as well as political and economic efforts to secure a foothold in the Holy Land. Perhaps the most vivid example of such an undertaking is the sermon that Pope Urban II delivered at Clermont in 1095, which indeed launched the Crusades (Upton 2007).

In fact, the medieval Christian imagination unceasingly accentuated the Holy Land, not least the reverence of Jerusalem as the city of peace (*visio pacis*) and a fortress for waging "spiritual warfare" (Southern 1995). Between 1095 and 1291, R.H. Southern notes, Christendom was so "obsessed" with the Holy Land that monks would "have been just as comfortable discussing the sacral nature of Mount Zion from the Old Testament as their scholarly peers at Oxford or Chartres would have been imagining the Jerusalem Temple of the Gospels" (102–33). While the extensive medieval discourse that inspired this mindset is beyond the scope of this monograph, the argumentation is clearly manifest in the period's Catholic texts (Long 2003).

The image of Jerusalem and the Holy Land persisted in the religious discourse, but many and manifold competing sites of veneration emerged in, say, Rome and Constantinople. Alongside a decentralized and ever diversifying faith, a variety of towns and sites increasingly cut into the Holy Land's religious market share. From the nineteenth century onwards, places like the Virgin of Guadalupe in Mexico or "Our Lady of Lourdes" in France have attracted throngs of pilgrims. In light of these developments, the Christian significance of the Holy Land has waned. As Mark Twain observed on a visit to Palestine in the late 1800s, political tensions and the hardships of the road further impinged on its status as a pilgrimage destination.

Amidst this growing competition, various agents – be they communal religious leaders, states, or corporations – have been globally promoting specific holy venues. In the case of the Holy Land, the establishment of the State of Israel ushered in a bevy of new religious sites and archeological finds that were compatible with the Zionist narrative. Owing to the winds of modernization and commodification, both government agencies and corporations set out to improve the country's tourist appeal (Shoval 2000). An integral part of this effort was to popularize and enhance the pilgrim experience.

Though widely viewed as a catalyst of devotion, pilgrimage is not a mandatory precept for most Christians but rather a volitional activity for the pious or a rite of passage for certain elites (Bowman 1991). At any rate, pilgrimage is becoming an ever more commonplace activity. Its growth – either as a devotional pursuit or a form of tourism – has been accelerated by the development of mass infrastructure around sacred places, such as tourism companies, hotels, and affordable transportation. What is more, various faith-based institutions have begun to regularly organize and actively push spiritual-cum-educational trips to far-flung holy sites.

Over the past few decades, it has even become standard practice for local churches to run community-led pilgrimages. Several months before departure, the church gives classes designed to prepare devotees for the trip (Fleischer 2000; Ron 2009). In this respect, pilgrimage has become a fillip for communal engagement, as it involves leisure activities, religious study, and devotional experience. Before the rise of the digital age, the flock's perception of holy sites was by and large the handiwork of the local clergy's sermons and programs. Nowadays, the pilgrimage enterprise is augmented by centralized global online media strategies aimed at countering rival groups. These efforts have taken on a greater importance, as conversion movements threaten to cut into the base of established faith institutions.

4.3 Conceptual Framing: Umberto Eco, Indexicality, and Digitized Holy Sites

In producing videos, religious institutions seek alluring content with which to burnish their credentials and ramp up the flock's devotion on a global scale. To this end, these bodies have tapped into the well-established tradition of pilgrimage and public veneration. Not surprisingly, many of these videos revolve around holy sites. For the sake of gauging the meaning-making aptitude of these sorts of works, a semiotic analysis will be conducted of their indexical properties. Drawing on the foundations that Umberto Eco laid down in *A Theory of Semiotics*

(1976), above all his notion of indexicality, we will take stock of how the meanings of sacred venues are transmitted to networked religious publics.[1] As Eco phrased it, indexicality is a mode of sign construction that puts a "sentence (or the corresponding proposition) in contact with an actual circumstance by means of an indexical device" (1976, 163). Put differently, the indexical sign links an object (or *perceptum*) to a narrative. This can take the form of a proclamation, true or false, that identifies the object with accepted knowledge. The object, which was heretofore deemed external and arbitrary, becomes a significant trace, for it is connected to both a narrative and other vestige of the same event. In this sense, multiple traces concomitantly substantiate each other's authenticity and validate the narrative (Violi 2012).

Believer experiences at a holy site are constructed through indexical markers of an imagined divinely inspired event. A case in point is the Foundation Stone – the cynosure of the Dome of the Rock in Jerusalem. Also known as the Pierced Stone, the venerated object is considered an imprint of a miraculous occurrence. However, different religions maintain their own narratives of what exactly transpired on this spot. Jews traditionally believe that it is the site of Isaac's binding (Gen. 22, 1–19). In addition, they consider the rock to be a spiritual junction between Heaven and Earth. While Muslims also consider the rock a spatial and temporal interchange, they maintain that it is where the Prophet Muhammad ascended to Heaven. The online representations of this site further expose viewers to this indexically charged environment.

Religious meanings are not an inherent part of any expanse. To acquire the status of "holy," places must first be recognized and interpreted as such (Eco 1976). Only then are traces identified and arranged to fit, corroborate, and ultimately validate a specific narrative. For pilgrims, the biblical story is a prism through which they construe the venerated landscape. That is to say, visitors dip into their childhood reservoir of hallowed images, accounts, and protagonists. Upon contemplating a site, pilgrims attempt to establish a link between physical spaces and objects. In what Eco (1976) refers to as the construction of "imprints," they hunt for and "point" to "clues" for the purpose of associating newly encountered objects with their repository of meanings. That is to say, people are constantly interpreting reality and searching for indicators that comport with their symbolic worlds, which are the product of their semiotic socialization (Zerubavel 1997, 71–2).

Following in Eco's conceptual footsteps, we aver that devotees can bond with holy sites by watching online videos. In determining how the legitimacy and centrality of such places are reconstructed in such material, we will identify the semiotic markers (indexical texts) in the digital content that is manufactured and disseminated by the Catholic Church.

4.4   Background and Methodology

The focus of this chapter is on videos created and uploaded to the internet by the media arm of Canção Nova in Israel/Palestine. A direct outgrowth of the 1975 encyclical *Evangelii Nuntiandi* (Evangelization in the Modern World), Canção Nova (New Song) is a monastic Catholic community that was founded in Brazil some three years later. In 2014, the Church officially entrusted this group with a ministry specializing in social network communications. Riding the wave of the Catholic Charismatic Renewal, Canção Nova extended its activities to the European Union (e.g. Portugal, Italy, Greece, France, and Cyprus) and beyond (e.g. Israel, India, the United States, and Paraguay) within a few decades (Carranza and Mariz 2013). Members practise a variety of celibate lifestyles, ranging from priesthood to devout couples (without children). Whatever the case, most of the community resides in gender-segregated dormitories and adheres to a pious daily *regimen*, which is informed by well-defined regulations governing its activities (e.g., prayers, shared domestic chores, and economic contributions).

In Israel, the Canção Nova runs its mission through the Christian Media Center (CMC) – a joint venture with Custodia Terrae Sanctae (a venerable Franciscan organization entrusted with safeguarding the region's sacred places). The main objective of the Christian Media Center (cmc-terrasanta.com) is to forge a direct ecumenical bond between the Holy Land and Christians the world over, regardless of denomination. As it stands, the CMC offers the following products: online HD documentaries and, above all, videos of religious events (e.g., sermons and masses) in English, French, Italian, Arabic, and Portuguese; live coverage of major Catholic celebrations (via online streaming or satellite broadcasts); and 24/7 live feeds of important holy sites in the region (a project still in its nascent stages). Owing to the group's rising stock in evangelical circles, our disquisition on Canção Nova is likely to enhance our understanding of religious new media.

Part of a larger ethnographic study of the CMC, its monastic staff, and operations, the topic of this particular chapter is the media organization's online videos. Field research was conducted at monasteries and other holy sites in Israel/Palestine, primarily the Galilee and the Jerusalem area. For instance, a substantial portion of the CMC's production activity took place at the Church of the Transfiguration and the Basilica of the Annunciation in Tabor and Nazareth, respectively. Conversations with staff members helped us design the various stages of our research, which are outlined over the next few pages.

(1) Field Mapping, Preliminary Coding of Videos and Visual Analysis. Between 2016 and 2017, we assembled a representative sample of sixty-eight videos on the subject of pilgrimage (as tagged by the media outlets) that were posted to the Franciscan Media Center (fmcterrasanta.org), Terra Sancta Blog (terrasanctablog.org), and the CMC Facebook Page (facebook.com/ChristianMediaCenter). Our selections were based on informant recommendations and the works' popularity, as per the Christian Media Center's staff, managers, and stakeholders as well as web-traffic sites like alexa.com and compete.com. Each of the three websites hosting the videos was mapped for the sake of comprehending its digital and semiotic structure. Drawing on Herring's web content analysis methodology (2009), the pages were monitored and documented throughout the research period. The selected videos were analyzed with the objective of ascertaining shared discursive traits and representational dynamics (see Pauwels 2015). Recurrent iconography and rituals were documented and coded (via Camtasia and Dedoose software, respectively). Indicators for the audiovisual analysis are enumerated in the coding scheme (see table 4.1).

(2) Post-Fieldwork Data Analysis, Identification of Patterns, and Comparison. Following the selection of videos, we developed an audiovisual analysis to glean both self-representations and media-related behavioural patterns in accordance with the following visual coding protocols: syntax, semantic taxonomy, and visual signifiers. The results were then compared with interviewee accounts. Thereafter,

Table 4.1 | Audio-visual analysis coding scheme

Objectives	Themes	Observations	Code	Audio-visual indicators
(1) To understand the emergence of monastic webmasters, particularly their innovations in proselytization through online video-sharing platforms.	Dissemination	Social media	CS-SM	References to social media (e.g., hashtags, links, and Facebook)
		Livestreaming	CS-LS	References to around-the-clock online broadcasts
		Television	CS-T	References to TV outlets
		Web-TV	CS-WT	References to web-TV
	Media products	Weekly news	MP-WN	References to the case study's newscast (i.e., Terra Sancta News)
		Online events	MP-OE	References to contemporary Christian events
		Documentaries	MP-D	Non-biblical accounts with educational/moral objectives
		24/7 livestreams	MP-24	References to the case study's continuous feeds from holy places
(2) Explicating the adoption of visual digital technologies by religious factors, not least collaborations on videos between monastic webmasters and traditional clergy.	Religious cooperation (between the Franciscan Custody and Canção Nova)	Working communications	RC-IC	Joint presence/venture of both religious groups
		Ecumenical relations	RC-ER	Shared rituals (e.g., prayer services)
		Group distinction	RC-CC	Separate displays of each monastic organization

Management	Canção Nova	PM-CN	Presence of hierarchical markers
	Franciscan Custody	PM-FC	Presence of hierarchical markers
	Media staff	PM-ET	Visibility of the media crew
Self-representation	Arab staff	DL-AS	Visibility of Arab staff members
	International staff	DL-IS	Visibility of international staff members
	Clergy	DL-C	Discernible media activities of monks
	Partnerships	C-DL	Discernible cooperation with external media factors
(3) Ascertaining how online video production and dissemination reinforce or challenge traditional worldviews, while creating alternative spaces for learning and community engagement.			
Biblical imagery	Affirmation	BI-A	Content derived from traditional Catholic visuals
	Deviation	BI-D	Modern imagery (e.g., shopping malls and technology)
Holy Land	"The birthplace of the Church"	HL-CB	References to the Church's founding narrative
	"Land of Jesus"	HL-LJ	References to the New Testament narrative
	Pilgrimage	HL-P	Visibility of pilgrims
	Local community	HL-LS	Visibility of local Catholic Arabs
	Conciliatory narrative	HL-AC	References to religious co-existence

Objectives	Themes	Observations	Code	Audio-visual indicators
	Biblical narrative	Fiction	BN-F	Fictional reenactment of biblical accounts
		Biblical performances	BN-BP	Biblical reenactments at canonical sites (e.g., baptism in the Jordan River)
		Biblical landscape	BN-BL	Visibility of sites mentioned in the biblical lore
		Icons	BN-HI	Presence of icons
(4) To elucidate the sanctioning of communications and information technologies as evangelical tools.	Mission	Canção Nova	M-CN	Explicit references to the Canção Nova's evangelical mission
		Custodia Terrae Sanctae	M-FC	Explicit references to the Franciscans' custodial mission
		Local community	M-LC	References to the role of Arab Christians
		Monastic personnel	M-MP	Self-view of media-producers qua evangelists
	Videos as part of the devotional environment	Affirmative/negative	RV-A RV-N	Presence of videos in religious contexts (e.g., smartphone use at holy sites and monitors in churches)
	Video-mediated religious experiences	Affirmative/negative	VE-A VE-N	Testimony of religious experiences

	Visual media	Ambience	VM-A	Emotional/expressive strategies (e.g., music and lighting effects)
		Unambiguity	VM-SE	Showing (rather than telling) in order to build trust
		Offline/online	VM-OO	Addressing the online circulation of the produced videos
		Spiritual dimension	VM-SPI	Addressing online viewers qua ritual participants
(5) Grasping Catholicism's strategic responses to emergent and/or competing religious movements, sects, and cults.	Political engagement	Affirmative/negative	PE-A PE-N	Visibility of contemporary political events, figures, or institutions
	Other religions	Judaism	OR-J	Visibility of Jewish institutions, symbols, and figures
		Orthodox Christianity	OR-OC	Visibility of Orthodox institutions, symbols, and figures
		Islam	OR-I	Visibility of Islamic institutions, symbols, and figures
	Adversarial religious media-groups	Affirmative/negative	CM-A CM-N	Explicit references to competing media groups and productions
	At-risk Christian communities	Affirmative/negative	EC-A EC-N	Explicit references to endangered Christian communities in the Middle East (e.g., Syria and Egypt)

observational, interview-derived, and other field notes were uploaded into our qualitative analysis software (Dedoose), coded, and compared with previous coding of the online content. Codes were formulated on the basis of topics that surfaced amid the fieldwork, especially issues pertaining to religion, authority, outreach, and community. By virtue of these steps, we were able to identify key categories in the religious-media narrative. The coding scheme and its attendant themes are outlined in table 4.1. Three independent researchers assessed the data (Strauss and Corbin 1998) and duly produced three sets of categories. Upon comparing and presenting their output (Marshall and Rossman 2014), differences and disagreements were resolved through dialogue. These steps ultimately led to a high inter-rater reliability (Olesen, Droes, Hatton, Chico and Schatzman 1994). To ensure accuracy and improve our understanding of posts, we applied member-checking techniques. First and foremost, discussions were held with media managers of Catholic orders that produce and disseminate visual content for devotional-cum-educational purposes. Last but not least, we will compare the findings to those in the relevant literature.

4.5   Findings

Our analysis of the Christian Media Center's videos uncovered four sources of legitimacy that account for the prominence of Holy Land religious sites.

Scriptural legitimacy affirms the centrality of holy sites, foremost among them institutionalized venues that host contemporary pilgrims on a regular basis, by means of constant references to the Bible.

Experiential legitimacy highlights the pilgrims' involvement. Under this heading, the venues' importance and sacredness are affirmed by on-site accounts of devotees. Furthermore, the motivations behind pilgrimages are expressed by lay persons, rather than clergy and stakeholders.

Journalistic legitimacy involves the adoption of basic discursive modes, aesthetics, and values of the modern news industry (e.g., objectivity and a focus on current events), with the objective of validating the holy sites and the pilgrimage rite.

Ritual legitimacy is the fruit of communal practices that are observed at sacred places. Videos prompt users to contemplate these sites as expanses that are relevant to contemporary faith. This sort of content implies that rituals performed at these venues generate holistic religious experiences.

4.5.1 Scriptural Legitimacy

This traditional form of legitimation puts a stress on venerating the Holy Land through the prism of scripture. In the videos under review, we discerned four indexical strategies that fall under this heading: biblical landscape, textual references, iconography, and performance.

a) Biblical Landscape. The most salient visual theme in our corpus is exotic, captivating footage of Holy Land landscapes. All the videos complement these "optics" with voice-overs that connect between a site's visage and its theological merits. Needless to say, this strategy involves biblical references to the featured locale. A case in point is a video titled "The Gospels' Trail" (uploaded 6 December 2011):

> The path starts from Nazareth, where Jesus spent his childhood and adolescence, passing through Magdala, the town of Mary Magdalene, along the shores of the Sea of Galilee, and until Capernaum. Here, the Gospels tell us, Jesus made his home, turning this city of fishermen into the centre of his ministry. Capernaum, where Christ performed many miracles, is reached via the Mount of Beatitudes, the site of the famous Sermon on the Mount – one of the most remarkable moments of his life.

This narration expounds on the sites that the camera presents, discussing their relevance to the biblical accounts of Jesus. While serving as filler, the voice-over also builds on the user's pre-existing knowledge. In aggregate, the visuals and audio put a contemporary sheen on an ancient tradition.

b) Textual References. Many of the videos interject textual references to the Bible for the sake of augmenting and embellishing the visual content. Scripture is often viewed as a prop for religious authority

(Gifford 2010). Likewise, graphic and narrational inserts are mixed into the videos for the sake of elucidating their religious message and linking visual content to the "story line." Unlike the previous indexical strategy, in which the media-operator takes charge of the narrative and actively shapes the commentary on the featured landscape, in this category the Bible is cited *verbatim* without the mediation of a third party. As such, the video and scriptures overlap, implying a direct link between the canonical narrative and the particular locale. Due to its content and mediation of the sublime, the video acquires a sacred aura of its own.

c) Iconography. Besides constituting sacred objects in their own right, icons are a symbolic materialization of religious lore or the divine. For this reason, they are a well-established means for conveying mythological narratives to the flock. Whereas some faiths and Christian denominations object to visual representations of the sacred, iconic paintings, carvings, statues, and the like are an integral part of the Catholic experience.

Though video iconography has been sanctioned by the Church and its followers for quite some time, the transference of icons to the digital realm poses challenges of its own. For instance, while icons are viewed as venerated objects that mediate the believers' connection to the divine, its mediatization may complicate the position of the user to the transcendental. Nevertheless, the videos under review offer footage of "real" icons depicting canonical events, such as the Last Supper. Though disseminated via modern channels, the icons in our corpus retain their traditional value. Similar to the content in the prior strategies, the icons are graphically juxtaposed to and/or associated with a holy site, thereby augmenting their relevance.

d) Performance. In many of the study's videos, pilgrims are captured reading from scripture in the locale where a biblical event purportedly occurred. At museums or archaeological sites, educational, ideological, economic, or religious stakeholders endeavour to communicate their interpretation of the expanse. Ben-Yehuda (1996) demonstrates how Masada, a Herodian fortress in the Judean Desert,[2] is packaged to foster a Zionist ethic, hosting ceremonies of the Israel Defense Forces and youth movements that espouse this ideology. Over the years, tour guides and pastors have sought to cultivate Holy

Land venues for Christian pilgrims. To this end, rites have been developed for specific sites that comport with these agents' worldview. Although these "performers" are beyond the scope of this monograph, they can be interpreted as an amalgamation of rituals, not least memorial-cum-mnemonic ceremonies, and pilgrimage experiences. As we shall see, this same mix also informs the videos produced by the Christian Media Center.

Our analysis of the "scriptural videos" revealed a number of modes through which users are invited to approach the sublime. The attendant indexical strategies represent a triangular process for generating meanings that are supposed to connect between a locale and biblical passage by means of a video. While the camera acts as an indexical pointer that directs the viewer's attention to revered places, the sacred narrative is transmitted by means of voice-overs, chyrons, iconography, and footage of pilgrimage activities (see figure 4.1). By dint of these elements, the active outreach of the video upgrades an already established holy site. In turn, the video itself is publicly acknowledged as a legitimate outreach tool fit for religious consumption by virtue of the place's standing.

4.5.2 Experiential Legitimacy

The strategy of experiential legitimation undergirds a host of videos offering peer testimonials. In other words, lay pilgrims enthusiastically vouch for the Catholic way of life while recounting their Holy Land visit. As part of our analysis, we identified four prevalent themes that come up in these sorts of videos: life-changing experiences, personal motivations, a call to pilgrimage, and pilgrim testimonies (see figure 4.2).

a) Life Changing Experience. A large share of these videos accentuates the deep impact that a pilgrimage had on a participant's life. While international travel is quite commonplace in this day and age, visits to holy sites are idealized as pinnacle events. For instance, a couple featured in "The Pilgrimage to the Holy Land: A Life Experience" (uploaded 9 March 2016) gushes that their trip was "a unique experience in [our] life. I love Christmas and I particularly love Christmas Day, but today I felt the birth of Jesus in my heart ... and I could not stop

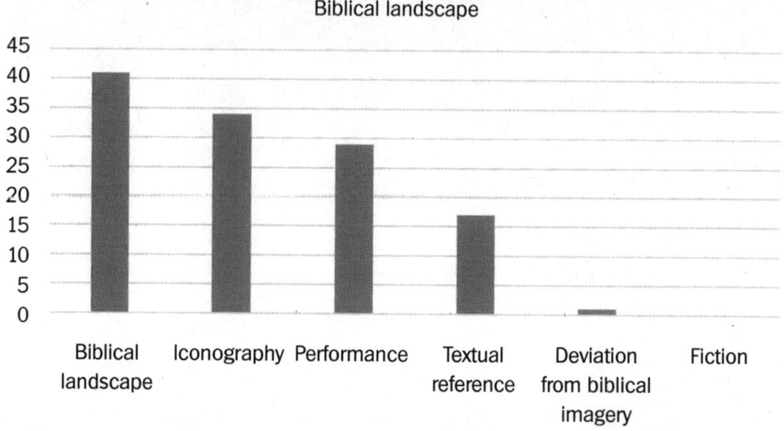

Figure 4.1 | Indexical strategies of scriptural legitimacy by frequency.

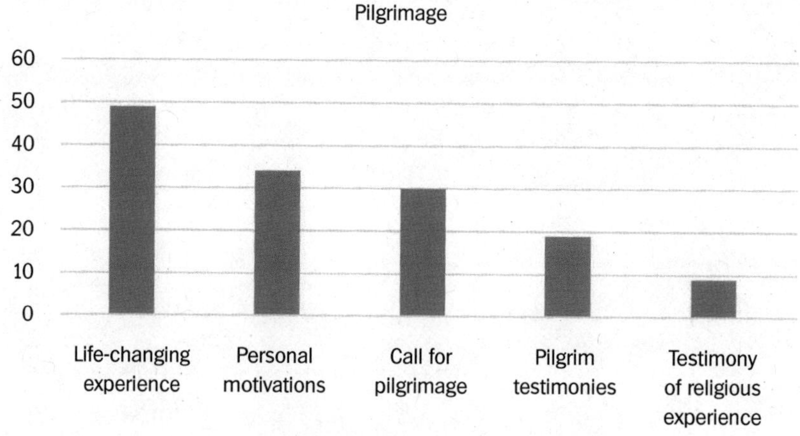

Figure 4.2 | Primary themes in pilgrims' videos by frequency.

'feeling' His love, 'feeling' Him. I cannot describe this moment … It is indescribable." In "A Life-Changing Experience: A Pilgrimage from Peru to the Holy Land" (21 June 2016), a visitor similarly remarks how the journey transformed his outlook:

It was a life-changing experience, from the first moment we arrived. From now on, every time we will hear the Gospels, our mind will come back here, to these places that we saw, where we prayed and sang, where we listened to our guide's elucidations, where we listened to the Gospel … [T]his is important to strengthen our faith and at the same time to pass it on to others.

The testimonies of "randomly selected" lay persons lend credence to the bottom-up perspective of holy sites.

b) Personal Motivations. Another form of bottom-up legitimacy turns up in videos exploring the personal motivations behind these pilgrimages. In their testimony, participants discuss the spiritual benefits that drew them to the Holy Land in the first place. An illustrative example of this is the video "Pilgrims from the United States to the Holy Land" (uploaded 27 May 2015). This work places the spotlight on a Californian visitor who states that the impetus behind his trip was "to have intimacy with the Lord and walk where he walked." In "A Luminous Moment in Everyone's Life" (uploaded 31 May 2017), a young couple maintains that "We decided to make this particular wedding trip to the Holy Land because we want to entrust our marriage to the Lord, and what better place than here?" Their reflections can perhaps be understood as a tacit critique of the generic leisure-driven honeymoon.

In these sorts of works, the meaning of the Holy Land is contemplated from a lay perspective. The subjects' unconventional motives ("intimacy with the lord" and consecrating a marriage) further entice the audience to embark on this special journey, either by coming to Israel/Palestine or continuing to watch such videos.

c) Call for Pilgrimage. Quite a few of the videos are direct appeals by clergy to join a Holy Land pilgrimage. In "A Luminous Moment in Everyone's Life" (uploaded 31 May 2017), Fr Francesco Patton urges believers to "Come … renew your faith, for here is the source of our experience of faith." Within this category are also efforts to lay to rest some prevalent fears about Israel/Palestine. For instance, Fr Donald Calloway, an American priest, grapples with security concerns in "Pilgrims from the United States to the Holy Land" (27 May 2015):

Many people, before we came, told me, "Father I cannot go there; it is dangerous." And I said, "It is not any more dangerous than going to Los Angeles or New York!" Now that I put the photos on Facebook every day, [devotees can see that] "we are here; we are here; we are doing this," and we are having fun, and we are smiling, and there are no problems. Many people say "I should have come! I should do this trip! I should've gone on this trip! I should've believed it!" I think that people should not be worried.

Breaking "the fourth wall," Calloway avails himself of Facebook to stress the rewarding experience that pilgrims had or the regret of those that stayed home. As we can see, different rhetorical approaches are used to convince the flock to join Holy Land tours, from traditional calls to strengthening the faith to citing rave reviews of past trips on social media.

d) Pilgrim Testimonies. A fair share of the videos document pilgrims in the midst of their journeys summing up their impressions thus far. While many of these testimonies are by lay pilgrims, the works often lean on clergy to accentuate the pilgrimage's religious significance and bolster its traditional legitimacy. A case in point is this excerpt from an interview with Jeanne D'Arc, a nun belonging to the Franciscan Sisters of the Eucharist, in the video "At the Source of Faith: Pilgrims in the Holy Land" (30 August 2016):

My experience here is different than I expected … [I]t is very peaceful, quiet, and relaxed. During the long journey, I was nervous, wondering how it would be like to be in Jerusalem … But … there is a serenity in the places where Christ was present, and that serenity is in the stones … and … in the ground. Being in the holy places, in Bethlehem, it is a great gift of the Mercy of God, who came to earth to be with us.

It bears noting that in the Christian tradition, serenity is viewed as a blessing, especially for members of the cloth.

In "The Lenten Desert" (21 February 2013), Emanuele Corti, a priest at a North Italian diocese (Como), homed in on another facet of the Holy Land pilgrimage: "[All] the faithful today [have] the opportunity to live … go back, and relive during these few hours the Israelites' forty years in the desert, and it certainly becomes a more concrete experience." Put differently, the trip is an opportunity to revisit, imagine, and possibly experience canonical events. By embracing the Bible or highlighting mental states like "serenity," which are associated with religious virtuosos, pilgrims can reach new spiritual heights.

The CMC's monastic webmasters endeavour to paint trips to the Holy Land as a meaningful experience for both cyber and boots-on-the-ground visitors. To this end, they reach out to and motivate the flock by interviewing trustworthy sources – either local clergy or lay devotees – as opposed to senior church figures or professional commentators. This turn to the lower echelons of the Catholic hierarchy betrays an effort to build a sense of familiarity and trust with the audience. Moreover, this kind of account is grounded on personal experience, which is characterized by both a proximity to the numinous (Otto 1954) and a joy for the more worldly delights of travel. The synthesis between well-known Catholic content and down-to-earth impulses behind Holy Land pilgrimage elicits a sense of authenticity and direct participation, even if the experience is confined to the cyber realm.

4.5.3 Journalistic Legitimacy

Hoping to win over the public's trust in the videos under review, the webmasters often draw on the journalistic style (see Marrone 1998). The medium assumes the format of a typical news program from the standpoint of both aesthetics and journalistic practices. For the most part, the content is delivered as a short news piece on a specific occurrence with voice-over, interviews, superimposed text, distinctive digital layout, opening graphics, a soundtrack, closing credits, and a recurring organizational logo. The Christian Media Center's modern studio, which is located near Jerusalem's Old City (see figure 4.3), well illustrates this point. Needless to say, this approach is not the sole preserve of the Franciscan–Canção Nova venture. For example, South Korea's leading Pentecostal movement, Assemblies of God, has a similar facility in the denomination's flagship church in Seoul (see figure 4.4).

Aesthetics aside, a major priority of journalism is reporting on controversies and other issues of public concern. In our corpus, we noticed myriad references to conflicts that have engulfed Christian minorities.

Figure 4.3 | Christian Media Center in Jerusalem, 2017.

Figure 4.4 | Studio for religious news broadcast at the Yoido Full Gospel Church in Seoul, 2016.

For instance, the Israeli–Palestinian struggle, the Syrian civil war, and the plight of Lebanon are all recurring themes. The coverage of these stories is freighted with inner tension between competing goals. On the one hand, there is a focus on impediments at Christian places of worship, such as access problems and threats to community members. On the other hand, there is occasionally a marked effort to downplay the region's violence and portray the holy sites as inviting, safe, and open to pilgrims.

Following an Israeli military operation in the Gaza Strip in 2012, the CMC posted a video, "Pilgrims' Serenity" (22 November 2012), describing the situation:

> The truce has been signed. The ceasefire started on Wednesday, November 21st at 8 PM, and a cautiously optimistic peace has descended on God's land. Pilgrims keep strolling through the ancient streets of the Holy City. Some are nervous about the events of the last few days, but in general the tourists who come to the *shuk* (marketplace) are quite calm.

While acknowledging the violence in Israel/Palestine, this report stressed the cessation of fighting, thereby implying that the area was safe for visitors. "Indians Marching for Christmas" (23 December 2013) also broaches this topic:

> In this procession, we will pray for peace in the Middle East, as Pope Francis has asked, to pray especially for Syria and all the other countries that are experiencing hardship. We want to pray for all Christians, religious sisters and brothers, who were attacked and killed, and for all those who are working toward peace in the Middle East. We want to pray for Palestine and Israel that they may find a peaceful and lasting solution.

In mentioning Syria and other hot spots, this account reminds viewers of the imperiled Christian communities in the Middle East. Moreover, it underscores the Christians in the region that are spreading the Church's ethos of peace and goodwill onto others. Apart from the

Holy Land, an emphasis is also placed on Christian values, prayers, the flock's bond with God, and the Holy See's guidance.

This same message is expanded on in a report, "Pilgrimage to Help God's Land" (8 January 2015), which was filed by Claudia Koll, the spokesperson of ATS Pro Terra Sancta Association, a Franciscan NGO:

> On the topic of the current situation [in the Middle East], I think that the presence of Christians in the Holy Land is important because Christians offer forgiveness, mercy, and therefore they are a link between Jews and Muslims. And with their gentleness and their sweetness and by proposing the Gospel of Jesus Christ, they can be an important seed in this land torn apart by war and hatred.

Like the other videos discussed in this section, Koll refers to the Israeli–Palestinian struggle in religious terms (Jews/Muslims). Moreover, she highlights the role of Christians as worthy emissaries of peace owing to their neutrality and the pacifist tenets of their faith.

In sum, webmasters try to enhance their videos' credibility by drawing upon journalism conventions, such as the profession's aesthetics, values, and subject matter. At one and the same time, the pieces always tap into Christian discourse. For instance, the spotlight is often directed on the travails of the Arab faithful in the hopes of fostering a sense of solidarity across the entire Catholic world.

4.5.4 Ritual Legitimacy

Within our cross section of videos, a substantial number depict Catholic clergy, prayers, and other rituals. These highly familiar subjects are placed within the more exotic context of the Holy Land. In consequence, these works buoy the spiritual-cum-religious pertinence of the area's venerated sites.

Many of these videos employ an anonymous voice-over describing rituals that take place in the Holy Land such as Christmas, Easter, the Via Delarosa procession. To demonstrate, a video referring to a rosary prayer taking place in Nazareth is narrated as follows (4 February 2016):

On Saturday night in Nazareth, some lights still illuminate the city where Jesus grew up. Near the basilica where the angel's Annunciation to Mary took place, the faithful recite the Rosary in a torchlight procession. Presided by the warden of the basilica and with the presence of the local Franciscans, the procession carries the image of Our Lady of Nazareth. While carrying the candles, each mystery of the Rosary is recited by the faithful in a different language, such as Arabic, Italian, Spanish, and Portuguese.

The narrator ties the Rosary Prayer to its back story. In so doing, he romanticizes this well-known ritual and amplifies its experiential meaning. Furthermore, an emphasis is placed on the late-night procession's multicultural flavour.

Another segment of this video features Susan Volpini, an American pilgrim, commenting on her ecumenical experience at this ambulatory service:

I converted to Catholicism, and I love being here in Jesus' sites. It is great to recite the Rosary and hear it being recited in other languages, like French, Italian, Arabic … The procession used to be a privilege only for those who were able to come to the Holy Land, but now even those who are far away will be able to follow it. As of January 2016, the prayer is transmitted by the Franciscan Custody Web TV and will arrive to other countries through Canção Nova Television and Telepace.

As a convert, the pilgrim is evidently all the more grateful for this opportunity to walk in Jesus's footsteps. In highlighting the procession's international colour and mediatization, she intimates that the ritual is enriched by its global popularity.

By dint of its granular references to Middle Eastern politics, "The Christmas Celebrations in Gaza" (uploaded late 2018) has a more local feel. This clip documents an all-but-unknown procession from the Church of the Holy Family in Gaza City. In his homily before a packed crowd at this Gazan house of worship, the apostolic administrator of the Latin Patriarchate of Jerusalem underscores the importance of this community and notes that its members "are not forgotten." Likewise, the voice-over narrative, including its allusions to Scripture, centres on the Vatican's efforts to reach out to this afflicted community, which is pinned down in the crossfire of the Israeli–Palestinian struggle.

By focusing on rituals, the webmasters reaffirm the Holy Land's prominence in the Catholic tradition. In the process, the tension between the familiar and the alien comes to a head. The standardized liturgy, the inclusion of youth, and audience participation are all mainstays of the Catholic religious experience. Placing these familiar scenes in a Holy Land setting only enhances the videos' significance and allure. What is more, these works cast doubt on the somewhat pervasive notion that the Middle East has stagnated into a comatose museum of the ancient Christian past by portraying its shrines as vibrant institutions that continue to attract both local devotees and foreign pilgrims. A plethora of televised broadcasts, radio feeds, videos, and podcasts allow believers to partake in rituals (e.g., Christmas Mass) at storied venues from afar. The mediated pilgrimages discussed herein certainly fit this bill. Apart from touting the Holy Land, the videos that feature areas outside of Israel's jurisdiction, not least the Gaza Strip, indicate that the Franciscan Custody's geographical ambit is more expansive than generally believed.

4.6   Conclusion

The present chapter has shed light on videos that are intended to reaffirm the Holy Land's status in the Christian faith. Within this framework, we assayed the meaning-making processes of content producers – a Catholic monastic media group – and sought to understand how the webmasters reflexively legitimize their works from the perspective of online viewers.

By adopting scriptural, experiential, journalistic, and ritualistic strategies, webmasters are reaffirming the prominence of holy sites in the digital realm. These efforts have sparked a dialectic process in which the content and the medium sanction one another. The first of these strategies, *scriptural legitimacy* (biblical landscape, textual references, iconography, and biblical performance), draws on central religious texts to magnify scared places. In these sorts of videos, the medium is presented as a "mere" conduit – the online mouthpiece of well-established religious institutions – for god's word. *Experiential legitimacy* strategies (life-changing experiences, personal motivations, calls to pilgrimage, and visitor testimonies) tout these venues and their rites by way of on-site believer testimonies. Put differently, the webmasters furnish a medium that allows for believer-to-believer communications. *Journalistic legitimacy* utilizes basic news-industry discursive modes, styles, and values to impart videos with an air of credibility. The final strategy, *ritual legitimacy*, involves a synthesis between a familiar practice, a trusted clergy member, and a venerated holy site. By transmitting a significant devotional performance to audiences across the globe, the video serves as an arbiter of ritual meaning.

By dint of these semiotic strategies, the webmasters construct the Holy Land's meaning for their online audience. As per Umberto Eco's theory of indexicality, each of these strategies takes advantage of *legitimation markers*. That is to say, signs and symbols are chosen to highlight and endorse a social, political and/or religious worldview. While pilgrimage to remote destinations is certainly a time-honoured practice, until the postwar era it was the sole preserve of what Weber termed "the religious aristocracy" (see Silber 1995, 25), that is well-endowed or fervent believers, like monks, who demonstrated their elevated social status and/or pious faith through arduous voyages to far-off, mysterious-cum-exotic destinations. However, the sharp drop in transportation costs over the past century has, among other things, expanded the international tourist circuit to religious sites. The digital revolution has added yet another dimension to the pilgrimage experience, as livestreaming, social media, and other platforms have brought this hitherto exclusive pastime to the masses.

To expand their "market share," the promoters of holy sites must not only remind believers of their product's lofty standing, but convince them that the places are relevant to their own lives. Furthermore, the webmasters endeavour to suit their content to the audience's media sensibilities. Through a combination of journalistic elements, traditional rituals, first-hand accounts, and established religious narratives, online users are invited to approximate a boots-on-the-ground pilgrimage. This simulation is rendered possible by validating indexical signs. For instance, webmasters emphasize the connection between the locale and the Holy Scriptures. In the videos of the Christian Media Center, this bond is forged via a strategic interplay between the camera (indexical pointer) and the four above-mentioned strategies. These steps elevate, *inter alia*, old churches, stones, and travellers into holy sites, genuine altars, and fervent pilgrims, respectively.

Videos offer faith-based movements new tools, or perhaps a new "language," of religiosity that capitalize on modern norms of media consumption and cinematic affordances, like those that are popular on YouTube. While televangelists certainly employ different strategies for generating leadership charisma, the focus on sacred places and their attendant rituals (e.g., processions) are at the forefront of our case study. In this chapter, we have taken stock of how Holy Land practices are animated and dramatized to suit online viewers. Thanks to these videos and various other efforts on the part of major stakeholders, the region's pilgrimage destinations are back in the Catholic limelight.

Against this backdrop, researchers are encouraged to delve into the macro and micro ramifications of these new media strategies. From a macroscopic standpoint, the impact of media-constructed centres of faith on religious communities around the globe warrants scholarly attention. In our estimation, the initiators of these sorts of projects are aspiring to create innovative forms of ecumenism and interfaith (or inter-denominational) dialogue, from which new religious praxes and leaders can emerge. On a meso level, the videos under review can be seen as educational tools that revolve around an experience of the viewer or a more abstract view of religious experience. While it is now commonplace for such videos to be screened in churches before and during services, this type of material is now consumed in less formal venues as well. A case in point is remote learning within the framework of online "self-educating communities" (Burbules 2006). What is more, our findings may induce microscopic studies on what this phenomenon reveals about the believer and his or her worldview. More specifically, the following questions beg asking: How do these videos fit the users' media and information-consumption habits? Within this digitalized reality, how do believers select, navigate, and endorse such content? Yet another related topic is profane stakeholders with an interest in advancing religious venues for the purpose of, say, increasing tourism or mobilizing migrant populations.

Throughout this chapter, we have focused on webmasters' efforts to bolster the credentials of the Catholic Church in the eyes of an imagined cohort of believers by means of online videos. The semiotic approach that we developed for the case study can be replicated by scholars gauging the utility and impact of comparable outreach programs of other religious bodies.

PART 3

Bolstering Religious Authority through Visual Content

5 Virtual Authenticity: Livestreaming Religious Sites

On a hot August day in 2017, we attended the Catholic Feast of the Transfiguration of Jesus on Mount Tabor, which many Christians believe to be the site of this iconic biblical event. Upon our arrival, we noticed banners commemorating the eighth centennial of the Custody of the Holy Land. Despite the onerous winding footpath leading to this remote venue, the Transfiguration Church would be filled with devotees by the time the service began.

As we approached the Franciscan house of worship, media crews were setting up their gear. Staff of the Christian Media Center were removing equipment from a room near the entrance to the main sanctuary. Elderly attendees had already taken a seat, and media members were positioning themselves to cover the event. In parallel, a mixed crowd of all ages was filing into the hall. Many of the believers were local Christian Arabs. Although the building offered some respite from the oppressive heat, the arrivals fanned themselves as they scanned the aisles for chairs or room to sit or stand on the floor. A robed monk directed them to find "the right place." Several key vantage points were reserved for camera operators filming "the main stage" and the dignitaries (foremost among them, the head of the Custody), the organ player, officiators, the youth choir, and the rest of the audience.

The ceremony began with a priest welcoming the attendees and greeting viewers from around the globe. While the former were by and large native Arabic speakers, the prayers were recited in several languages. From atop the stage, a dark-toned young woman read from the gospel in Portuguese. After a musical interlude courtesy of the aforementioned choir, a short sermon was delivered in Arabic. This

Figure 5.1 | Media crew setting up gear before the transfiguration feast ceremony on Mount Tabor, August 2017.

was followed by another hymn and a brief homily in English. Alongside the traditional Latin liturgy, parts of the ceremony were also conducted in Spanish, Italian, and Arabic. Professional cameramen were strategically arrayed at favourable shooting angles throughout the hall. For instance, a few camera operators stood on tables, and some tracked the ecclesiastical "players" from the altar (see figure 5.1). What is more, quite a few worshipers recorded the event on their mobile phones and other devices. The festivities opened and closed with a procession from and to a historic oratory on the compound's premises, which was videoed by a drone overhead.

While the event was certainly held in a specific venue and catered to local worshippers, its mediatization by lay participants and, all the more so, Church-sponsored media crews was pronounced. In contrast to other public events, like concerts or ballgames, the camera operators were hardly an "invisible" presence. Although the Transfiguration Feast is not a major occasion (compared to, say, Christmas Eve in Bethlehem), its organizers simultaneously targeted two distinct audiences: pilgrims and local congregants, on the one hand; and international viewers, on the other.

Given the dearth of summer events on the liturgical calendar, the Transfiguration Feast constitutes a big draw for both the Catholic traveller and internet surfer. While much of the footage taken was for future editing and usage, the ceremony was also streamed live to public assemblies and home viewers around the world. Major religious institutions are increasingly turning to livestreaming venerated expanses – be they specific events or continuous twenty-four-hour feeds – as a form of international outreach. As we shall see, the Western Wall in Jerusalem and Our Lady of Lourdes in France are among the holy sites with these sorts of feeds.

Against this backdrop, the present chapter assays the efforts of organized religion to maintain its base and win over new hearts via livestreaming. We will explore the motivations and key agents behind such novel enterprises, as well as clerical responses to this phenomenon. To this end, a theoretical construct has been formulated that draws heavily on Walter Benjamin's concept of the aura. Our findings suggest that devotional feeds are restoring the centrality of sacred expanses in the public imagination. Moreover, these livestreams are bolstering the global outreach campaigns of traditional denominations. Last but not least, the adoption of these media tools is elevating the status of webmasters within the ecclesiastical hierarchy.

5.1 Capturing, Sharing and Invigorating Experiences: Livestreaming in Comparative Contexts

Instilling a sense of authenticity and identification with an external event is a challenge faced by producers of various digital formats, from computer games, like Second Life, to chatrooms. Livestreaming has been a popular communicative strategy for meeting these objectives. By virtue of the immediacy and presence of livestreams, users feel as though they are participating in the broadcasted event and belong to the host community. The excitement of taking part in a live gathering creates a meaningful experience. Moreover, livestreaming injects a lecture, political demonstration, rock concert, or football match with an intensity that eludes, say, a YouTube video. This stimulation not only boosts the user's motivation to learn, cultivate a political identity, and join a leisure activity, but can indirectly inspire social solidarity and zeal.

Livestreaming in a wide array of fields is gradually netting research attention. In Luo, Hsu, Park, and Hancock's estimation (2020), this technology ratchets up the viewer's emotional involvement by allowing them to watch with others and comment on developments in real time. Building on Durkheim's theory of "collective effervescence" (1995 [1912]), these scholars hypothesize that face-to-face engagement in public rituals is emotively arousing. Accordingly, Luo, Hsu, Park, and Hancock contend that their subjects "feel happier" and more excited when viewing televised events, such as the World Cup, together with family and friends, than alone. Parsing a voluminous dataset of comments posted to news and media happenings on YouTube, they found that, all things being equal, live reactions are more intense than posterior comments across all the event types they researched.

Drawing on the respected Uses and Gratifications Theory, Hilvert-Bruce, Neill, Sjöblom, and Hamari (2018) examined the popular gaming website Twitch (N = 2227). By dint of multiple and ordinal linear regression, this cohort identified six primary factors that attracted users to this livestreamed platform: social interaction, community feel, meeting new people, entertainment, obtaining information, and loneliness. In a similar vein, Haimson and Tang (2017) recorded viewers' experiences as they livestreamed events on Facebook Live, Periscope, and Snapchat Live Stories. On the basis of their subjects' responses, the scholars uncovered four qualities that hooked in audiences: immersion, immediacy, reciprocity, and sociality. Depending on their technological affordances, outlets possess varying degrees of these characteristics. At any rate, Haimson and Tang determined that the livestreaming experiences afford real time interaction and sociality in a manner that, for example, YouTube, does not. In the researchers' estimation, this ability to deliver meaning and affect is indicative of the medium's prowess.

Livestreaming is also a verified source of income. In their seminal paper, Lu Jia et al. (2020) demonstrate that there is a strong correlation between the level of user donations and the "atmosphere" stimulated on real-time chats accompanying events on Facebook-Live, You-Tube-Live, and Twitch. As a result, they concluded that the design of such interactive platforms is vital to triggering audience enthusiasm and spending.

Indeed, livestreaming has merited quite a bit of attention from human-computer-interaction (HCI) scholars. More specifically, they have described how state-of-the-art technology and well-designed live mixed-media can be used to optimize the feeds and reinforce communal behaviour (Diamant-Cohen and Golan 2016; Hamilton, Garretson and Kerne 2014; Sripanidkulchai, Maggs and Zhang 2004).

In other fields, studies have focused on these feeds' educational and political utility. Shephard (2003) emphasizes how streaming online resources in class settings can improve the face-to-face student–teacher encounters. More recently, pedagogic works have discussed the benefits of remote learning via livestream platforms. Abdous and Yoshimura (2010) even claim that these learning frameworks are as effective as traditional modes of instruction.

With respect to the political sphere, Thorburn (2014) has focused on a student-operated livestream television channel that broadcast police activities during the Quebec student strike of 2012. By conveying a sense of authenticity, Thorburn concludes, this bottom-up technology spurred on resistance to government violence. Gregory (2015) describes how Brazilian activists use livestreaming to narrate their accounts and keep a distant audience abreast of the situation on the ground. In doing so, they ramp up the audience's level of involvement and occasionally manage to recruit them for social initiatives. Furthermore, he demonstrates how such broadcasts allow far-flung audiences to share a common experience.

For decades, families and communities have often assembled to watch live religious events, such as Christmas Day Mass, on television. Over the past fifteen years or so, podcasts have been added to the mix. Owing to the unique properties of livestreaming, we contend that its viewing experience differs from that of other outlets. As Martini (2018) has shown, user activity changes in relation to the means of communication. Whereas online videos elicit low-intensity user-to-user interactions, not least prolix messages and numerous replies, livestreaming reportedly triggers a powerful sense of communion. Building on this theory, we argue that webmasters leverage the properties of livestreaming to shape viewers' relationship with holy sites.

5.2   Livestreaming Holy Sites

With the mass proliferation of broadband online services, livestreaming has emerged as a popular outlet. Among the objectives behind such webcasts is the mediatization of holy sites (see figures 5.2 and 5.3).

For the purposes of this book, livestreaming is defined as content delivered synchronically over the internet. Needless to say, there is a wide range of livestreaming genres. We have identified six "ideal type" characteristics (in the Weberian sense, Weber 1968, 20–2) of this platform. Though not necessarily the most popular features of livestreaming, in our estimation they set this outlet apart from the rest:

1   Audiovisual Communication. For users, livestreaming generally emphasizes a sensual multimedia experience (even for intellectually driven content), rather than a studious undertaking per se, such as in written text.

2   Real Time. Unlike other online formats, livestreaming is synchronous. In other words, it is produced and consumed at one and the same time. Consequently, viewers are unable to control the flow of information by, say, hitting fast-forward, pause, or replay.

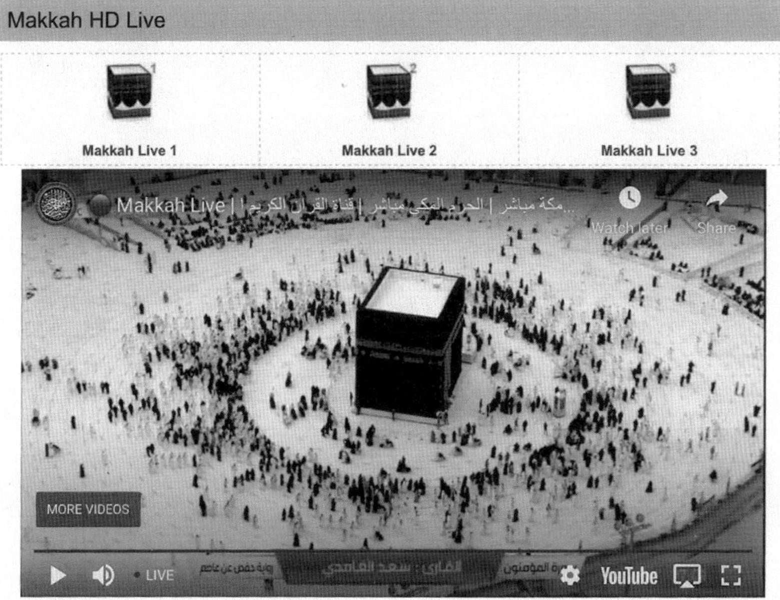

Figure 5.2 | 24/7 livestreamed feed of the Kaaba, provided by Makkah Live (an Islamic organization based in the United Kingdom).

3 Evanescence. In contrast to videos or filmed media, livestreaming yields a short-lived and non-retrievable outcome. This ephemeral nature underscores the infrequency of the event. Moreover, its transitory essence bears an implied supremacy vis-á-vis recorded events.

4 "Raw Feed." While media productions usually involve extensive editing at the service of a preconceived narrative, livestream broadcasts are produced on the fly. In consequence, they are highly dependent on the way the event unfolds, and the editing tends to be veiled.

5 Constant Accessibility. Like other new media content, livestreaming can be accessed via most mobile devices at home, in public, or on the go.

6 Ubiquity. Quite a few livestreaming outlets are broadcast around the clock. This characteristic allows users to develop a

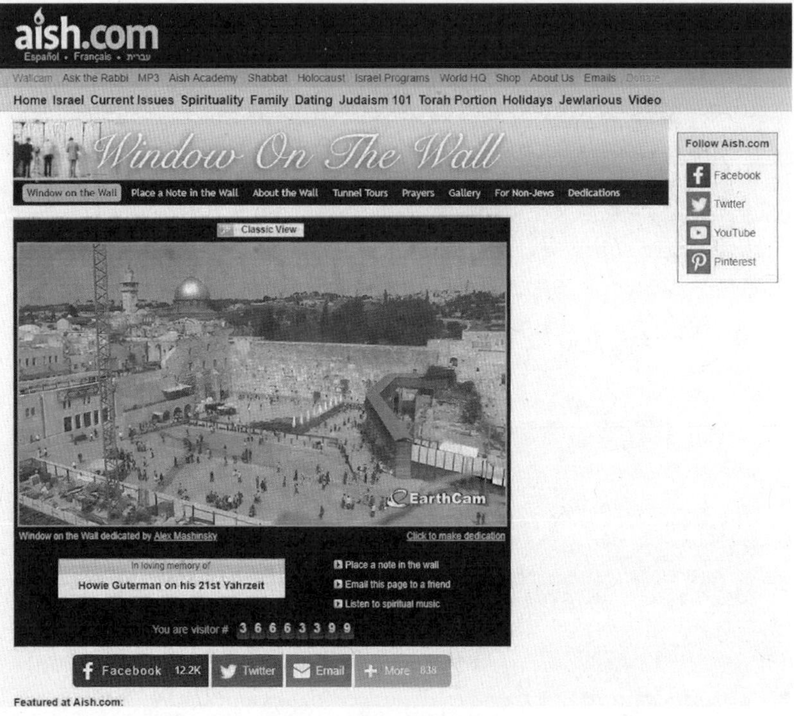

Figure 5.3 | 24/7 livestreamed feed of the Western Wall, provided by Aish HaTorah (a Jewish Orthodox educational NGO).

permanent and synchronized relationship with distant sites, actors, and occurrences.

These six mediatized components vary in the different sub-genres of livestreaming (e.g., sporting events or reality shows), but in aggregate they create a meaningful experience of the streamed venue that appears to resemble that of actual visitors. Believers view livestreamed religious media not only in the privacy of their living room but on monitors placed in stores, hospitals, prayer houses, and lounges of retirement communities. Ethnographers have stressed the paradox of pilgrims journeying to far-off lands in order to deepen the identities that they maintain back at home (Kaell 2014, 13). While underscoring the holy expanse's significance, livestreaming might alleviate this contradiction. A historic forerunner of this outlet is the photographic representation of sacred places. More recently, other forms of technological engagement have entered the devotional marketplace. In the late 1990s, for example, Aish HaTorah (an institution dedicated to persuading Jews to "return" to the Orthodox fold) enabled believers to perform the traditional custom of inserting a note into the Western Wall via fax. This service is currently available online at the Aish.com website (see figure 5.3 above). Taking a page out of the Aish HaTorah playbook, a Hassidic website (chabad.org) invites users to send a *kvittel* ("small note") to the grave of Menachem Mendel Schneerson, the highly venerated grand rabbi of Chabad. In the Catholic world, remote worship services are provided by numerous websites. A case in point is conventopadrepio.com, which lights candles for online devotees at the burial chamber of Saint Padre Pio (an Italian friar renowned for displaying stigmata). These offerings reflect the growing phenomenon of believers connecting to sacred places through the internet. Moreover, they open a window onto the struggle of religious organizations to find innovative, non-canonical ways to the public's heart. The demand for these services is indicative of a physical or even material dimension of faith, which is mediated and enlarged by new media tools.

While this phenomenon involves the mediatization of holy sites, the platforms' allure stems from a structural tension. On the one hand, these places are venerated on account of their specific location (e.g., shrines in Jerusalem, Mecca, and Lourdes) and their ingrained connection to the divine in the religious imagination. On the other hand, cyberspace can be viewed as an ephemeral and non-territorial realm. It is the convergence between these two seemingly antithetical properties that engenders new channels for religious activity. In addition to prayer and contemplation, prominent religious organizations are increasingly advising the faithful to cultivate mediatized relationships with major holy sites.

The proliferation of institutional livestreamed feeds that are operated for devotional purposes raises the question of how worldviews are shaped, and meaning is negotiated by these sorts of products. With this question in mind, we have delved into a joint Catholic media venture that streams live from holy places in Israel/Palestine. Launched by the Franciscan order and the Brazil-based Canção Nova movement, this collaboration has already yielded a 24/7 feed of the Basilica of the

Figure 5.3 | 24/7 livestreamed feed from the Grotto at the Basilica of the Annunciation in Nazareth.

Figure 5.5 | Behind the scenes: the production studio at the Basilica of the Annunciation in Nazareth.

Annunciation in Nazareth (see figures 5.4 and 5.5). Furthermore, the two groups are working on similar projects in Jerusalem and Bethlehem. Our field study of this enterprise offers a firsthand look at the nascent stages of a religious livestreaming initiative.

In the pages that follow, we will elaborate on our study of this Catholic co-production. Our fieldwork included comprehensive interviews with the venture's webmasters, a thorough examination of their media productions, and participant-observation fieldwork at holy sites and media production studios. Building on the religion-cum-media literature and the attendant Catholic discourse, we developed a theoretical framework that draws heavily on the scholarship of Walter Benjamin. Over the course of our fieldwork, we uncovered three principal goals behind this collaboration: evangelizing youth, fostering affinity towards the Holy Land, and maintaining a constant presence of the transcendental. These findings will be analyzed through the prism of Benjamin's concept of the "aura." In the process, we hope to discern how the feed from Nazareth endows viewers with a sense of proximity to the divine. We contend that livestreaming has transformed devotional experience and imparted webmasters a secondary authority onto ecclesiastical webmasters. Succinctly put, our case study attests to the emergence of new roles in the Catholic Church and novel forms of religious engagement in the digital age.

5.2 "Catholicism Live": Taking the Leap from "Old" to "New" Media

The turn to livestreaming can be viewed as a new phase in the Catholic Church's efforts to deepen its connection with the flock via media tools. Its traditionist leanings aside, the Church has gradually integrated media into its outreach strategies. According to some researchers, this approach dates back to the 1920s. The International Catholic Organization for Cinema and the International Catholic Association for Radio and Television were indeed founded in 1928. Eight years later the *Vigilanti Cura* papal encyclical of 1936 identified the cinema's potential as a platform for disseminating Catholic ideals (Ortiz 2003, 182). In 1948, the Pontifical Commission for Social Communications was formed to address concerns about the challenges that the dawn of the audiovisual era presents for religious educators (Campbell 2010, 36).

Whereas some religious groups view social media as irredeemable lairs of transgression (Golan and Campbell 2015), the Catholic position is that these outlets can be used on a daily basis to advance the following goals: to spread core religious values and authentic expressions of devotion, and to entrench religion at the forefront of the public domain. To these ends, the Church has indeed broadcast and provided footage to the media of public events since the 1950s.

Rome's promotion of the Holy Land, though, has lagged behind other new media projects. Early video productions included the globally disseminated footage from Pope Paul VI's historic visit to Israel/Palestine in 196, and the Israel Broadcasting Authority's annual coverage of the Christmas Mass in Bethlehem. A recurring broadcast which has extended for several decades. Thus, church initiatives to produce religious content have for the most part been limited to print offerings, photographs, and documentaries. Largely owing to the substantial economic investment and technological obstacles that this entailed, video footage was only provided of peak events (i.e., Christmas rites and papal pilgrimages). As a result, most Catholics were only sporadically engaged with the Holy Land.

5.3　The Three-Pronged Temporality of Livestreaming

Similar to cinema and literature, the internet invites users to experience a formatted construction of time, namely a realm in which time is sequenced in a different manner. Patterns of temporal compression and expansion are indeed an established characteristic of films and novels (Rimmon-Kenan 1983). Above all, scholars point to a discrepancy between the audience's "real time" and the time span of the narrated/edited framework. From the 1990s onward, the literature has pointed to a similar distinction in online content, especially between synchronous and asynchronous modes of communication (Rafaeli and Sudweeks 1998; Danet 2001). In our estimation, there are three corresponding temporal realms in audiovisual communications that dictate the viewers' experience:

1　Time of Context. This dimension refers to the user's whereabouts during the media experience (e.g., at the movie theatre or on the living room couch). Owing to technological advances, this realm is in a constant state of flux. While the theatre, for instance, was the lone option for watching cinema throughout the first half of the twentieth century, the emergence of television and, more recently, mobile communications have redefined this practice. These sorts of developments have had a substantial impact on the organization of society in all that concerns the modal and temporal possibilities for consuming information. A fine example is the change in the way people get the news. Rigid TV newscast schedules had structured daily life since the 1950s, but the advent of the VCR, cable television, DVR, and news apps have transformed viewing habits.

2   Time of Narration refers to the duration of the narrative process. While the length of, say, a movie or YouTube video is basically predetermined by its producer, new technologies have given users a measure of control over this realm. A case in point is the nigh ubiquitous option of pausing, rewinding, and skipping. As linear consumption gives way to fragmented "viewage," creators often opt for a modular narrative that is more amenable to the user's preferences. For instance, many YouTube videos provide narrative indexes in the "About" section that enable consumers to watch the content in a nonlinear and partial manner.

3   Time of Story. As discussed in the narratology literature, this dimension consists of the time span that is propagated by the narrated events. Unrelated to the previous strands, time of story is essentially the narrated time in which the plot unfolds. Needless to say, its duration can appreciably vary from one work to the next. Depending on the literary devices the author employs, it may or may not be linear. For example, the time of the story could encompass one day or an entire century. Moreover, the narrative can be structured by flashbacks, slow motion, and leaps forward. The time of story is impervious to contextual influences, but technological developments may have some impact on its actual duration. For instance, a feature film often conforms to technological considerations

and industry standards (e.g., a running time of 90–120 minutes). In a similar fashion, broadcasted events will adhere to the preferences and/or constraints of the media (i.e., duration, time zones, and equipment issues).

While livestreaming may fall under the category of audiovisual communications, this sub-genre possesses distinct qualities. Be that as it may, the three temporal dimensions also apply to livestreaming. In fact, the relations between these realms can be configured in a more specific manner. The "time of story" in livestream feeds is linear and tightly linked to the "time of context" via the "time of narration." For instance, a typical soccer match lasts ninety minutes (time of story). Excluding the halftime intermission, the broadcast is also ninety-minutes long (time of narration). Consequently, the viewer will have to set aside at least ninety minutes to watch the entire game (time of context). In these sorts of cases, the opening minute of the story utterly corresponds to the first minute of narration and consumption. Popularly known as "real time," the synchronization between the temporal strands may occasionally impose certain difficulties for audiences in different time zones. Live broadcasts of peak events, such as the midnight mass in Bethlehem, may be uncomfortable for spectators in California where the ceremony begins at 2:00 pm. On the other hand, this feed implicitly offers an "authentic" construct of the event, as it coincides with the start time in the home of the nativity. The argument can be made that the wider the gap between the believers' time zone and that of the venerated object (what Lacan dubbed "*Objet petit a*"), the greater the mystique and journey of the imagination.

5.4 Approaching the Divine in Real Time: Walter Benjamin and Livestreaming

While the relation between holy sites and devotional experiences has merited considerable scholarly attention (Badone 2004; Coleman and Eade 2004), the relation between the former and media tools, especially livestreaming, has barely registered in the literature. Walter Benjamin's seminal work on art reproduction can perhaps enhance our understanding of livestreaming's potential as a gateway to the "numinous"

(Otto 1958 [c1916]). Most notably in *The Work of Art in the Age of Mechanical Reproduction*, Benjamin (2008 [c1931]) discusses the extent to which art reproductions exude the authenticity of their originals. The intellectual defines the aura of natural objects as "the unique phenomenon of a distance, however close it may be" (285). Moreover, Benjamin contemplates the distance between a real experience and an artistic approximation thereof. In contrast to other art forms, he contends that photographs *qua* reproductions diminish and "weaken" the aura.

Benjamin's critique of photography raises questions concerning distance and practice. In his estimation, an artwork's proximity to the original experience determines its significance to the viewer. Photography, though, is reproductive by its very definition. In consequence, an experiential discrepancy is interposed between the authentic-cum-inspiring original and its imitation, thereby diminishing the importance of the experience.

In recent years, the topic of aura has come up in the discourse on the wherewithal of popular films, television programs, virtual reality, and new media products to replicate the original experience (Bolter, MacIntyre, Gandy and Schweitzer 2006). Examining the relations between a believer and religious sites, articles, and artworks is vital to comprehending his or her experiences. Owing to their capacity for inspiring awe, their proximity to the transcendental, and their devotional roles, such items and venues appear to have a powerful "auratic existence." Holy sites are perceived as being closest to the divine, for they are not reproductions. If so, the meaning of devotional livestreaming and its relation to physical space is of utmost importance to the discussion at hand. By exploring the outlook of webmasters on digital productions and computer-mediated pilgrimage, we hope to shed light on this phenomenon.

5.5   An Insider's Look at the Production of Religious Livestreaming

The focus of this chapter is on the production of livestreamed content on the part of the Christian Media Center – the joint media venture between the Franciscans and the Canção Nova – in the Holy Land between 2015 and 2017. Over the course of our fieldwork, we identified two product categories that the centre offered. The first is a continuous raw feed of live images from a sacred place. To date, the CMC is only mediatizing one site in this fashion: The Basilica of the Annunciation in Nazareth. However, our informants mentioned plans to add two venues in Jerusalem: Gethsemane and, if possible, the Church of the Holy Sepulchre. The second product is scheduled religious events. This sort of broadcast involves cutting-edge technologies, more staging, and coordination with the administrators of the holy sites. In the hopes of explicating these productions, we surveyed live feeds of major holidays, like Christmas, Easter, and the Feast of St Francis of Assisi, from Israel/Palestine.

For the purposes of this chapter, webmasters are defined as religious internet-cum-technology staff, entrepreneurs, and other stakeholders in the creation of online content. To grasp how the Christian Media Center's webmasters regard their media productions, both in terms of their worldviews and individual roles, we designed a mixed-method approach that leans on the ethnographic data gathered in the field. Accordingly, we attended ceremonies in various monasteries and prominent shrines in Israel/Palestine that were broadcast by the CMC. Among the sites that we canvassed were the Basilica of the Annunciation (Nazareth), the Church of the Nativity (Bethlehem), the Holy Sepulchre Church (Jerusalem), and the Cenacle (Jerusalem). Additionally, twenty-five in-depth interviews were conducted with Franciscans and members of the Canção Nova. Most of these interviewees were volunteers, monks, and other clergy serving on webmaster production teams. During these sessions, we broached the following sort of questions:

How does the "visuality" of livestreaming suit your evangelical
   mission?
How does the global reach of this medium fit your objectives?
Does broadcasting rituals online enhance their standing?
Are there any religious limitations on videoing ceremonies and
   sacred places?
Can an online feed convey holiness?
Is there competition between faith-based groups over
   representing the Holy Land?
In the long run, will live digital media become part and parcel of
   officially sanctioned Christian practice?

In the run-up to our ethnographic inquiry, we watched a balanced sample of Franciscan and Canção Nova productions. These transmissions were broadcast on a number of websites, such as the Franciscan Media Center (fmcterrasanta.org) and the TV Canção Nova Facebook Page (facebook.com/tvcancaonova). Familiarity with this content enhanced our discussions with webmasters and our understanding of their objectives.

By comparing these videos, our field notes, and interview transcripts, we gained insight into how our subjects perceive their media activities.

"Dedoose" mixed-method analysis software was used to thematically code the interviews according to the topics that emerged over the course of our fieldwork. We were especially sensitive to issues of authority, religion, pilgrimage, outreach, and community. It also bears noting that ethical concerns were addressed. Haifa University's Institutional Review Board (IRB) granted its approval on 8 August 2015.

5.6 Catholic Media Entrepreneurship Online: The Franciscan/ Canção Nova Initiative

Canção Nova boasts a proven track record in new media outreach. Founded by Brazilian Catholics in 1978 in direct response to the *Evangelii Nuntiandi*, an encyclical by Pope Paul VI,[1] Canção Nova is a monastic community (Cachoeira Paulista). The evangelical mission and method of this community is, however, unconventional for monastic standards. Indeed, their approach and practice reflect in various ways the encyclical's idea that "modern man has passed beyond the civilization of the word, which is now ineffective and useless, and that today he lives in the civilization of the image. These facts should certainly impel us [the Catholic Church] to employ, for the purpose of transmitting the Gospel message, the modern means which this civilization has produced" (*Evangelii Nuntiandi*).

In recent years, the Vatican has entrusted this organization with an evangelical ministry, which revolves around social communications. Riding the wave of the Catholic Charismatic Renewal, Canção Nova has expanded its activities to Western Europe (i.e., Portugal, Italy, Greece, France, and Cyprus) and beyond (Israel, India, the United States, and Paraguay) within just a few decades (Carranza and Mariz 2013).

Sharing a commitment to the evangelical mission, Canção Nova members in the Holy Land practise a variety of pious lifestyles, ranging from traditionally dressed celibate monks to devout married couples without children. Most of them reside in gender-segregated dormitories and adhere to elaborate rules governing the community's daily routine (e.g., prayers, shared domestic chores, and the economic management of the collective).

Within Israel/Palestine, the Canção Nova operates under the aegis of the Christian Media Center (CMC), in conjunction with the Franciscan Custody of the Holy Land. The centre's primary mission (cmc-terrasanta.com) is to cultivate a direct bond between Christian denominations throughout the world and the Holy Land. At present, the Canção Nova offers three sorts of media products to its international audience: (a) online documentaries and videos of religious ceremonies in high definition, sermons, and the like in English, French, Italian, Arabic, and Portuguese; (b) live coverage of big Catholic events, via online feeds and satellite TV; and (c) livestreaming from a number of holy sites, including the aforementioned 24/7 operation at the Basilica of the Annunciation. Given the Canção Nova's rising global prominence in evangelical outreach, studying this group opens a window onto how age-old religious institutions are employing new visual media tools.

5.7 Digital Gateways to the Transcendental: Livestreaming to Networked Publics

Our frequent visits to holy sites that are livestreamed by the CMC afforded us a glimpse of the production processes behind two categories of programing: a stationary camera feed that provides 24/7 coverage of the venue (see figure 5.1 above); and broadcasts of major events (figure 5.2) to a networked public. According to the webmasters' own testimony, their mission is to re-establish the Holy Land as a centre of Christian worship. Moreover, these initiatives are helping the Franciscans and Canção Nova redefine their position and bolster their authority within the Catholic world. Our findings revealed three underlying goals behind their efforts to place the Holy Land back at the centre of the Christian stage:

Evangelizing Youth. Pushing the boundaries of religious socializ-
ation in order to "speak the language" of contemporary youth.
Re-Establishing Affinity towards the Holy Land. Forging a
close bond between the flock and biblical sites.
Maintaining a Constant Presence of the Transcendental.
Rendering sites that are viewed as intercession points with
God readily accessible to the general public.

5.7.1 Evangelizing Youth

The ubiquity of media devices, particularly among the younger generation, is of grave concern to the religious establishment. A case in point
is Pope Francis's encyclical narratives emphasizing the new media's
impact on socialization processes. Additionally, this topic reared up
time and again in our conversations with informants. For instance, a
young female webmaster affiliated with the Canção Nova opined that

> Nowadays, there are groups you cannot reach if you don't have a
> media [presence] because all of society is engulfed by it, espe-
> cially the new generation. So I think that if we want to reach
> the new generation, we need to get with the times. The media
> is an efficient tool for evangelization, for reaching the coming
> generations … If you don't embrace these means, you cannot
> reach people. Their lives are totally into it. Youth, children … So
> we need to get with the program if we want to evangelize, if we
> want to save more souls for Jesus. (personal interview, translated
> from Italian)

Our interlocutor underscores generational shifts. In her view, young
people have developed a subculture that highly values information
from new media sources. Moreover, they are oblivious to other channels of communication. As a result, she believes that youth are recep-
tive to new forms of religious teaching. With this in mind, she calls for
an educational reform in which new media is used to connect young
audiences to traditional teachings."
In a similar vein, a prominent Franciscan described the advantages
of livestreaming:

The target of Catholic television is the middle-aged and elderly population, which is not familiar with livestreaming. Livestreaming is for young people. At first, the reason we streamed live from Nazareth was outreach to nursing homes and hospitals … so that old people could see Nazareth, the cave; they could see it and pray – recite the Rosary in front of the Grotto. That was the idea. Then, of course, you want to expand to liturgies, processions, torch light … These new things will be starting in the months ahead. (personal interview, translated from Italian)

According to this interviewee, different age groups require different outlets. In an effort to replicate past successes with established media outlets, he posits, the Church should target the young via livestreaming.

A Canção Nova seminarian explained the key role that new media play in his group's efforts to cultivate a positive image of the Catholic Church among millennials:

Lots of young people who are using drugs and those kinds of things can now see the Word of God – an image of the Holy Land – and see how beautiful it is and how it can change your life. These young people are not the same as the youth of our grandmothers' [generation]! Back in the day, our grandmothers were going to church and praying at home. Today … the youth aren't praying at home. When they look at the Church, they say: "This is passé; I want something new." So, for me, social media is a key to delivering a new type of religious experience to the youth. When they come to a prayer service at our [i.e., the Canção Nova] community, they see that is young! "How beautiful," [they exclaim,] I didn't know it was like this. Is this what being Catholic [is all about]?" Yes, it is. I believe that social media works like this: you cannot go to the Church, so the Church will come to you. Or the Holy Land. You cannot come to the Holy Land, so … the Holy Land … will come to you. How? Through social media. On TV and on the internet. (personal interview, translated from Italian)

This seminarian paints a negative image of his fellow millennials ("using drugs") to accentuate the importance of engaging youth (cf.

Cohen 1987). Furthermore, he asserts that the Canção Nova has managed to connect with this generation by enticing them with access to the sublime ("how beautiful the Holy Land is"), transformative messages ("change your life"), and a relevant environment ("the Church is young") – all by means of online technologies.

Taking into account the media-saturated environment of today's youth, our interviewees stress the importance of using new media to instill religious values in the new generation. Correspondingly, the webmasters avail themselves of these same tools to counter the perception that the Church is an anachronistic institution. They believe that their online content is quite meaningful to viewers, as it enables the latter to experience the awe that inheres the Holy Land's biblical sites.

5.7.2   Re-Establishing Affinity towards the Holy Land

Scholars of pilgrimage, ideological excursions, and museology (Badone 2004; Coleman and Eade, 2004; Ben David 1997; Shenhav 2013) demonstrate how guides convey meaning by knitting together specific historic times and places with the objective of creating a sense of affinity between their audience and an event or site. In a similar fashion, the Christian Media Center has turned to livestreaming in order to connect viewers with biblical sites.

A Palestinian cameraman and video editor discussed the significance of his work:

> When we are doing the live broadcast, it is really important
> because there are a lot of people staying at home and watching
> the mass from the place where Jesus Christ was. In Capernaum,
> for example, or we [also] had one two weeks ago in Deir Rafat –
> Our Lady of Palestine [a monastery near Beit Shemesh, in
> central Israel]. So, the people are waiting, they are waiting to see
> the mass. They are staying in their home just to watch the mass
> from the place of Jesus. (personal interview)

In other words, the video editor perceives a sense of anticipation for the livestreamed feeds of big events. Moreover, he implies that these webcasts help strengthen the viewer's relationship with Jesus, which is indeed a key facet of his mission.

Similar ideas came up in a discussion on Canção Nova's global outreach with one of the group's webmasters in Israel/Palestine:

Our project is to bring more and more holy places to the people [via the internet]. For this, we work in cooperation with the Custody of the Holy Land. The first Basilica where we built this communication system [a 24/7 live-stream feed] was here [in Nazareth]. The Custos of the Holy Land [the major superior of the Custody] has already told us that the next one should be the Gethsemane. And little by little, I think we will have the possibility to broadcast a mass, to have ... livestreaming [infrastructure] in all the sanctuaries of the Holy Land, [so as] to bring these places all over the world in the easiest way possible. But my personal dream is to do something in the Holy Sepulchre. It is the most important place for us. Here in Nazareth, it was a first attempt to see how it worked [*sic*]. (personal interview)

Over the course of the interview, the operator lists a number of holy places that the CMC is intending to stream live. He defines the feed from Nazareth as a pilot for future projects throughout Israel/Palestine, foremost among them the Church of the Holy Sepulchre.

A founder and senior policymaker at the CMC also discussed this mission:

Livestreaming makes you live the actuality of the event. In the videos, you see something which has happened before [*sic*]. In my opinion, this influences the ways a person can participate in an event, especially from an emotional point of view ... [W]hen you watch a livestreaming, you are living the same moment of what is happening in front of your eyes. Videos are not something dead, of course, but they show something which happened before, not in the same moment. We think that livestreaming makes people live the emotion of the celebration in a stronger way [*sic*]. (personal interview)

Besides other advantages over standard videos, the policymaker claims, live feeds captivate their audiences. Furthermore, he attributes the superiority of livestreaming to its temporal dimension, which charges the viewer experience with emotion. In sum, the second objective behind the Franciscan–Canção Nova partnership is to strengthen the flock's bonds with the Holy Land. Our informants pointed out that livestreaming provides meaningful real-time experiences. More specifically, they enable believers to tap into biblical sites on a daily basis from their home environments.

5.7.3   *Maintaining a Constant Presence of the Transcendental*

While artifacts and sacred places are widely accepted channels for engaging with the transcendental (Stadler 2015; Eliade 1958), livestreaming allows believers to access these mediums on their own terms, albeit through electronic means. A Canção Nova priest and media operator reflected on how these feeds sustain devotees' relationships with God:

> When you think of a program or a celebration, you have a place and you have a time. But, for example, I am not happy today and I want to pray. Yesterday when I arrived in my house, my brother told me, "Father, a family came here [to Nazareth], and they wanted to pray in the church. We opened the door and they prayed there, and we prayed with them." And I said "Thanks God, because you were here and they could pray in the church." When you make a livestreaming, you are doing this: keeping the doors of the church open. Also, Pope Francis he also told this in a letter: "We want the doors of the church open." And with the livestreaming, we are doing this. Any time that a person wants to pray and feel near to God, you can access your computer or cellphone or iPad and you can see there, and you can pray there, not just to see … But you receive the opportunity to leave your soul to see God here, here [*sic*]. (personal interview)

This interviewee correlates between worshiping at a holy site and participating in a service there via a live feed. Citing a papal communication, he avers that these technologies are legitimate means for pursuing religious goals and approaching the divine.

A prominent leader of the Canção Nova's media activities in Israel/ Palestine shared his enthusiasm for livestreaming:

To give people a glimpse of the life in this sanctuary [i.e., the Basilica of the Annunciation]. To connect [with God] – there! There [Nazareth] is the place where the Annunciation, where the Word Incarnate [was issued forth]. So, people have an opportunity to go there, see it for five, ten [minutes], perhaps an hour. They can contemplate the place where the mystery transpired, contemplate, admire, meditate. There, looking at that image of the Grotto, your mind will venture to the episode [discussed] in the [biblical] passage. Then you take the Bible, you go to the Gospel, to the passage of the Annunciation, and you … meditate. And then that meditation becomes a prayer, your communication with God, and then God performs His work. So, this is the reality of streaming, of sharing your personal moment. Can this be done with a community? Yes, it can, but I believe it is more personal. You can go there in the second it takes you to click [on a mouse] and summon [the Basilica] to your computer screen. Today we have the Smart TVs. Therefore, you can also reach the Annunciation Grotto, the Church of St Joseph, the upper part of the Basilica of Annunciation on your home TV. This is the [CMC's] first project; it is a pilot. But other sanctuaries in the world [are] already [being streamed live] … This is not something new nor is this the lone site. Other sanctuaries have [also] set up [a feed] to allow people to have this interaction. (personal interview, translated from Portuguese)

This interlocutor described how at any moment, a bevy of devotional activities are only a few clicks away. By virtue of livestreaming, an individual can remotely access a holy site and connect to the divine from the comfort of home. Furthermore, he claimed that believers can secure divine intervention ("and then God performs His work") through these feeds. Thus, he regards livestreaming as a tool available to believers to intervene in the world through otherworldly means.

A webmaster, who also works as a simultaneous translator at livestreamed events, underscored the personal experience:

In today's world, most people are looking for support, for a haven. To this end, [livestreaming] is crucial. For instance, do I want to recite the Rosary? I can watch a [feed from] the Basilica of the Annunciation, [and] see the grotto … For me, it is important from this standpoint: if a person wants to pray, that person can enter the Basilica, stay there, contemplate, observe. From my perspective, the beauty of livestreaming [is that it] brings the people inside sanctuaries. (personal interview, translated from Italian)

This webmaster views live feeds as a gateway not only to prayer ("recite the Rosary"), but to immerse oneself in the special environment of a holy place.

In summation, the webmasters have a wide range of ideas concerning the types of experiences that livestreaming can facilitate. Although the impact from viewing a site in this fashion does not measure up with that of hands-on experiences, livestreaming offers a surrogate means for connecting with God and fulfilling spiritual aspirations. Much like prayer and contemplation, these digital activities are also believed to secure divine intervention for the believer's worldly pursuits.

5.8   Livestreaming and the Religious Experience

Throughout this chapter, we have explored how religious institutions endeavour to shape the flock's worldviews and experiences by streaming live from holy places. Over the course of our fieldwork on a joint Catholic media venture in the Holy Land, we uncovered three underlying objectives behind the webmasters' mediatization of renowned shrines. The first, evangelizing youth, is a primary goal of countless clergy. By adjusting to the digital literacy and inclinations of the new generation, the Church hopes to stimulate awe-inspiring encounters with the biblical narrative that ultimately enable the flock to connect with the numinous. The second goal, arousing affinity towards the Holy Land, indicates that the webmasters deem livestreaming to be an unfiltered outlet for inducing experiences that were once the sole preserve of those who embarked on "real" pilgrimage. The final objective, maintaining a constant presence of the transcendental, can be interpreted as the desire to allow believers to interact with God whenever and wherever they please. In other words, the Christian Media

Center is building outlets for attaining divine intervention via the contemplation of livestreamed images that are accessed through quotidian devices, like smartphones and tablets.

Walter Benjamin's conception of the "aura" enhances our understanding how webmasters grasp livestreaming. The aura of holiness is quite often the fruit of centuries of veneration in a specific locale (e.g., the Ka'bah, the Western Wall, and Golgotha). Drawing on the authority of scripture, this aura has been persistently cultivated by the sites' ecclesiastical custodians and lay supporters (Gifford 2010). In parallel, these same factors endeavour to make traditional beliefs relevant to contemporary audiences. Leaning on Benjamin's ideas, we suggest that each particular experience can be "ranked" in accordance with its proximity to the sacred. Similarly, the holiness of a venerated site appears to reverberate to other, more distant satellites, from religious articles and works of art (e.g., icons) to livestreaming feeds and other cybernetic outlets (websites or digital games).

The rise of livestreaming and online devotional representation has created new opportunities for mass cultural transmission. That said, can widely dispersed, remote audiences find meaning in such "auratic" religious experiences? Or does Benjamin's theory of the diminished significance of reproduced art extend to the case of devotional live feeds? The webmasters we interviewed feel that these broadcasts are less influential than firsthand pilgrimage. However, they also stressed their efforts to mitigate this loss through improvements to the livestreaming experience itself, rather than other forms of mediation (documentaries, art, photographs, brochures, and pilgrimage literature). This, then, implies a hierarchy of religious proximity to the divine. What is more, we have discerned that livestreaming transforms the social structure around holy places and their derivatives. Gravitating around the actual venues, which occupy the top echelon, are clergy, digital actors, stakeholders, agents, and believers (see figure 5.6).

Following Water Benjamin's train of thought, livestreaming has some of the characteristics of mechanical reproduction, such as a photograph. By evoking a sense of proximity to a holy site, the broadcast mediates its aura. The process improves both the venue's standing as a centre of worship and the transmitting institution – in our case, the Catholic Church – owing to its privileged relationship with the

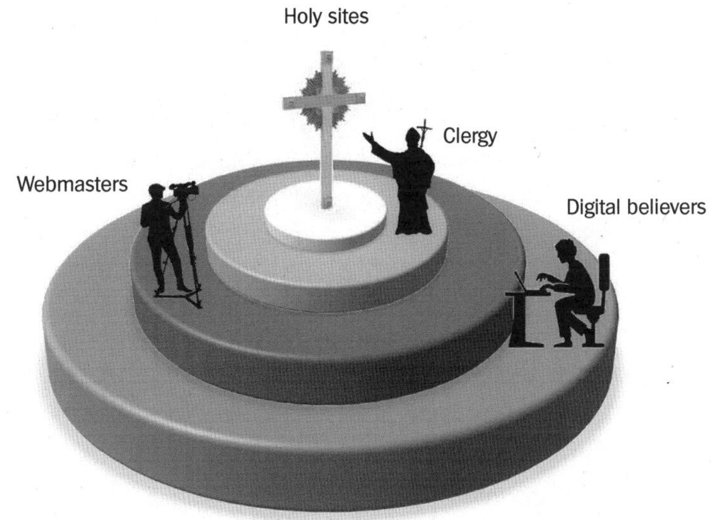

Figure 5.6 | Mapping the role and status of religious actors as they relate to the mediatization of holy sites.

venerated site. What is more, live steaming has elevated webmasters, perhaps unexpectedly, to the rank of secondary authorities within ecclesiastical hierarchies.

The question of authority has always stood at the very heart of the sociology of religion (cf. Gifford 2010). In Caplan and Stadler's riveting anthology (2011), the contributors have illuminated various ways in which contemporary Jewish ultra-Orthodox (Haredi) society has developed alternative authority agents. This legitimacy is a by-product of complementary, secular forms of knowledge (e.g., medicine and pedagogy) that were acquired at non-ultra-Orthodox institutions. For all intents and purposes, these factors compete with the rabbinical elite for the trust of community members. For example, in Caplan and Stadler's edited volume, Vered Bagad Elimelech discusses the Haredi cinema as an emergent source of moral guidance, albeit delivered by means of informal entertainment (a theme also investigated in the work of Matan Aharoni 2014). In a similar vein, Golan and Mishol-Shauli (2018) discuss the emergence of web-journalists as power brokers and gatekeepers of knowledge in the Haredi community.

In the case at hand, webmasters similarly undertake to establish their leadership credentials, albeit through their media expertise. As opposed to the external credentials of the emergent Jewish authority figures, our subjects' enterprise falls under the purview of the Catholic Church. Though the potential exists for internal subversion, the webmasters openly promote the Vatican. It stands to reason that they are competing with the lower ranks of the Church's outreach apparatus (e.g., local clergy and catechists), for they are "moving into their territory" as mediators of religious knowledge that espouse their worldviews before a mass audience. In consequence, the webmasters' authority derives from both the Church's standing and their personal influence on the flock. For example, they varnish their popular legitimacy by displaying the venerable Franciscan insignia on their videos; at one and the same time, they advance up the Church hierarchy by virtue of their direct access to rank-and-file believers (cf. Golan and Campbell 2015).

As noted in the introduction, Catholic livestreaming activities can be viewed as part of a heated global struggle for Christian hearts. In this context, maintaining the allegiance of devotees, foremost among them young people, is a growing concern for religious institutions. To strengthen the appeal of the *Ritus Romanus*, the Church is turning to livestream feeds and other digital means for the purpose of ratcheting up the veneration of Catholic-controlled biblical sites.

Given the long history of factionalism within the Christian world, the partnership between the Canção Nova and the Franciscan order can be viewed as an attempt to establish a unified front for the sake of revitalizing a commonly held belief system. The turn to digital tools affirms Eisenstadt's (2000) notion of "dynamic conservatism," namely the spread of traditional content by means of new institutional partnerships and modern operations. Over the ages, these sorts of enterprises have redrawn the boundaries and altered the identity of faith-based groups.

6 The Pope on Instagram: Managing Religious Authority and Globalized Charisma in the Digital Age

6.1 Introduction

"Pray for Me." With this caption, which appeared in multiple languages, Pope Francis launched his official Instagram account on 19 March 2016. In the inaugural image, the pontiff is seen kneeling alone in prayer, seemingly unaware of being photographed. As such, this post shares a private moment of devotion with millions of believers around the world. Be that as it may, the image is obviously the handiwork of a professional photographer and a sophisticated public-relations team. The tension generated by this sort of public/private duality is rather commonplace among the social media offerings of public figures.

Although the Vatican already had a presence on social networks like Twitter, the opening of the Instagram account netted a great deal of public attention, for the confluence of new technologies and religion is still quite a draw. To mark this hybrid occasion, the Holy See invited Kevin Systrom, Instagram's chief executive, to the public inauguration in Rome. Facing a crowd of journalists, Francis uploaded his initial post and declared that "I am beginning a new journey to walk with you along the path of mercy and the tenderness of God."[1] Moreover, he announced his intention of ratcheting up the pontificate's presence on social media. According to Vatican officials, the Instagram launching was especially promising given the wherewithal of images "to unite people across cultures and languages."

Over the past twenty years, the use of religious social media has grown by leaps and bounds. These networks have emerged as robust platforms that drive the discourse, practice, and modes of leadership.

By virtue of their devotional content, these frameworks have also become online venues for communal interaction.

Though quite a few members of organized faith-based groups have lauded these networks, others raise concerns about the proliferation of new forms of religious authority that are liable to challenge the establishment. In fact, scholars have recently suggested that there is a correlation between these diverse online offerings and the mounting volatility of religious affiliation. For example, a recent survey conducted by the Pew Research Center projects that by 2050, Europe's Christian population will have plummeted by about 100 million and that 23 per cent of the continent's inhabitants will be religiously unaffiliated. In South America, mass conversion has transformed what was once a fairly stable religious environment (Lehmann 2013), as Catholics have declined from 90 per cent of the population in the 1960s to a mere 69 per cent by 2014. Two-thirds of these proselytes have joined new charismatic Christian movements (Pew Report 2014).

In light of the above, the challenge of affirming and popularizing ecclesiastical leadership (particularly its charismatic elements) has become a major concern for religious institutions in the digital age. This chapter broaches the question of how online religious authority is constructed, preserved, and wielded online by these bodies. As per our findings, religious institutions are increasingly resorting to cyber means for developing a public image that is specifically designed to bolster the charismatic bona fides, as opposed to the traditional or bureaucratic credentials of their upper echelons.

In an effort to comprehend how religious institutions are managing their social media outreach, we have taken stock of the above-mentioned papal Instagram feed. This account offers images of Francis carrying out his apostolic duties. For example, they capture the pope officiating key Vatican ceremonies, leading visits around the world, and conducting interfaith meetings. Moreover, it allows the flock to respond to their shepherd's posts. Throughout the pages of this book, we will place the spotlight on organized religions' struggles in today's competitive devotional landscape. Among the challenges that these groups face are outreach drives, the emergence of alternative sources of religious authority, far-reaching socio-religious change, and a major upswing in personal discretion on matters of faith.

6.2   Religious Authority and the Nature of Charisma

The literature has accentuated the somewhat "soft," elusive nature of religious authority. For instance, senior clergy are deemed to have an informal sway over the flock. Drawing on Weber's insights, Gifford (2010) views scripture, tradition, and charisma to be proven catalysts of authentic-cum-inspirational religious experiences. The scriptural component, he avers, includes symbolically charged artifacts (e.g., the *mezuza*, prayer beads, and arabesque decorations) that are used to sanctify religious ceremonies and adorn holy expanses. In Gifford's estimation, these objects supplement the literal meanings of canonical texts (e.g., the Qur'an and Bible), which primarily serve as moral guides. Furthermore, both the texts and their related artifacts serve to bolster the charisma of devotional leaders.

The question of authority has always stood at the heart of the sociology of religion. In *Economy and Society* (1978), Weber points to three channels of authoritarian legitimacy: traditional, bureaucratic-legal, and charismatic. While the credentials in traditional and modern societies may differ, the notion of power emanating from a community of believers has endured. Legitimacy derives from the popular-cum-informal acceptance of a figure's knowledge and wisdom (Turner, 2017). As in the case of, say, *ulama* in the Arab world or the Israeli Rabbinate, this standing is often conferred upon individuals by state bureaucracies.

According to Weber (1978, 241–2), charisma is "a certain quality of an individual personality by virtue of which he is considered extraordinary and treated as endowed with supernatural, superhuman, or at least specifically exceptional powers or qualities." Legal and traditional leadership, he postulated, are permanent structures that sustain the everyday needs of the community, but charisma is a formidable source of authority that can be attributed to a wide range of social actors, including religious figures, demagogues, and even criminals (Bendix 1962, 299). Such a leader often comes to the fore in times of crisis. Though potent, Weber noted, charismatic appeal tends to be short lived. However, its shelf life can be prolonged by the "routinization of charisma." Put differently, charismatic leadership is capable of assuming a more bureaucratic form in which the leader's teachings are canonized, his or her values are codified into law, and personal authority is vested in de-personalized positions (Stark 1965). Owing to legal and traditional restraints on power, leaders aspiring to expand their purview and clout may go the charismatic route.

Following in Weber's footsteps, researchers have approached charisma from many different angles. A handful of studies have focused on the mass embracement of charismatic leaders. This camp delves into the psychoanalytic-social dimensions of this phenomenon (Adorno, Frenkel-Brunswik, Levinson, and Sanford 1950) such as the fierce, irrational loyalty that such figures command (Lindholm 1990; 2013). In Kets de Vries's estimation (1988), charisma is an emotive trait that is attractive to individuals looking for surrogate parental figures to boost their sense of personal security, especially during times of crisis. Other researchers have explored the institutional dimensions of charisma and the ways it is marketed. They accentuate conceptions of power that are symbolically manifest by charismatic figures or holy sites (Geertz 1973; Shils 1975).

Shils (1975, 127) postulates that charisma "is the quality which is imputed to persons, actions, rules, institutions, symbols, and material objects because of their presumed connection with 'ultimate,' 'fundamental,' 'ritual,' and order-determining powers." However, this definition seems to be lacking. As Tambiah (1984 326) contends, there is an underlying bifurcation in Weber's treatment of this subject. While charisma is inherently unstable, volatile, and "revolutionary," it is also institutionalized, a constitutive part of social endeavours, and interwoven into concrete situations. Regardless of whether charisma is institutionalized, it possesses emotional, expressive, and communicative attributes. Antonakis, Bastardoz, Jacquart, and Shamir (2016, 304) define it as "values-based, symbolic, and emotion-laden leader signaling." Consequently, they place a strong emphasis on the representation of the leader, beyond his or her actual accomplishments or personal qualities.

In exploring the visual aspects of the pope's authority, it is only natural that we revisit the topic of charisma, with the following objectives in mind: fathoming charisma's new online presence; and determining how symbols and signalling constructs are strategically employed to ramp up a leader's popularity. The aim of this chapter is not to add yet another full-length explication of charisma to the extensive literature on this topic but to assay a particular sub-genre of this phenomenon: the strategic efforts to instil a leader-centred outlook of reality in the public consciousness via "image-mediated charisma." As discussed below, this sort of enterprise is the outgrowth of an animated mode of interaction between leaders and their constituency.

6.3 Charisma, Leadership, and Authority in the Digital Sphere

Researchers have variously chosen to either study charisma in close-knit organizational settings or explore charismatic appeal that is generated from afar. The literature on the mechanisms of this allure highlights the concept of "leader distance," namely the level of inter-action and proximity between charismatic figures and their adherents. A handful of scholars emphasize the advantages of direct leadership in all that concerns securing popular legitimacy and esteem. Unmedi-ated charismatic authority is built on a relationship of trust in which the figure's conduct, level of inspiration, and interaction with devotees is constantly under evaluation. Conversely, other researchers note the potential of building a romanticized and meaningful paradigm of leadership by means of remote and looser ties with followers. In fact, the populace is more likely to attribute "superhuman" or "larger-than-life" characteristics to these sorts of figures than those adopting a hands-on approach (Shamir 1995). Paradoxical as it might be, then, a lack of familiarity with a leader's daily conduct and activities is fer-tile ground for charismatic attraction. This sort of charismatic appeal relies on image-building, for the results of this public relations work constitute the adherent's primary means for grasping the disposition of the leader.

A key concept in this area of research is "socio-psychological dis-tance." Over the past twenty years, scholars have revisited the manner in which this notion is framed through the lens of "construal theory" (Eyal and Berkovich 2018; Trope and Liberman 2010). This theoretical framework stresses the current positioning of objects or events vis-à-vis the leader, as the distance between them determines the extent to which the objects are abstracted or reified. Scholars (Fiedler 2007; Trope and Liberman 2010) point to five realms of distance that are pertinent to leadership:

Temporal – the proximity in time to a given event.
Spatial – the sense of distance from the leader.
Social – the sense of affinity to a figure or group.
Hypothetical – the perceived certainty that an event will occur.
Affective – the emotional connection to a subject of reference.

Antonakis and Atwater (2002) discuss two independent benchmarks: the physical distance between the leader and follower, and the perceived social propinquity. In aggregate, these seven factors of proximity are viewed as basic components from which myriad configurations can be devised to explain such relations. Building on these insights, scholars have focused on the increasingly mediatized relationships between leaders and adherents on electronic platforms. As part of these efforts, they have coined the idea of a virtually proximate "e-leadership" (Avolio, Kahai, and Dodge 2001; Avolio, Sosik, Kahai, and Baker 2014). Employing Antonakis and Atwater's said terminology (2002), this style of leadership is characterized by an inherent tension between appreciable "physical distance" and low levels of "perceived social distance," which is an outgrowth of frequent interactions. In our estimation, the quality of the communications also impacts the sense of intimacy between the two.

Since the rise of the cinema and, all the more so, television, the literature has underscored the importance of visual communication to the branding of leaders. Perhaps the earliest work of this kind was the Frankfurt School's research on the means of communication adopted by fascist regimes. This was followed, *inter alia*, by scholarship on the American public's responses to the first wave of televised presidential debates. The spread of visual communications to the digital realm, especially owing to the popularity of YouTube and social networks at the turn of the millennium, have only intensified this facet of leader interactions with the public. To wit, nearly every politician – local, national, or global – has at least some online presence. From LinkedIn pages describing the users' career paths to organizational webpages, a vast array of professionals (e.g., business managers, educators, medical doctors, and legislators) utilize visual communication as part of their effort to manage their public image.

The immense growth of online manifestations of leadership aside, there is a dearth of scholarship on this emergent form of authority. An examination of the visual strategies that are adopted to cultivate public images is bound to improve our understanding of the creation and maintenance of charisma in the digital age.

6.4 The Evolving Visual Language of Faith

The study of religion extends to its visual manifestations in works of art and ritual objects, like rosary beads. While such objects may have long been popular with believers, their status has often been contested by ecclesiastical authorities. For instance, Islam and Protestant streams raise the banner of iconoclasm. With the growth of new media, and what appears to be the legitimization of photographing devotional content, further research attention should be paid to online visual communications.

To date, scholars have focused on the textual dimension of religious content. Our study of the visual aspects of faith-based digital outlets has revolved around a semiotic analysis. Moreover, we have drawn heavily on the literature concerning the social impact of shared digital images. Adopting a socio-semiotic outlook, Rose (2016) asserts that image producers confer meanings that establish and reinforce social categories, stereotypes, opinions, and cultural capital. Following in Rose's footsteps, a handful of social network researchers have discussed Facebook's impact on its users' relationships, both on and offline. Ellison, Steinfield, and Lampe (2007) demonstrate how college students use this network to manage their social capital. According to Tonks (2012), students in New Zealand promote themselves by uploading "drinking photos" onto social-networking services (SNSs). Mourning practices have also been translated into the language of visual communication. Leaver and Highfield delve into the "book-ends" of online identity, placing the spotlight on images of birth and death uploaded onto Instagram. In their estimation, this platform is characterized by a set of expectations and institutionalized normative patterns that undergird its content. For example, discussions on bereavement tend to accentuate personal expressions of loss, rather than collective commemoration. Plumbing visual expressions of grief, Gibbs, Meese, Arnold, Nansen, and Carter (2015) further emphasize this negotiation and usage of the internet's architecture. They examine the wherewithal of such visual posts to build rapport between members of online social networks through informal mediation – a sharp contrast to the more rigid and structured physical ceremonies.

Babis (2020) has investigated expressions of mourning on Facebook. While less interested in the differences between social media platforms, she is nonetheless conscious of the particular affordances of each one with respect to social capital. Babis depicts a community of foreign live-in caregivers residing in Israel who have developed a visual culture on social networks. The main issue that she contends with is how these migrants convey their grief on digital platforms. Scouring through reams of photos, Babis explicates the outcomes of image sharing. While this fieldwork is reminiscent of Leaver and Highfield's above-cited article, she finds that in a brick-and-mortar community threatened by departures, posting images is conducive to fostering a sense of togetherness. These topics also turn up in studies on devotional uses of images, visual symbolism, and new media. Although much work remains to be done, a few scholars have begun to weigh in on the consequences of digital visualization on religious practice, identity, symbolic exchange, and veneration.

Following along these same lines, Nardella (2012) has explored the interspersal of religious symbols into Italian advertisements. He concludes that the populace's devotional imagination begets a "religious field" that is easily transferred to other spheres of meaning. For instance, references to biblical events and figures are prevalent in various cultural expanses, including commercials. Nardella (2012, 237) also mentions the importance of religious symbols in the Eastern Orthodox tradition, where icons are believed to manifest divine energies that provide the beholder with access to the invisible world of the spirit. As featured in Stadler's monograph on Greek Orthodox rituals and processions in Jerusalem (2020), devotional art can trigger an emotionally charged experience.

The transition of visual language from mass media to the digital realm has opened technological affordances to both devotees and agents of organized religion, both of whom "capture" images for the sake of presenting or sharing them on social networks. Needless to say, this practice is highly encouraged by the media culture and corporate platforms (John 2017).

For example, as Schwartz notes (2009), digital cameras are such prevalent technologies-of-the-self that public religious ceremonies are routinely shared on various outlets. Visual imagery thus plays a major role in choreographing rituals and reflexive customs. In fact, the circulation of digital images, which relies on a synergy between cameras and online platforms, is leaving an ever-deeper mark on contemporary religion. Most of the literature on this phenomenon concentrates on Islam. Mejova and Benkhedda (2017) discuss Instagram posts that centre around Halal products. Scouring a vast dataset, the researchers highlight visual-cum-textual posts that laud such dietary practices in Muslim countries.

Conducting fieldwork in Indonesia, Nisa (2018) discusses the Instagram posts of Muslim youth. Focusing on outreach (*da'wa*) practices, she argues that her subjects turn to images with the objective of evincing their piety and becoming social media influencers. On Instagram, Nisa demonstrates, young Muslim women can serve as agents of proselytization in the hopes of earning plaudits from their community. By embracing new media tools that are popular among young women, her subjects advance traditional ideals of faith. Beta (2019) also explores young Muslim influencers operating on Instagram. Driven by a mélange of religious, political, and commercial motives, these activists endeavour to shape the identity of young women in accordance with a conformist vision of Islam.

Peterson (2020) also reflects on the sway of religious social media influencers through the prism of Leah Vernon's trolling campaign on Instagram. An American-Muslim social activist and "plus size Hijabi model," Vernon undertakes to publicly disrupt Islamic fashion. Documenting these activities, Peterson takes stock of digital activism and a religious woman's critique of her community's mainstream aesthetic culture on social networks. In so doing, he offers an alternative image of Muslimhood and femininity.

The literature on the ability of new media visual communications to disseminate religious ideas underscores the principal agents – social media influencers. However, there is a dearth of scholarship on this rapidly growing field, especially the transition of senior establishment clergy to the digital sphere. Filling this void, we will home in on the burnishing of clerical authority through visual communications. Morgan (2018) observes how devotional images draw on a belief system and entice believers into responding to its primary meanings. For example, lonesome bachelors turn to pictures of saints in the hopes of finding a companion. What is more, these sorts of representations are credited with working miracles, such as overcoming barrenness and poverty. Bilu (2020) discusses the ways in which members of Habad, an ultra-Orthodox movement, revere the image of their deceased spiritual leader – Menachem Mendel Schneerson. Quite a few devotees hang the rabbi's picture in their homes. Now and again, they speak to the photograph and testify how the *"rebbe"* gazes back at them. Both Morgan and Bilu discuss the putatively miraculous and transcendental meanings of such images. Moreover, they demonstrate how these venerated items affirm seniority within the circles under review. Building on these findings, we will scrutinize the visual language of Pope Francis's Instagram account.

6.5 Instagram, Catholicism, and Pope Francis's Account

Launched as an image-sharing network in October 2010, Instagram boasts more than 500 million active users around the globe (Instagram 2017). As a subsidiary of Facebook, Instagram is well connected to leading SNSs. However, the company stresses its niche position as a key facilitator of online visual communication. In contrast to other SNSs, like Facebook and Twitter, the platform's architecture only enables members to post photographs and short videos. Heretofore overlooked, the app is steadily gaining the attention of researchers (Russmann and Svensson 2016).

According to the Pew Research Center, Instagram has been the fastest growing social network in the United States since 2012. Strongest among the eighteen to forty-nine-year-old segment, more than 28 per cent of the American adult population has opened accounts with this network. Instagram's main function is the dissemination of personalized images that serve as technologies of the self. For instance, users regularly post selfies documenting their experiences (Schwartz 2009) on mobile phones and tablets. More so than browser-based platforms, the activity on Instagram takes place around the clock in an immersive atmosphere. This personal usage is augmented by communal sharing (either *ad hoc* or ongoing). All in all, these functions have spawned a web 2.0 public that responds to current events primarily through hashtags, such as #GOT or #MeToo (Highfield and Lever 2015).

Though personal posts account for the majority of traffic on Instagram, public entities are increasingly turning to this network for marketing and outreach purposes. This includes corporations (e.g., Coca-Cola and BMW), governmental agencies (the NYPD and the Louvre), NGOs (Amnesty and Greenpeace), and religious movements (Chabad and Canção Nova). While institutional websites display the images of their leaders and staff in a hierarchical manner, Instagram offers a less structured approach in which posts are arranged chronological order. For this reason, there is not necessarily any logical connection between successive posts. However, followers manage to get a feel for developments in the subject's life.

The launching of Pope Francis's official Instagram account continues a legacy of media appropriation that has been evident throughout the Church's history and in official papal communications since the 1920s (Campbell 2010; Ortiz 2003). Since the mid-twentieth century, the Vatican has been regularly broadcasting and providing footage of public events to news organizations, with the objective of raising its public profile. Although a number of faith-based groups have written off social media as an irredeemable source of transgression (Golan and Campbell 2015), the Catholic position is that these outlets can play a valuable role in transmitting religious values and giving authentic voice to pious behaviour. Accordingly, the pontificate encourages believers to use social media on a daily basis for the purpose of spreading the Christian gospel and entrenching religion at the forefront of the public domain. To this end, Pope Benedict XVI initiated the Holy See's engagement with online social networking by posting his first Twitter message in December 2012. Benedict's account, @Pontifex, has continued to serve the papacy after his resignation.

Departing from the Twitter model of titularly labelling the account (Pontifex), the papal Instagram account (@franciscus) was named after the reigning bishop of Rome himself. In an interview for Vatican

Radio, the prefect of the Secretariat for Communications, Mgr Dario Edoardo Viganò, commented on the rationale behind the opening of Francis's Instagram account:[2]

> The pope has stated that images speak volumes to him and explained this by saying: "When a child meets me, they give me a drawing. I ask them questions about the drawing and as I ask these questions, the child slowly begins to express what they intended to show in their drawing." So, images are not just a copy of reality, they communicate much more: a detail, an aspect of the pope's caress, a blessing … The idea is to recount the papacy through images, to enable all those who wish to accompany and know more about Pope Francis's pontificate to encounter his gestures of tenderness and mercy.

This official's positive approach towards Instagram exemplifies the Holy See's candid recognition of this image-laden medium's communicative power. The pope embraced this platform despite its frequent non-verbal and non-scriptural nature and despite its identification with profane and even licentious content. While Francis indeed manages to come across as an authentic leader in the press (Lundgren 2017), less is known about the strategic management of his image on digital platforms.

6.6   Collection and Analysis of Visual Data

Within the framework of our research on Pope Francis's Instagram posts, material was gathered using the grounded ethnographic approach to digital "data capture" (Boellstorff, Nardi, Pearce and Taylor 2012; Golan and Babis 2017; Kozinets 2010). The material was then used to identify and elaborate on the Catholic Church's *modus operandi* in all that concerns the implementation of its visual communication strategies.

Our dataset was assembled by scrutinizing all the content on Francis's Instagram account for the first sixteen months of its existence (20 March 2016 through 23 July 2017. A qualitative content analysis of the 429 photos and videos that were uploaded during this period was

Figure 6.1 | Headline of Pope Francis's Instagram profile.

carried out using Dedoose software, and all these images were coded in a grounded fashion. More specifically, we took note of the semiotic and informational messages that each item conveys to viewers, not least its portrayal of Francis's enterprise. To this end, we identified the main topic of every image, the documented papal activity, and any embedded theological information. Codes were used to record the setting (the ritual and/or location) and communicative format (video or stills) of each post.

The coding process leaned on Glaser & Strauss's comparative analysis principles (1967). Three independent researchers scrutinized the entire corpus of Francis's Instagram account (Strauss and Corbin 1998) and formulated data categories. Upon comparing their results (Marshall and Rossman 2014), disagreements were resolved via dialogue. These measures netted a high inter-rater reliability level among the team members (Olesen, Droes, Hatton, Chico, and Schatzman 1994). To bolster the findings' credibility and explicate the posts, we held discussions with media managers of Catholic orders that produce visual content for devotional and educational purposes. In addition, we compared the data with the literature on charisma and leader distance.

6.7   Framing the Pope: The Construction of Religious Leadership

Upon opening Francis's Instagram page, visitors encounter the network's standard format for user profiles. However, seasoned Instagrammers may be surprised by the non-reciprocal nature of the feed: while more than five million users are openly registered as the pope's followers, he does not keep tabs on any account whatsoever (see figure 6.1).

From their initial encounter, then, users are reminded of the vast distance between themselves and the pontiff, as the latter is exclusively an imparter of information. That said, believers are invited to engage with the pope by simply hitting "follow," no pun apparently intended. With the click of a button, the bishop of Rome is integrated into their mobile phone, tablet, and/or PC experiences.

By plumbing the entire corpus of Francis's account, we discerned four major facets of his visual representation on Instagram: hierarchical positioning; geographical locales; haptic engagement; and visual focus.

6.7.1 Hierarchical Positioning

This element refers to the online representation of authority figures within the framework of their affiliated organization. In the Catholic setting, cardinals, bishops, and other players all hold leadership positions at different rungs of an established hierarchy. This pecking order might lead one to assume that the pope would frequently be depicted on his Instagram feed with his immediate subordinates (e.g., cardinals). On the basis of our in-depth survey of this account, it turns out that Francis appears in 96.2 per cent of the uploaded images. Moreover, the pontiff is consistently shown wearing distinctive-cum-traditional papal attire,[3] thereby affirming his elevated status. That said, he is rarely depicted interacting with elites, as other members of the cloth merit scant exposure (3 per cent of images). On those rare instances in which posts incorporate clergy, they are relegated to support roles in, say, the officiation of public ceremonies. In two of the images, clergy receive blessings from the pope.

Bypassing the clergy's historic role as intermediaries, the papal feed offers lay believers a direct channel to the very top of the Catholic pyramid. To a greater extent than other networks, Instagram posts reduce "the space between two social groups" (Henderson, Fujita, Trope, and Liberman 2006). The institutional hierarchy that forms a protective social barrier around the pope is by and large suspended in the digital realm, as the flock enjoys direct access to their shepherd.

6.7.2 Geographical Locales

Geographical locales are the physical context in which the pontiff and his followers are displayed on Instagram. Of the 429 images we exam-

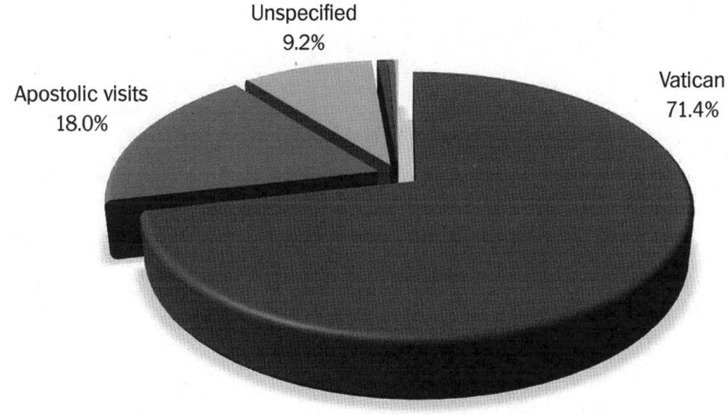

Figure 6.2 | Geolocalization of Pope Francis's Instagram images.

ined, the vast majority frame the pope – with the help of a caption – in a specific venue.

As illustrated in figure 6.2, the Vatican is easily the most popular location on Francis's account (71.4 per cent of the images). This focus on the Eternal City not only underscores its importance to the pontiff and the Catholic faithful but affirms and, at least for some users, introduces the centrality of, say, St Peter's Square and the Sistine Chapel as principal settings of papal awe.[4] A much smaller, but nonetheless significant, portion of the images (18.0 per cent) are apostolic visits to Catholic communities the world over. For most of the far-flung believers, the Vatican is a geographically remote locus of veneration. Therefore, pictures of Francis's international missions symbolically mitigate this distance (see Trope and Liberman 2010). By accentuating locales, the pope bridges the gulf between far-off parishes and Rome – the spiritual heart of Catholicism.

These images of papal trips also imply that Francis might some day visit the average devotee's own hometown. In this case, it is the hypothetical distance that is shortened, as there is a greater likelihood of meeting the pope (Armor and Sackett 2006). Symbolic as it might be, following this Instagram feed provides users a daily encounter with the revered pontiff.

6.7.3 *Haptic Engagement*

This category consists of images that show Francis physically touching devotees or objects of interest. The pope is represented thus in approximately half of the posts under review (see figure 6.3). Roughly a quarter of these images feature lay followers, nine feature ritual objects, more than 12 per cent non-ritual objects, and a mere 3.1 per cent include other clergy. Pictures of one-on-one exchanges with lay Catholics serve to humanize the exalted bishop of Rome.

As opposed to these interactive scenes, half of the images depict Francis on his own, say, delivering a speech (19.5 per cent) or engrossed in thought (12.4 per cent). These scenes underscore the pontiff's role as a grand master of ceremonies and mediator of the transcendental. Needless to say, these functions set him apart from the masses.

The combination of approachable and lofty representations engenders a balanced image of the Catholic leader. In the former, scenes of direct contact with the rank and file temporarily suspend and thus reaffirm the established hierarchy. Furthermore, the interplay of both haptic and solitary images gives voice to a wide range of emotions. This heterogeneity creates a drama-filled tension that betrays an "affective distance" (Fielder 2007). For instance, Francis is smiling in some of the pictures and frowning in others. Papal sermons or moments of quiet contemplation are essentially strategic representations of affective distance that appear to convey a sense of inaccessibility. However, this distance is tempered by haptic images that evoke a "warm" and direct relationship between the pontiff and his flock.

6.7.4 *Visual Focus*

Visual focus refers to the captured gaze of the leader in a particular video or photo. Simply put, it describes what the pope is looking at. The following targets were the object of his attention in nearly three-quarters of the images: devotees, the camera, icons or ritual objects, and clergy (see figure 6.4). A much smaller percentage of the images (11.0 per cent) display Francis in a meditative state, with his eyes closed. In almost a quarter of the posts, the focus is unspecified. For example, the pontiff is delivering a sermon to an audience outside the frame.

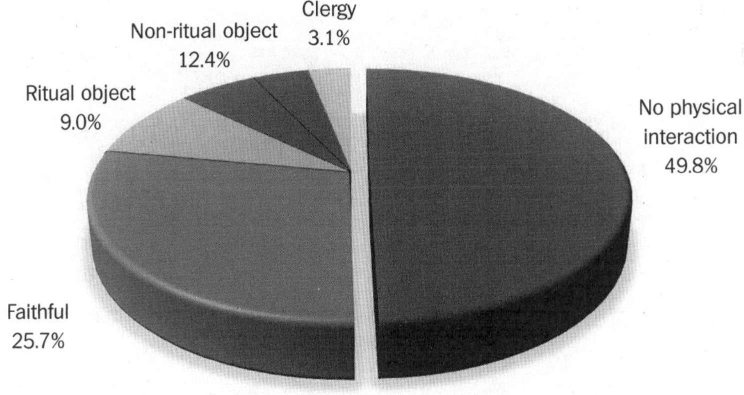

Figure 6.3 | Physical contact in Pope Francis's Instagram images.

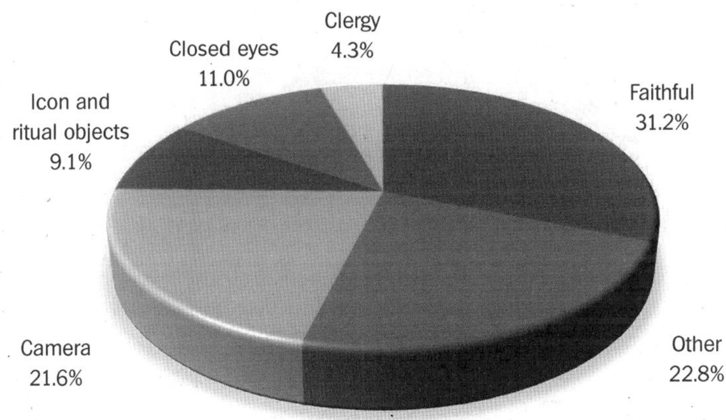

Figure 6.4 | Pope Francis's visual focus in his Instagram feed.

All told, the objects of Francis's attention can be divided into three main categories: proximate devotees; online followers that he engages by facing the camera and "breaking the fourth wall"; and the transcendental, which is expressed by a meditative posture or a focus on devotional items.

In our estimation, there is a dissonance between images where the pope's distant gaze is on believers and those in which it is turned to the camera and an invisible (online) audience. It stands to reason that these situations parallel the tension between those in which the pontiff addresses a mass audience at, say, rallies or ceremonies and his face-to-face encounters with individuals. Strung together on the Instagram feed, these images are part and parcel of Francis's efforts to build an intimate, if symbolic, relationship with his myriad followers. In other words, photos and videos in which he peers directly at the viewer can be seen as a mitigation of hypothetical distance, for these images dangle the prospect of a personal relationship with the bishop of Rome. What is more, this personalization of the online relationship shortens the affective distance between the pope and his flock, thereby invoking a sense of warmth. These cases also sharply diverge from awe-inspiring scenes of an elevated figure pondering the sublime.

Through a combination of hierarchical positioning, geographical locales, haptic engagement, and visual foci, these Instagram posts engender a binal user experience in which the pontiff is seen as both an approachable figure and a lofty man of God. In so doing, the Vatican strategically avails itself of online social distance to "balance" the way its leader is perceived.

6.8 Conclusion

This chapter has explored the manner in which religious institutions construct, re-affirm, and leverage their leaders' authority via social media. Focusing on the pope's Instagram account, we discerned the social categories that emerge from the images his PR specialists, photographers, and webmasters upload onto the feed. A grounded survey of the entire corpus of papal Instagram videos and photos enabled us to identify four elements of the strategic management of the pontiff's "leader distance" that have facilitated the construction of his authority and shored up his clout: hierarchical positioning, geographical locales, haptic engagement, and visual focus.

Similarities were found between these elements and several concepts that were raised in the literature on manufactured charisma and socio-psychological distance. More specifically, hierarchical positioning corresponds with insights on social distance, and discussions on spatial and hypothetical distance mirror our notion of geographical locales. What is more, Fiedler's analysis of affective distance (2007) as well as Trope and Liberman's work on spatial and hypothetical distance (2010) were relevant to our findings on haptic engagement and visual focus. Showcasing multiple forms of interrelated social-psychological distance, Trope and Liberman's construal level theory elucidates the social scheme of the pope's Instagram account. Unlike earlier studies, we found that psychological distance is neither a straightforward dichotomy between close and far nor a spectrum with measurable wave lengths of proximity. Instead, this distance is capable of functioning as a synthesis between the two, allowing for the coexistence of different and even contradictory orientations (e.g., near/far and amiable/aloof).

In terms of hierarchical positioning, our findings indicate that social distance was reduced by circumventing ministerial representation, highlighting the pontiff, and downplaying other church figures. At one and the same time, other images accentuated the pope's propinquity to the divine, thereby evincing a greater sense of social distance vis-à-vis his followers. A hallmark of Francis's Instagram feed, then, was the counterintuitive concurrence of down-to-earth and remote ties with his flock. In the case of geographical locales, there was dissonance between images taken at the Vatican, which evince the pontiff's sublime authority, and those taken on visits around the globe, in which he comes across as an approachable figure that is present in the daily life of his flock. By raising the possibility of a meeting with the bishop of Rome, these scenes reduce the hypothetical distance between the leader and individuals. A similar duality informs the other two facets – haptic engagement and visual focus – of the user experience with the pontifical Instagram account.

In this ambiguous setting, believers can formulate a variety of different conceptions that suit their existing or evolving notions of the pope, religion, and God. The feed is a social construct whose properties and dynamics are more akin to informal or educational frameworks (see Kahane 1997) than traditional religious or authoritarian hierarchies (Adorno et al. 1950).

Honing in on social distance from the perspective of construal theory, we would expect a consistent level of separation between the pope and his devotees, as elevated figures tend to cultivate a distanced form of leadership across the board, be it in the social, spatial, affective, or hypothetical sphere. That said, our findings show that the distance is not ontologically fixed. Instead, it is a relative construct that delegates agency onto both the pontiff's image makers (e.g., those running his Instagram feed) and individual followers, who are allowed to negotiate their own relative positions. Moreover, the platform enables users to introduce Pope Francis into their lives with a single click of the mouse. This accessibility shortens their hypothetical distance as well. In other words, the believer is afforded an opportunity to trim his or her physical, social, temporal, and affective distance vis-à-vis the bishop of Rome.

Avolio, Kahai, and Dodge (2014) have documented the ability of leaders to truncate social distance via digital technology. Building on their conclusions, we show how social media platforms alter hypothetical distance by offering members of a religious denomination an assortment of videos and photographs depicting the leader maintaining a wide array of relationships with believers, running the gamut from tight to remote. Owing to the managed nature of the Instagram experience, the papal account creates an image of what scholars refer to as a "distant charismatic leadership." This symbolic form of idealized leadership runs counter to direct charismatic models, which revolve around the figure's perceived dedication to lofty standards of virtuous behaviour. Within this framework, the leader serves as an exemplar for his followers, who observe his or her actions on a firsthand basis (Shamir 1995; Antonakis et al. 2016). Conversely, Instagram furnishes an edited profile devoid of variances from the idealized image. For this reason, habitual consumption of papal Instagram images can bestow transcendental meaning upon its followers. Moreover, the feed allows them to engage with the Catholic mission, tap into key manifestations of the faith (e.g., annual ceremonies and iconic sites), bask in the Church's glory (e.g., remotely participate in mass gatherings), and satisfy their more concrete desire to maintain a semi-tangible relationship with the pope.

Drawing on Bilu and Ben Ari's insights on manufactured charisma (1992), we contend that the Holy See accentuates Francis's own charisma on his Instagram feed as part of its struggle to prevent the rationalization and institutionalization of the papacy. As Weber has shown, the routinization of charisma hinders the leader and the institution's clout. Since the end of the Second World War, the Catholic Church's power has steadily eroded. This trend is epitomized by the departure of erstwhile devotees, particularly in Latin America, to competing streams and by ongoing challenges to key social tenets of the Catholic creed on issues like gender, sexuality, and labour (Napolitano 2016). Against this backdrop, the Instagram experience offers a new set of tools for sustaining and enhancing the pope's appeal. For the most part, his authority stems from ex-territorial, non-temporal, and circuitous (or vague) power relations with the flock, which are largely dependent on voluntary acceptance of the Church's province. By dint of its stress on user agency, Instagram overcomes its ephemeral traits to represent the pontiff's leadership in a meaningful way.

It bears noting that the focus of this book is limited to the images themselves, rather than how users shape their own perception of Francis when visiting his Instagram feed. There is indeed a lacuna in the scholarship concerning the experiences of believers, as well as leaders and their representatives, on social networks. In addition, future works should explore the similarities and differences between users' online experiences and other encounters with religious institutions or traditional forms of outreach. While the present study has turned the spotlight onto the Catholic Church, less centralized religions (e.g., Buddhism among the established religions and new faith-based movements like Neopaganism) also deserve attention. Lastly, it is incumbent upon us to take stock of the way Muslims and Jews use visual media outlets, for their religions have much different attitudes on image veneration.

The limited purview of *Sacred Cyberspaces* aside, our findings point to the emergence of image-generated charisma and digital distance. In this chapter, we have argued that the latter explains the former. At any rate, both concepts warrant future investigation not only with respect to faith-based leaders but their counterparts in the political and cultural spheres. The insights yielded by our analysis of image-generated charisma and digital distance mesh neatly with the arguments of construal theory. What is more, they attest to a falloff in leader distance owing to online communications and a strengthening of the agency of both mid-level clergy and lay devotees alike.

Conclusion: Catholicism, Rupture, and Media Efforts

In the study of Christian movements and new media, there has been a bias as Protestant and Charismatic groups received more attention than their more "invisible" Catholic counterparts. This bias may be attributed to the zeal and excitement that Protestant growth has entailed in perhaps unexpected regions, such as Latin America, and its strength in dominant Western states, most notably the US or Germany: places where the fervency of Protestant growth was accompanied by religious media expansion, including televangelism, YouTube video representation, and such (Rosenthal 2007; Schofield Clark 2002). In contrast to their Catholic counterparts, Protestant groups were seen as flexible in the sense that they embraced and honed the craft of disseminating their religious beliefs through the creation of mass spectacles that connected the informal aspects of entertainment to the fundamental aspirations of belief. In their heyday, Evangelical and fundamentalist leaders remained committed to a conservative theology that embraced television as a means to spread the word of God. A mission they continue today. While many mainline leaders may not have anticipated the growing importance of television, particularly in American culture, these leaders garnered relative success in religious broadcasting, as they fostered the creation of an active audience, which would promote further growth in its publics, attracting family members, friends, and communities. All of which bolster their cause culturally and politically. In this book, we examined the response to the emergent medium as it occurred in the Catholic movement: its top-down leadership, mid-range clerics, and, to a lesser extent, its grassroots believers.

Despite scholars' inclination to underscore Protestant activity, including their media efforts, recently, a growing amount of scholarly attention has been given to the rise of religious media among Catholics. For example, in December 2019, *Problemi dell'informazione* published a special issue, edited by Carlo Nardella and Guido Gili, dedicated to the relationship between Pope Francis and the media. While not an isolated publication, this return to engagement in Catholic scholarship from a social scientific perspective, rather than a theological or historic prism, is not incidental. In recent years, numerous scholars have invested efforts towards reintegrating Catholicism back into the larger fold of comparativist anthropology and sociology of religion. Most notable in this effort is the collection *The Anthropology of Catholicism* (2017), a volume that discusses the endurance of Catholicism amid winds of crises.

Indeed, Catholic communities and the Holy See are threatened by forces that can potentially rupture their way of life, and erode the institutional, social, and cultural fabric of the Church and its popular following. Beyond the usual suspects that challenge religion, namely that of secularism and modernity at large (Stolz et al. 2016; Asad 1999; Casanova 2008), significant competitors have emerged in the religious market that offer enticing and meaningful ways to express their relation to the transcendental. This includes new age religious movements (Hanegraaff 2018), the growth of Pentecostal movements and the aforementioned evangelicals that have led to massive conversion, particularly in South America, which challenged religio-political identities (Burdick 2013).

Back in the 1960s and 1970s, scholars noted sparks of Catholic enthusiasm that accompanied the re-engagement with pilgrimage and "folk-syncretic practice." However, this enthusiasm was short-lived, and by the 1980s the interest waned while disengagement from the Church was growing on a global scale (Noget, Napolitano, and Mayblin 2017, 5). This trend is connected with larger secularization movements. In a 2018 study issued by the Université libre de Bruxelles and the Observatory of Religions and Secularism (ORELA), it was found that the Catholic Church in Europe is suffering from a decline in attendance. Accordingly, in most EU countries, the downward trend in church attendance is continuing, despite the fact that occasional (holy days) practice rates remain higher and that popular manifestations like pilgrimages draw a significant crowd, partially connected with growing rates of mass tourism on a global scale (Sägesser, Nelis, Schreiber, and Vanderpelen-Diagre 2018, 12–13). A disengagement that fostered a growing sense of apathy towards the Catholic church and a sense of its stagnation, particularly compared to alternative and emergent religious movements. To all of this, by the 1990s, Catholic Church sexual abuse cases began to receive significant media and public attention in countries including Canada, the US, Chile, Australia, Ireland, and much of Europe. Publications that fostered a negative image of the Church as corrupt and protecting deviant behaviour, with baffled and entailed contradicting responses by clerics and Holy See leadership. In light of these developments, it would seem that the church would be direly wounded and hard to recover. Nevertheless, multiple efforts have emerged to fortify the Church, restore its influence and invigorate its believers. In this book, we have aimed to follow these efforts as they manifest, albeit through new media platforms, and highlight how the church has demonstrated resilience, despite its rupture and multiple pressures.

In the book's preface, we set off the study's key agenda of exploring how religious institutions shape users' worldviews by means of digital communication. Furthermore, we set out to examine the ways that religious institutions, most notably through the case of the Catholic church, revitalizes its clout through the use of new media. Thus, we suggested that examining what could arguably be seen as the largest-scale religious institution, offers an outlook of the ways that long-standing conflicts over power, influence, and legitimacy within religious organizations are being waged in the digital sphere.

Exploring the ways that the Catholic church invigorates its believers, we focus on four key challenges that the Church, much like other faiths, faces, and the ways that media activity is set to address these predicaments. This includes the following:

1 The Problem of Religious Proselytization. Religious outreach is not only a key tenant in Christian philosophy and praxis, but also can be seen as a necessary activity for fortifying religious communities and expanding their publics. Furthermore, studies ranging from the 1970s to the 2000s indicated a problem of young American Catholics' identity formation and

socialization. These studies highlighted the rise of a flexible or diffuse form of identity that is more individualistic, selective in its traditional praxis, less involved in the Catholic church as an institution and downplaying it among other identities (Smith, Longest, and Christoffersen, 2014). Accordingly, commitment to the church and its teachings is fluid and unstable, thus prompting consistent exposure and learning to fasten trust towards the church and adherence to its teachings.

2   Sacred Sites. Sacred sites offer believers access to the transcendental as well as to key religious narratives and have thus become focal points for historic power struggles. However, these sites often undergo ebb and flow periods of popularization and disinterest as global publics often turn to alternative venues to address their religious aspirations. Given the rise in localized sites of religious fervor, interest in the Catholic Church's historic sites of claim may be threatened. Furthermore, the geographic and cultural distance between indigenous believers and key Catholic sites can be an impediment to their connection and finally, in light of a growing multiplicity of religious attractions (e.g. processions, communal events) of Catholic and non-Catholic groups the relevance of religious sites is questioned. Thus, a powerful experiential mechanism of affiliation to the Catholic Church is diminished.

3   The Problem of Authenticity. Believers continuously yearn to translate their beliefs to an experience that connects them with the divine. This includes critical moments of connection at a church, holy grave, confessional box, or otherwise. These practices can be seen as a yearning for authentic belief. Thus, authenticity is here understood as an affinity with narrated religious anecdotes (e.g miracles, saint involvement), that are materialized through a relic, image, or locale. Given the *longue durée* and magnitude of the Catholic church, much of these spaces and objects of veneration are standardized, idealized, and routinized on a global scale and, over time, may lose their charismatic appeal. Thus, threatening a key tool for believers' affinity to the Church.

4 The Problem of Leadership. Religious leaders have always struggled with a pursuit for relevance, legitimacy and power. However, in a massive transnational movement, such as that of the Catholic Church, its key leaders (headed by the pope) undergo a threat of distance and inaccessibility as well as stagnancy that stems from the deeply embedded institutional nature of the Church and the Holy See. Church leadership is often challenged by an inadequate inclination to address current issues, thus, seeing their teachings as idiosyncratic to ever changing circumstances. A problem that is compounded by the growth of alternative religious practices that involve young and charismatic clerics that compete with the Catholic apparatus and leadership. Finally, as aforementioned, there is a large-spanning distrust in mid-range clergy, stemming from the highly publicized scandals. Ergo, the Church seeks to enhance its leaderships' attraction and uncover additional means to facilitate its growth.

These challenges are significant from a theological, institutional and sociological standpoint as it involves believers' religious creed and the Church's legitimation as their leading institution of faith. We argue that the Catholic Church, and its various sub-movements, have developed mediatized formats that address these issues. In this book, we have explored these communicative actions.

Addressing *the problem of religious proselytization*, we focused on the emergence of webmasters. These media agents can be seen as an emergent form of religious emissaries that are dedicated to the creation of vibrant digital sites to appeal to believers. In chapter 2, we offer a bird's-eye view on the significance of webmasters and their various channels of online religious expression as they become mobile apps operators, website administrators, YouTubers, and more.

Religious webmasters are increasingly becoming key players that invisibly operate as content providers that edit, design, create, and orient the perspective of devotional websites. In chapter 2 we explore their emergence and discuss their significance for Catholicism. Indeed, in times of social and technological change, occupational roles are challenged by anomie, thus driving religious webmasters to form their professional creed, praxis, and legitimation. To explore the proliferating roles of the webmaster as they gain footing in the religious world, chapter 2 turns to discuss the life histories of these emergent media agents. Simply put, we aimed to understand who are the religious webmasters and how is their activity institutionalized to establish a (semi) professional role. Findings reflected the emergence of webmasters acting as entrepreneurial loners that develop religious products which are often experimental: an app for bedtime prayer, a rosary app, and the like. Simultaneously, findings indicated a separate modality of players involved in sizable establishments, most notably that of the Catholic church. In both modalities, webmasters were found, by and large, to lean upon their esoteric knowledge on computing and technological/communicative training, rather than a theological prowess to establish their positions.

These findings led us to consider the motivations that underpinned the workings of webmasters. To this end, in chapter 3, we examined what drove the webmasters of the Canção Nova/Franciscan media venture in the Holy Land. Drawing on interviews from active webmasters we found this to be a yearning to create a meaningful virtual experience that will draw believers to the divine and Catholic teachings. Furthermore, they see their work as fostering a global Catholic community that shares an affinity with the faith, its symbols, and venerated sites. Accordingly, the Holy Land serves as a platform of agreement that is accessible through the alternative medium of digital pilgrimage. Through our exploration of Catholic webmasters' motivations, findings alluded to a re-alignment of the social structure around the sacred and its manifestations. This includes not only the holy places themselves but a mélange of digital actors, stakeholders, brokers, and devotees. The webmasters attempt to reprise an "aura of authenticity" by invoking a proximity to the sacred. Through these efforts, webmasters are fostering new forms of religious experience and becoming key players in proselytizing Catholicism, thus enhancing Catholic influence and elevating their own status as advancers of the faith.

Facing the challenge of sacred places, of their centrality and significance, our study unveiled Catholic media efforts to enhance the primacy of holy sites with an emphasis on those of the Holy Land. In chapter 4, we draw an in-depth analysis of videos created by the Christian Media Center in Jerusalem and distributed through its websites and media partners. Through a semiotic analysis that draws upon principles set forth by Umberto Eco, we suggest that several social strategies of legitimation are invoked (scriptural, experiential, journalistic, and ritual based). It was found that religious activities that are performed in the Holy Land are not only animated and dramatized for the benefit of online viewers but are also used to re-appropriate these spaces as epicentres of belief – thus not only bolstering the Catholic creed but also serving the interests of key stakeholders who are invested in these sites. By transmitting a significant devotional performance to audiences across the globe, the video serves as an arbiter of ritual meaning and ownership of the Catholic church, thus serving as a way to reignite global belief that these sites offer a connection to the transcendental and a channel to a (re)enchanted worldview: a worldview that connects the sacred history of biblical narrative to contemporary sites via video viewership.

Another major problem faced by the Catholic Church centres upon the religious experience or, as previously articulated, *the problem of authenticity*. Given the standardization and routinization of modes of engagement with the transcendental, audiovisual means were found to be useful tools to transmit Catholic ideas, rekindle the religious experience for many, and foster a sense of Catholic authenticity. These tools can be useful for older generations seeking to revisit their personal and collective imagination of religious experience, as well as a means of connecting to millennials on social media. Through interviews with Catholic webmasters, in chapter 5 we reviewed efforts made by these content producers to enhance a sense of authenticity among believers. This is aimed at evangelizing youth, invigorating an affinity towards the Holy Land and maintaining a constant presence of the transcendental through smart technologies. To this end, the mode of livestreaming is widely employed. Whether in Lourdes, Nazareth, or the Vatican, livestreaming is characterized by features that enhance the sense of authenticity and counter its impediments. This includes livestreamings' audio-visual appeal, its ubiquitous accessibility on mobile devices, and its connection to holy sites and religious activities in real time. The emergence of webmasters as mediators triggered a transformation in the traditional Catholic organigram to include religious webmasters as legitimate agents of the faith and unintentionally empowered these agents as interpreters of various facets that frame current belief.

Finally, addressing *the problem of leadership*, as aforementioned, high clerics, led by the Holy See, face challenges of distance, low accessibility, and relevance. To this end, in our study (chapter 6), we investigated Pope Francis's Instagram postings. Through our sixteen-month data collection, we uncovered the strategies employed by webmasters to hone the charismatic appeal (beyond bureaucratic and traditional sources of legitimation) of the pope, to enhance his visibility on the religious stage, and to increase his relevance by addressing current issues. While Twitter and other media may also play a significant role, this groundbreaking study examines the visual communicative language of the Holy See through the lens of leadership theory.

Notes

Introduction

1 See Arthur Ntembula, "Cyberspace – A New Environment for Worship," Vatican News, 30 March 2020, https://www.vaticannews.va/en/africa/news/2020-03/cyberspace-a-new-environment-for-worship.html.
2 By code, we mean deeply ingrained principles, as opposed to practices *per se*. Cf. Kahane (1997).

Chapter One

1 Gore delivered his famous speech concerning the internet's vast potential on 21 March 1994. See http://vlib.iue.it/history/internet/algorespeech.html. Accessed 24 May 2020.
2 Lawrence Lessig examines these developments, as well as related laws, *Code, Version 2.0*. Also see Segev (2010), *inter alios*.
3 Analyzing a state website is an extremely time-sensitive research activity, due to the frequent content updates. Nur's study of vaticanstate.va, in November 2019, identified key attributes that are germane to present and future discussions on religious media.
4 It bears noting that this section is now in plain view, albeit consigned to the bottom of the page. Accessed 19 April 2020.
5 Although vaticannews.va merits a more comprehensive investigation, this book's purview limits us to an account of several key properties.
6 For a look at non-religious sourcing, see Barzilai, Tzadok, and Eshet-Alkalai (2015); Hendriks, Kienhues, and Bromme (2015).
7 In evangelical circles, "spiritual" and "social" tend to be intertwined.
8 See https://play.google.com/store/apps/details?id=com.lamachi.clicktopray&hl=en. Accessed 24 May 2020.

Chapter Three

1 See http://www.vatican.va/content/pius-xii/en/encyclicals/documents/ hf_p-xii_enc_08091957_miranda-prorsus.html. Accessed 24 May 2020.

2 Over the past decade, the See of Rome has regularly broached issues pertaining to communications and the Internet. On papal proclamations concerning the latter, see Pope Benedict XVI, "The Priest and Pastoral Ministry in a Digital World: New Media at the Service of the Word," 16 May 2010, https://w2.vatican.va/content/benedict-xvi/en/messages/ communications/documents/hf_ben-xvi_mes_20100124_44th-world-communications-day.html. Pope Benedict discussed social media's potential for helping the Church realize Catholic ideals in "Social Networks: Portals of Truth and Faith; New Spaces for Evangelization," 12 May 2013, http://w2.vatican.va/content/benedict-xvi/en/messages/ communications/documents/hf_ben-xvi_mes_20130124_47th-world-communications-day.html.

3 At present, it appears as though this narrative is being obfuscated by elements within the Canção Nova leadership.

4 Kahane (1997) elaborates on dualism in informal educational settings. For a comprehensive look at diachronic dynamics in religious contexts, see Eliade (1958).

5 Established in the seventh century, the Maronite church is an Eastern community that is affiliated with the See of Rome. While the heart of the present-day Maronites is in Lebanon, they have branches in Israel/ Palestine, Syria, and Turkey. Given the modest resources of the Palestinian Maronites, the Christian Media Center in Jerusalem provides an institutional umbrella for Youssef's web activities. Eyal Zisser (1995) expounds on this collective.

Chapter Four

1 "Networked religious publics" are online collectives that advance a sense of imagined belonging and restructure existing religious groups by means of socio-technological affordances. Cf. "networked publics" as used by Papacharissi (2014); Boyd (2010).

2 During the First Jewish-Roman War, Judean rebels managed to capture this mountaintop redoubt. According to the accounts of first century Roman-Jewish historian Flavius Josephus, towards the end of the campaign, the victorious Romans laid siege to Masada and its 960

men, women, and children. After several months of operations, the troops breached the defences. Upon entering the fortress, the vanguard discovered that rather than surrender, the occupants had committed mass suicide.

Chapter Five

1 Papal encyclicals, also known as apostolic exhortations, are official documents launched by the pope to high-ranked clergy. These documents indicate doctrinal guidelines concerning issues of public and religious concern. Since 1740, although with some exceptions, these messages in Latin are the official channel through which the pope indicates high priorities for the Catholic Christian community (Zängle 2014). Reflecting an attempt to establish not only transparency with regard to Catholic creed, but also a more direct communication between the pope and believers. Thus, supplementing mid-range clerical mediation, these communications are today available to the general public online in several languages.

Chapter Six

1 See the initial posting and a report thereon in Reuters, "Pope Launches Instagram Account," 19 March 2016, http://www.reuters.com/video/2016/03/19/pope-launches-instagram-account?videoId=367797183.

2 Mauro Pianta, "Viganò: 'Instagram Will Help Recount the Papacy through Images,'" *Vatican Insider*, 18 March 2016, http://www.lastampa.it/2016/03/18/vaticaninsider/eng/news/vigan-instagram-will-help-recount-the-papacy-through-images-KXQw7n YCF9PIFjH0UVzD6H/pagina.html.

3 Pope Francis is repeatedly discussed by the news media as promoting a discourse of austerity. A case in point is his modest attire, which contrasts sharply with the lavish vestments favoured by his predecessors (Vallely 2013).

4 It bears noting that the papacy's official-cum-political dealings are rarely displayed on Instagram, as the emphasis is on Francis's direct, personal connection with believers.

References

Abdous, M.H., and M. Yoshimura. 2010. "Learner Outcomes and Satisfaction: A Comparison of Live Video-Streamed Instruction, Satellite Broadcast Instruction, and Face-to-Face Instruction." *Computers & Education* 55 (2): 733–41.

Adorno, T.W., E. Frenkel-Brunswik, D.J. Levinson, and R.N. Sanford. 1950. *The Authoritarian Personality.* New York: Harper & Brothers.

Aharoni, M. 2014. "Eliciting 'Kosher Emotions' in Ultra-Orthodox Jewish Women's Film." In *The Emotions Industry,* edited by M. Moshe, 95–116. New York: Nova Publishers.

Anderson, B. 1991. *Imagined Communities – Reflections on the Origin and Spread of Nationalism.* New York: Verso.

Antonakis, J., and L. Atwater. 2002. "Leader Distance: A Review and a Proposed Theory." *Leadership Quarterly* 13 (6): 673–704.

Antonakis, J., N. Bastardoz, P. Jacquart, and B. Shamir. 2016. "Charisma: An Ill-Defined and Ill-Measured Gift." *Annual Review of Organizational Psychology and Organizational Behaviour* 3: 293–319.

Armor, D.A., and A.M. Sackett. 2006. "Accuracy, Error, and Bias in Hypothetical Events." *Journal of Personality and Social Psychology* 91 (4): 583–600.

Asad, T. 1999. "Religion, Nation-State, Secularism." In *Nation and Religion: Perspectives on Europe and Asia,* edited by P. Van Der Veer and H. Lehmann, 178–96. Princeton, NJ: Princeton University Press.

Aumente, J. 1987. *New Electronic Pathways: Videotex, Teletext and Online Databases.* Newbury Park, CA: Sage Publications.

Avolio, B.J., J.J. Sosik, S.S. Kahai, and B. Baker. 2014. "E-Leadership: Re-Examining Transformations in Leadership Source and Transmission." *Leadership Quarterly* 25 (1): 105–31.

Avolio, B.J., S. Kahai, and G.E. Dodge. 2001. "E-Leadership: Implications for Theory, Research, and Practice." *Leadership Quarterly* 11 (4): 615–68.

Badone, E., and R. Roseman. 2004. *Intersecting Journeys: The Anthropology of Pilgrimage and Tourism.* Urbana: University of Illinois Press.

Baram-Tsabari, A., and A.M. Schejter. 2019. "New Media: A Double-Edged Sword in Support of Public Engagement with Science." In *Learning in a Networked Society*, edited by Y. Kali, A. Baram-Tsabari, and A.M. Schejter, 79–95. Cham, CH: Springer.

Barker, E. 2005. "Crossing the Boundary: New Challenges to Religious Authority and Control as a Consequence of Access to the Internet." In *Religion and Cyberspace*, edited by M. Hojsgaard and M. Warburg, 207–44. London: Routledge.

Barzilai, S., E. Tzadok, and Y. Eshet-Alkalai. 2015. "Sourcing while Reading Divergent Expert Accounts: Pathways from Views of Knowing to Written Argumentation." *Instructional Science* 43 (6): 737–66.

Barzilai-Nahon, K., and G. Barzilai. 2005. "Cultured Technology: The Internet and Religious Fundamentalism." *Information Society* 21 (1): 25–40.

Beard, F., and R.L. Olsen. 1999. "Webmasters as Mass Media Gatekeepers: A Qualitative Exploratory Study." *Internet Research* 9 (3): 200–11.

Becker, H.S., and A.L. Strauss. 1956. "Careers, Personality, and Adult Socialization." *American Journal of Sociology* 62 (3): 253–63.

Bekkering, D. 2011. "From 'Televangelist' to 'Intervangelist': The Emergence of the Streaming Video Preacher." *Journal of Religion and Pop Culture* 23 (2): 101–17.

Ben-David, O. 1997. "Tiyul (Hike) as an Act of Consecration of Space." In *Grasping Land: Space and Place in Contemporary Israeli Discourse and Experience*, edited by E. Ben-Ari and Y. Bilu, 129–46. Albany, NY: Suny Press.

Bendix, R. 1962. *Max Weber: An Intellectual Portrait*. New York: Anchor Books.

Benedict, X. 2011. "Truth, Proclamation and Authenticity of Life in the Digital Age." *Message of His Holiness Pope Benedict XVI for the 45th World Communications Day*, 2011: https://w2.vatican.va/content/benedict-xvi/en/messages/communications/documents/hf_ben-xvi_mes_20110124_45th-world-communications-day.html. Accessed 3 August 2013.

Beniger, J.R. 1987. "Personalization of Mass Media and the Growth of Pseudo-Community." *Communication Research* 14 (3): 352–71.

Benjamin, W. 2008. *The Work of Art in the Age of Mechanical Reproduction*. London: Penguin Books.

Ben-Yehuda, N. 1996. *Masada Myth: Collective Memory and Mythmaking in Israel*. Madison: University of Wisconsin Press.

Berkovich, I., and O. Eyal. 2018. "Help Me if You Can: Psychological Distance and Help-Seeking Intentions in Employee-Supervisor Relations." *Stress and Health* 34 (3): 424–34.

Berkowitz, D. 1990. "Refining the Gatekeeping Metaphor for Local Television News." *Journal of Broadcasting & Electronic Media* 34 (1): 55–68.

Bertuzzi, N. 2017. "Sessualità e stampa cattolica in Italia. Un confronto fra aree e riviste." *Religioni e società* 88: 49–62.

Beta, A.R. 2019. "Commerce, Piety and Politics: Indonesian Young Muslim Women's Groups as Religious Influencers." *New Media & Society* 21 (10): 2140–59.

Bhola, H.B. 1983. "Non-Formal Education in Perspective." *Prospects* 13 (1): 45–53.

Bilu, Y., and E. Ben-Ari. 1992. "The Making of Modern Saints: Manufactured Charisma and the Abu-Hatseiras of Israel." *American Ethnologist* 19 (4): 672–87.

Blondheim, M., and E. Katz. 2016. "Religion, Communications, and Judaism: The Case of Digital Chabad." *Media, Culture & Society* 38 (1): 89–95.

Boczkowski, P.J. 2010. *News at Work: Imitation in an Age of Information Abundance.* Chicago: University of Chicago Press.

Boellstorff, T. 2015. *Coming of Age in Second Life: An Anthropologist Explores the Virtually Human.* Princeton: Princeton University Press.

Boellstorff, T., B. Nardi, C. Pearce, and T.L. Taylor. 2012. *Ethnography and Virtual Worlds: A Handbook of Method.* Princeton: Princeton University Press.

Bolter, J.D., B. MacIntyre, M. Gandy, and P. Schweitzer. 2006. "New Media and the Permanent Crisis of Aura." *Convergence: The International Journal of Research into New Media Technologies* 12 (1): 21–39.

Bowman, R.M. 1991. *Understanding Jehovah's Witnesses: Why They Read the Bible the Way They Do.* Grand Rapids, MI: Baker Book House.

Boyd, D. 2010. "Social Network Sites as Networked Publics: Affordances, Dynamics, and Implications." In *A Networked Self,* edited by Z. Papacharissi, 47–66. New York: Routledge.

Bunt, G.R. 2009. *iMuslim: Rewriting the House of Islam.* Chapel Hill: The University of North Carolina Press.

Burbules, N.C. 2006. "Rethinking the Virtual." In *The International Handbook of Virtual Learning Environments,* edited by J. Weiss, J. Nolan, J. Hunsinger, and P. Trifonas, 37–58. Dordrecht: Springer.

– 2006. "Self-Educating Communities: Collaboration and Learning through the Internet." *Counterpoints* 249: 273–84.

Burdick, J. 2013. *Blessed Anastácia: Women, Race and Popular Christianity in Brazil.* New York: Routledge.

Burgess, J., and J. Green. 2009. *YouTube: Online Video and Participatory Culture.* Cambridge and Malden, MA: Polity Press.

Campbell, H. 2005. "Making Space for Religion in Internet Studies." *The Information Society* 21 (4): 309–15.

– 2010. *When Religion Meets New Media.* London: Routledge.

– 2013. "Religion and the Internet: A Microcosm for Studying Internet Trends and Implications." *New Media & Society* 15 (5): 680–94.

Campbell, H.A. 2017. "Surveying Theoretical Approaches within Digital Religion Studies." *New Media & Society* 19 (1): 15–24.

Cantoni, L., and S. Zyga. 2007. "The Use of Internet Communication by Catholic Congregations: A Quantitative Study." *Journal of Media and Religion* 6 (4): 291–309.

Caplan, K., and N. Stadler. 2009. *Leadership and Authority in Israeli Haredi Society*. Jerusalem: Van Leer and Hakibutz Hameuchad [Hebrew].

Carolus, A., J.F. Binder, R. Muench, C. Schmidt, F. Schneider, and S.L. Buglass. 2019. "Smartphones as Digital Companions: Characterizing the Relationship between Users and their Phones." *New Media & Society* 21 (4): 914–38.

Carranza, B., and C. Mariz. 2013. "Catholicism for Export: The Case of Canção Nova." In *The Diaspora of Brazilian Religions*, edited by C. Rocha and M.A. Vasquez, 137–65. Leiden: Brill.

Casanova, J. 2008. "Balancing Religious Freedom and Cultural Preservation." *The Review of Faith & International Affairs* 6 (2): 13–15.

– 2008. "The Problem of Religion and the Anxieties of European Secular Democracy." In *Religion and Democracy in Contemporary Europe*, edited by G. Motzkin and M. Fischer, 63–74. London: Alliance Publishing Trust.

Castells, M. 2002. *The Internet Galaxy: Reflections on the Internet, Business and Society*. Oxford University Press on Demand.

Chang, I., H. Tai, and F. Yeh. 2013. "A VANET-Based A* Route Planning Algorithm for Travelling Time and Energy-Efficient GPS Navigation App." *International Journal of Distributed Sensor Networks* 9 (7): 1–14.

Chesnut, R.A. 2009. "Charismatic Competitors: Protestant Pentecostals and Catholic Charismatics in Latin America's New Religious Marketplace." In *Religion and Society in Latin America*, edited by L.M. Penyak and W.J. Perry, 207–23. Mary Knoll, NY: Orbis.

Clark, L.S. 2002. "Overview: The 'Protestantization' of Research into Media, Religion, and Culture." In *Practicing Religion in the Age of the Media: Explorations in Media, Religion, and Culture*, edited by S.M. Hoover and L.S. Clark, 7–33. New York: Columbia University Press.

Cohen, E. 2014. *Jewish Youth around the World, 1990–2010: Social Identity and Values in a Comparative Approach*. Leiden: Brill.

Cohen, S. 1987. *Folk Devils & Moral Panics: The Creation of the Mods and Rockers*. Oxford: Basil Blackwell.

Cohen, S.M., and A.Y. Kelman. 2010. "Thinking about Distancing from Israel." *Contemporary Jewry* 30 (2–3): 287–96.

Cohen, Y. 2015. "The Israeli Rabbi and the Internet." In *Digital Judaism*, edited by H. Campbell, 183–204. London: Routledge.

Coleman, E.G. 2012. *Coding Freedom: The Ethics and Aesthetics of Hacking*. Princeton: Princeton University Press.

Coleman, S., and J. Eade. 2004. *Reframing Pilgrimage: Cultures in Motion*. New York: Routledge.

Coleman, S., and J. Elsner. 1995. *Pilgrimage: Past and Present in the World Religions*. Cambridge, MA: Harvard University Press.

Cowan, D. 2016. "New Religious Movements." In *Religions in the Modern World: Traditions and Transformations*, 3rd edition, edited by L. Woodhead, C. Partridge, and H. Kawanami, 379–406. London: Taylor & Francis.

Crompton, R. 1990. "Professions in the Current Context." *Work, Employment and Society* 4: 147–66.

Csordas, T.J. 2007. "Global Religion and the Re-Enchantment of the World: The Case of the Catholic Charismatic Renewal." *Anthropological Theory* 7 (3): 295–314.

– 2015. "A Global Geography of the Spirit among Catholic Charismatic Communities." In *The Anthropology of Global Pentecostalism and Evangelicalism*, edited by S. Coleman and R.I.J. Hackett, 129–43. New York: New York University Press.

Custodia Terrae Sanctae (website). The Franciscan Mission in the Holy Land. Accessed 14 March 2016. http://www.custodia.org/default.asp?id=2049.

Danet, B. 2001. *Cyberpl@y: Communicating Online*. Oxford: Berg.

De Abreu, M.J.A. 2009. "Breath, Technology and the Making of Community. Canção Nova in Brazil." In *Aesthetic Formations: Media, Religion, and the Senses*, edited by B. Meyer, 161–82. New York: Springer.

Deuze, M. 2003. "The Web and Its Journalisms: Considering the Consequences of Different Types of Newsmedia Online." *New Media & Society* 5 (2): 203–30.

Diamant-Cohen, A., and O. Golan. 2017. "Downloading Culture: Community Building in a Decentralized File-Sharing Collective." *Information, Communication & Society* 20: 1–18.

DiMaggio, P.J., and W.W. Powell. 1983. "The Iron Cage Revisited: Institutional and Collective Rationality in Organizational Fields." *American Sociological Review* 48 (2): 147–60.

Durkheim, E. 1964. *The Division of Labor in Society*. New York: Free Press.

– 1995. *The Elementary Forms of the Religious Life*. New York: The Free Press. [1912]

Eco, U. 1976. *A Theory of Semiotics*. Bloomington: Indiana University Press.

Eisenstadt, S.N. 1969. *Change and Continuity in Israeli Society: The Dynamic Conservatism of a Small "Revolutionary" Society.* Cambridge, MA: Harvard University, Center for Middle Eastern Studies.

El Marzouki, M. 2015. "Collaborative Media: Production, Consumption, and Design Interventions." *New Media & Society* 17 (10): 1756–7.

El Marzouki, M., and H.A. Campbell. 2015. "Strategic Management of Religious Websites: The Case of Israel's Orthodox Communities." *Journal of Computer-Mediated Communication* 20 (4): 467–86.

Eliade, M. 1958. *Patterns in Comparative Religion.* New York: Meridian.

Ellison, N.B., C. Steinfield, and C. Lampe. 2007. "The Benefits of Facebook 'Friends': Social Capital and College Students' Use of Online Social Network Sites." *Journal of Computer-Mediated Communication* 12 (4): 1143–68.

Elster, J. 1989. "Social Norms and Economic Theory." *Journal of Economic Perspectives* 3 (4): 99–117.

Eshet-Alkalai, Y. 2004. "Digital Literacy: A Conceptual Framework for Survival Skills in the Digital Era." *Journal of Educational Multimedia and Hypermedia* 13 (1): 93–106.

Ess, C. 2004. "'Revolution? What Revolution?': Successes and Limits of Computing Technologies in Philosophy and Religion." In *A Companion to Digital Humanities*, edited by S. Schreibman, R.G. Siemens, and J. Unsworth, 132–42. Maiden, MA: Blackwell.

Etzioni, A. 1969. *The Semi-Professions and their Organization: Teachers, Nurses, Social Workers.* New York: Free Press.

Evetts, J. 2003. "The Sociological Analysis of Professionalism: Occupational Change in the Modern World." *International Sociology* 18 (2): 395–415.

– 2011. "A New Professionalism? Challenges and Opportunities." *Current Sociology* 59 (4): 406–22.

Evolvi, G. 2016. "Is the Pope Judging You?" In *LGBTQs, Media and Culture in Europe*, edited by A. Dhoest, L. Szulc, and B. Eeckhout, 135–52. New York: Taylor & Francis.

Eyal, O. 2009. "Degeneracy, Resilience and Free Markets in Educational Innovation." *Systems Research and Behavioral Science* 26 (4): 487–91.

Eyal, O., and I. Berkovich. 2010. "National Challenges, Educational Reforms, and Their Influence on School Management: The Israeli Case." *Educational Planning* 19 (3): 44–63.

Fagerjord, A. 2015. "Humanist Evaluation Methods in Locative Media Design." *The Journal of Media Innovations* 2 (1): 107–22.

– 2019. "Toward App Studies." Accessed 16 February 2019. http://fagerjord.no/downloads/FagerjordAppstudiesIR13.pdf.

Fiedler, K. 2007. "Construal Level Theory as an Integrative Framework for Behavioral Decision-Making Research and Consumer Psychology." *Journal of Consumer Psychology* 17 (2): 101–6.

Fleischer, A. 2000. "The Tourist behind the Pilgrim in the Holy Land." *International Journal of Hospitality Management* 19 (3): 311–26.

Fournier, V. 1999. "The Appeal to 'Professionalism' as a Disciplinary Mechanism." *The Sociological Review* 47 (2): 280–307.

Freidson, E. 1994. *Professionalism Reborn: Theory, Prophecy, and Policy*. Chicago: University of Chicago Press.

Freston, P. 2010. "Reverse Mission: A Discourse in Search of Reality?" *Penteco-Studies* 9 (2): 153–74.

Friedrich-Silber, I. 1995. *Virtuosity, Charisma and Social Order: A Comparative Sociological Study of Monasticism in Theravada Buddhism and Medieval Catholicism*. Cambridge: Cambridge University Press.

Frizzo-Barker, J., and P.A. Chow-White. 2012. "'There's an App for That': Mediating Mobile Moms and Connected Careerists through Smartphones and Networked Individualism." *Feminist Media Studies* 12 (4): 580–9.

Fujita, K., M.D. Henderson, J. Eng, Y. Trope, and N. Liberman. 2006. "Spatial Distance and Mental Construal of Social Events." *Psychological Science* 17 (4): 278–82.

Garelli, F. 2016. *Religion Italian Style: Continuities and Changes in a Catholic Country*. London: Routledge.

Geertz, C. 1973. *The Interpretation of Cultures*. New York: Basic Books.

Gibbs, M., J. Meese, M. Arnold, B. Nansen, and M. Carter. 2015. "#Funeral and Instagram: Death, Social Media, and Platform Vernacular." *Information, Communication & Society* 18 (3): 255–68.

Gifford, P. 2009. "Religious Authority: Scripture, Tradition, Charisma." In *Routledge Companion to the Study of Religion*, 2nd edition, edited by J. Hinnells, 391–403. New York: Routledge.

Giorgi, A. 2019. "Mediatized Catholicism – Minority Voices and Religious Authority in the Digital Sphere." *Religions* 10 (8): 463.

Glaser, B., and A. Strauss. 1967. "Grounded Theory: The Discovery of Grounded Theory." *Sociology: The Journal of The British Sociological Association* 12: 27–49.

Golan, O. 2013. "Charting Frontiers of Online Religious Communities." In *Digital Religion: Understanding Religious Practice in New Media Worlds*, edited by H. Campbell, 155–63. New York: Routledge.

Golan, O., and A. Berger. 2021. "Evaluating Public Religious Knowledge: Sourcing Practices of Online Information among Jewish Modern Orthodox Learners." Paper for the ISMRC 2021 Conference, Sigtuna, Sweden.

Golan, O., and D. Babis. 2019. "Towards Professionalism through Social Networks: Constructing an Occupational Community via Facebook Usage by Temporary Migrant Workers from the Philippines." *Information, Communication & Society* 22 (9): 1230–52.

Golan, O., and H.A. Campbell. 2015. "Strategic Management of Religious Websites: The Case of Israel's Orthodox Communities." *Journal of Computer Mediated Communication* 20 (4): 467–86.

Golan, O., and M. Martini. 2018. "Digital Pilgrimage: Exploring Catholic Monastic Webcasts." *The Communication Review* 21 (1): 24–45.

Golan, O., and N. Mishol-Shauli. 2018. "Fundamentalist Web Journalism: Walking a Fine Line Between Religious Ultra-Orthodoxy and the New Media Ethos." *European Journal of Communication* 33 (3): 304–20.

Golan, O., and N. Stadler. 2016. "Building the Sacred Community Online: The Dual Use of the Internet by Chabad." *Media, Culture & Society* 38 (1): 71–88.

Gori, N. 2019. "A colloquio con il direttore delle Ville pontificie, modello di ecologia integrata." *L'Osservatore Romano*. 20 September 2019. Accessed 11 November 2019. https://www.vaticanstate.va/it/novita/item/456-a-colloquio-con-il-direttore-delle-ville-pontificie-modello-di-ecologia-integrata.html.

Gregory, S. 2015. "Ubiquitous Witnesses: Who Creates the Evidence and the Live(d) Experience of Human Rights Violations?" *Information, Communication & Society* 18 (11): 1378–92.

Grieve, G.P. 2015. "The Middle-Way Method: A Buddhist-Informed Ethnography of the Virtual World of Second Life." In *Buddhism, the Internet, and Digital Media*, edited by G.P. Grieve and D. Veidlinger, 23–39. New York: Routledge.

Haimson, O.L., and J.C. Tang. 2017. "What Makes Live Events Engaging on Facebook Live, Periscope, and Snapchat." In *Proceedings of the 2017 CHI Conference on Human Factors in Computing Systems*, 48–60. New York: Association for Computing Machinery.

Halbwachs, M. 1992. "The Legendary Topography of the Gospels in the Holy Land." In *On Collective Memory*, edited and translated by L.A. Coser, 193–235. Chicago: University of Chicago Press.

Halupka, M. 2017. "Scientology's Relationship with the Internet: The Struggles of Contemporary Perception Management." In *Scientology in Popular Culture: Influences and Struggles for Legitimacy*, edited by S.A. Kent and S. Raine, 279–300. Westport, CT: Praeger.

Hamadache, A. 1991. "Non-Formal Education: A Definition of the Concept and Some Examples." *Prospects* 21 (1): 111–24.

Hamilton, W.A., O. Garretson, and A. Kerne. 2014. "Streaming on Twitch: Fostering Participatory Communities of Play within Live Mixed Media." In *Proceedings of the 32nd Annual ACM Conference on Human Factors in Computing Systems*, 1315–24. New York: ACM.

Hanegraaff, W.J. 2018. *New Age Religion and Western Culture: Esotericism in the Mirror of Secular Thought*. Leiden: Brill.

Harper, D., and H.M. Lawson. 2003. *The Cultural Study of Work*. Lanham, MD: Rowman & Littlefield.

Hartman, T., and N. Marmon. 2004. "Lived Regulations, Systemic Attributions: Menstrual Separation and Ritual Immersion in the Experience of Orthodox Jewish Women." *Gender & Society* 18 (3): 389–408.

Haynes, N. 2013 "On the Potential and Problems of Pentecostal Exchange." *American Anthropologist* 115 (1): 85–95.

Heim, M. 1999. *Electric Language: A Philosophical Study of Word Processing*. New Haven, CT: Yale University Press.

Helland, C. 2005. "Online Religion as Lived Religion. Methodological Issues in the Study of Religious Participation on the Internet." *Online-Heidelberg Journal of Religions on the Internet* 1 (1): 1–16.

– 2014. "Virtual Tibet: From Media Spectacle to Co-Located Sacred Space." In *Buddhism, the Internet, and Digital Media: The Pixel in the Lotus*, edited by P.G. Greive and D. Veidlinger, 155–72. London: Routledge.

Henderson, M.D., K. Fujita. Y. Trope, and N. Liberman. "Transcending the 'Here': The Effect of Spatial Distance on Social Judgment." *Journal of Personality and Social Psychology* 91 (5): 845.

Hendriks, F., D. Kienhues, and R. Bromme. 2015. "Measuring Laypeople's Trust in Experts in a Digital Age: The Muenster Epistemic Trustworthiness Inventory (METI)." *PLOS one* 10 (10): e0139309.

Herring, S.C. 2009. "Web Content Analysis: Expanding the Paradigm," In *International Handbook of Internet Research*, edited by J. Husinger, L. Klastrup, and M. Allen, 233–49. Dordrecht: Springer.

Highfield, T., and T. Lever. 2015. "A Methodology for Mapping Instagram Hashtags." *First Monday* 20 (1): 1–11.

Hilvert-Bruce, Z., J.T. Neill, M. Sjöblom, and J. Hamari. 2018. "Social Motivations of Live-Streaming Viewer Engagement on Twitch." *Computers in Human Behavior* 84: 58–67.

Hirschkind, C. 2006. "Cassette Ethics: Public Piety and Popular Media in Egypt." In *Religion, Media, and the Public Sphere*, edited by B. Meyer and A. Moors, 29–51. Bloomington: Indiana University Press.

Hoover, S., and N. Echchaibi. 2014. "Media Theory and the 'Third Spaces' of Digital Religion." The Center for Media, Religion, and Culture. University of Colorado. Accessed 5 December 2021. https://www.researchgate.net/

profile/Stewart_Hoover/publication/287644204_The_Third_Spaces_of_Digital_Religion/links/567825d108aebcddaoebcb9f/The-Third-Spaces-of-Digital-Religion.

Hutchings, T. 2014. "Now the Bible Is an App: Digital Media and Changing Patterns of Religious Authority." In *Religion, Media, and Social Change*, edited by K. Branholm, M. Moberg, and S. Sjo, 151–69. London/New York: Routledge.

– 2017. "The Anglican Cathedral of Second Life." In *Creating Church Online: Ritual, Community and New Media*, edited by T. Hutchings, 140–67. New York: Routledge.

Instagram. 2017. "Our Story." Accessed 22 January 2018. https://instagram-press.com/our-story.

Israel Central Bureau of Statistics. 2018. *Society in Israel, Report No. 10: Religion and Self-Definition of Level of Religiosity*. Jerusalem: Central Bureau of Statistics.

Jacobson, D.C. 2004. "The Ma'ale School: Catalyst for the Entrance of Religious Zionists into the World of Media Production." *Israel Studies* 9 (1): 31–60.

Jenkins, H. 2006. *Convergence Culture: Where Old and New Media Collide*. New York: New York University Press.

John, N.A. 2017. *The Age of Sharing*. Hoboken, NJ: John Wiley & Sons.

Jonveaux, I. 2014. "Facebook as a Monastic Place? The New Use of Internet by Catholic Monks." *Scripta Instituti Donneriani Aboensis* 25: 99–109.

Kaartveit, B.H. 2013. "The Christians of Palestine: Strength, Vulnerability, and Self-Restraint within a Multi-Sectarian Community." *Middle Eastern Studies* 49 (5): 732–49.

Kahane, R. 1997. *The Origins of Postmodern Youth: Informal Youth Movements in a Comparative Perspective*, vol. 4. Berlin: Walter de Gruyter.

Kaplan, D. 2000. *The Silicon Boys and their Valley of Dreams*. New York: Harper Collins.

Keller, T., and J. Weibler. 2015. "What it Takes and Costs to Be an Ambidextrous Manager: Linking Leadership and Cognitive Strain to Balancing Exploration and Exploitation." *Journal of Leadership & Organizational Studies* 22 (1): 54–71.

Kets de Vries, M.F.R. 1988. "Prisoners of Leadership." *Human Relations* 41 (31): 261–80.

Kneip, J. 2007. "Library Webmasters in Medium-Sized Academic Libraries." *Journal of Web Librarianship* 1 (3): 3–23.

Kozinets, R.V. 2010. *Netnography: Doing Ethnographic Research Online*. London: SAGE.

LaFrance A. 2016. "Smartphones Rule the Internet." Accessed 3 July 2016. http://www.theatlantic.com/technology/archive/2016/05/smartphones-takeover/482880.

Lange, P.G. 2014. *Kids on Youtube: Technical Identities and Digital Literacies.* Walnut Creek, CA: Left Coast Press.

Leaver, T., and T. Highfield. 2018. "Visualising the Ends of Identity: Pre-Birth and Post-Death on Instagram." *Information, Communication & Society* 21 (1): 30–45.

Lee-Treweek, G. 2003. "Women, Resistance, and Care: An Ethnographic Study of Nursing Auxiliary Work." In *The Cultural Study of Work*, edited by D. Harper and H. Lawson, 297–414. Lanham, MD: Rowman & Littlefield.

Lehmann, D. 2013. "Religion as Heritage, Religion as Belief: Shifting Frontiers of Secularism in Europe, the USA and Brazil." *International Sociology* 28 (6): 645–62.

Lehmann, D., and B.B. Siebzehner. 2006. *Remaking Israeli Judaism: The Challenge of Shas.* London: C. Hurst & Co.

Lessig, L. 2006. *Code, Version 2.0.* New York: Basic Books.

Levi-Strauss, C. 1974. *Structural Anthropology.* New York: Basic Books.

Lindholm, C. 1990. *Charisma.* Oxford: Blackwell.

– 2013. *The Anthropology of Religious Charisma: Ecstasies and Institutions.* New York: Palgrave Macmillan.

Long, B.O. 2003. *Imagining the Holy Land: Maps, Models, and Fantasy Travels.* Bloomington: Indiana University Press.

Lövheim, M. 2012. "A Voice of Their Own: Young Muslim Women, Blogs, and Religion." In *Mediatization and Religion: Nordic Perspectives*, edited by S. Hjarvard and M. Lövheim, 129–45. Gothenburg: Nordicom.

Lu Jia, A., Y. Rao, H. Li, R. Tian, and S. Shen. 2020. "Revealing Donation Dynamics in Social Live Video Streaming." In *Companion Proceedings of the Web Conference*, edited by A.E.F. Seghrouchni, G. Sukthankar, T.Y. Liu, and M.V. Steen, 30–1. Geneva: International World Wide Web.

Ludlow, P. 1996. *High Noon on the Electronic Frontier: Conceptual Issues in Cyberspace.* Cambridge, MA: MIT Press.

Lundgren, K.J. 2017. "The Paradox of the 'People's Pope': Pope Francis and the Cult of Authenticity." *International Journal of Media & Cultural Politics* 13 (3): 303–12.

Luo, M., T.W. Hsu, J.S. Park, and J.T. Hancock. "Emotional Amplification during Live-Streaming: Evidence from Comments during and after News Events." *Proceedings of the ACM on Human-Computer Interaction*, vol. 4, 1–19. New York: Association for Computer Machinery.

Lynch, A.P. 2018. "Digital Catholicism: The Internet and the Vatican." In *Global Catholicism in the Twenty-First Century*, 31–46. Singapore: Springer.

Mariz, C.L. 2017. "From Brazil to the World." In *Religion, Migration, and Mobility*, edited by C.M. de Castro and A. Dawson, 52–151. New York: Routledge.

Marshall, C., and G.B. Rossman. 2014. *Designing Qualitative Research*. Thousand Oaks, CA: Sage.

Martini, M. 2013. "Reacting to Fitna: Performing Citizenship and New Forms of Online Video Activism." *Lexia* 13–14: 261–87.

– 2015. "Palestineremembered.com: A Virtual Homeland between Past and Future." *Carte Semiotiche* 14: 116–28.

McMullin, S. 2013. "The Secularization of Sunday: Real or Perceived Competition for Churches." *Review of Religious Research* 55 (1): 43–59.

McNelly, J.T. 1959. "Intermediary Communicators in the International Flow of News." *Journalism Quarterly* 36 (1): 23–6.

Mejova, Y., Y. Benkhedda, and K. Khairani. 2017. "#Halal Culture on Instagram." *Frontiers in Digital Humanities* 4 (21).

Mishol-Shauli, N., and O. Golan. 2019. "Mediatizing the Holy Community – Ultra-Orthodoxy Negotiation and Presentation on Public Social Media." *Religions* 10 (7): 438.

Morgan, D. 2018. *Images at Work: The Material Culture of Enchantment*. Oxford: Oxford University Press.

Mostaghimi, A., and B.H. Crotty. 2011. "Professionalism in the Digital Age." *Annals of Internal Medicine* 154 (8): 560–2.

Napolitano, V. 2016. *Migrant Hearts and the Atlantic Return*. New York: Fordham University Press.

Narbona, J. 2016. "Digital Leadership, Twitter and Pope Francis." *Church, Communication and Culture* 1 (1): 90–109.

Nardella, C. 2012. "Religious Symbols in Italian Advertising: Symbolic Appropriation and the Management of Consent." *Journal of Contemporary Religion* 27 (2): 217–40.

Nelson, A.J., and J. Irwin. 2014. "'Defining What We Do – All Over Again': Occupational Identity, Technological Change, and the Librarian/Internet-Search Relationship." *Academy of Management Journal* 57 (3): 892–928.

Nisa, E.F. 2018. "Creative and Lucrative Da'wa: The Visual Culture of Instagram amongst Female Muslim Youth in Indonesia." *Asiascape: Digital Asia* 5 (1–2): 68–99.

Noomen, I., S. Aupers, and D. Houtman. 2011. "In Their Own Image? Catholic, Protestant and Holistic Spiritual Appropriations of the Internet." *Information, Communication and Society* 14 (8): 1097–117.

Norget, K., V. Napolitano, and M. Mayblin. 2017. *The Anthropology of Catholicism*. Oakland: University of California Press.

Ntembula, A. "Cyberspace – a New Environment for Worship." *Vatican News*, Dicasterium pro Communicatione, 30 March 2020.

Ojo, M. 2007. "Reverse Mission." In *Encyclopedia of Mission and Missionaries*, edited by J.J. Bonk, 380–2. London, Routledge.

Oldenburg, R. 1989. *The Great Good Place: Café, Coffee Shops, Community Centers, Beauty Parlors, General Stores, Bars, Hangouts, and How They Get You Through the Day*. New York: Paragon House Publishers.

Olesen, V., N. Droes, D. Hatton, N. Chico, and L. Schatzman. 1994. "Analyzing Together: Recollections of a Team Approach." In *Analyzing Qualitative Data*, edited by A. Bryman and R.G. Burgess, 111–28. London: Routledge.

O'Reilly, T. 2009. *What Is Web 2.0*. California: O'Reilly Media, Inc.

Orgad, S. 2012. *Media Representation and Global Imagination*. Cambridge: Polity Press.

Oro, A.P. 2014. "South American Evangelicals' Re-Conquest of Europe." *Journal of Contemporary Religion* 29 (2): 219–32.

– 2019. "Transnacionalização evangélica brasileira para a Europa: significados, tipologia e acomodações. Etnográfica." *Revista do Centro em Rede de Investigação em Antropologia* 23 (1): 5–25. [Portuguese].

Ortiz, G. 2003. "The Catholic Church and its Attitude to Film as an Arbiter of Cultural Meaning." In *Mediating Religion: Studies in Media, Religion, and Culture*, edited by J.P. Mitchell and S. Marriage, 179–88. London: T & T Clark.

Otto, R. 1958. *The Idea of the Holy* (vol. 14). Oxford: Oxford University Press.

Palmisano, S., and A. Giorgi. 2021. "Le donne nel mondo cattolico e la pandemia. Un nuovo protagonismo?" Paper presented at the seminar series La Religione ai Tempi del CoronaVirus, AIS-Sociology of Religion, 19 February 2021.

Papacharissi, Z. 2014. "On Networked Publics and Private Spheres in Social Media." In *The Social Media Handbook*, edited by J. Hunsinger and T. Senft, 144–58. New York: Routledge.

– 2015. *Affective Publics: Sentiment, Technology, and Politics*. Oxford: Oxford University Press.

Paul VI. 1975. *Evangelii Nuntiandi: Catholic Social Thought: The Documentary Heritage*, 301–45.

Pauwels, L. 2015. *Reframing Visual Social Science: Towards a More Visual Sociology and Anthropology*. Cambridge: Cambridge University Press.

Petersen, J.A. 2005 "Modern Satanism: Dark Doctrines and Black Flames." In *Controversial New Religions*, edited by J.R. Lewis and idem, 423–57. Oxford: Oxford University Press.

Peterson, K.M. 2020. "The Unruly, Loud, and Intersectional Muslim Woman: Interrupting the Aesthetic Styles of Islamic Fashion Images on Instagram." *International Journal of Communication* 14: 20.

Pew Research Center. 2014. "Religion in Latin America: Widespread Change in a Historically Catholic Region." Accessed 5 December 2021. https://www.pewforum.org/2014/11/13/religion-in-latin-america.

Piraino, F. 2016. "Between Real and Virtual Communities: Sufism in Western Societies and the Naqshbandi Haqqani Case." *Social Compass* 63 (1): 93–108.

Pontifical Commission for Social Communications. 1971. *Pastoral Instruction: "Communio Et Progressio." On the Means of Social Communication.* Rome: Vatican Printing Press.

Rafaeli, S., and F. Sudweeks. 1998. "Interactivity on the Nets." In *Network and Netplay: Virtual Groups on the Internet,* 173–89. Palo Alto, CA, and Cambridge, MA: AAAI Press and MIT Press.

Rashi, T. 2013 "The Kosher Cell Phone in Ultra-Orthodox Society." In *Digital Religion: Understanding Religious Practice in New Media Worlds,* edited by H. Campbell, 173–81. London: Routledge.

Rheingold, H. 2000. *The Virtual Community: Homesteading on the Electronic Frontier.* Cambridge, MA: MIT Press.

Rimmon-Kenan, S. 1983. *Narrative Fiction: Contemporary Poetics.* New York: Methuen Press.

Rogers, A. 2004. *Non-Formal Education: Flexible Schooling or Participatory Education?* Hong Kong: The University of Hong Kong and Klewer Academic Publishers.

Ron, A.S. 2009. "Towards a Typological Model of Contemporary Christian Travel." *Journal of Heritage Tourism* 4 (4): 287–97.

Rose, G. 2016. *Visual Methodologies: An Introduction to Researching with Visual Materials.* London: SAGE.

Rosenthal, M. 2007. *American Protestants and TV in the 1950s: Responses to a New Medium.* New York: Springer.

Russmann, U., and J. Svensson. 2016. "Studying Organizations on Instagram." *Information* 7 (4): 58.

– 2017. "Interaction on Instagram? Glimpses from the 2014 Swedish Elections." *International Journal of E-Politics* 8 (1): 50–66.

Sägesser, C., J. Nelis, J. Schreiber, and C. Vanderpelen. 2018. "Religion and Secularism in the European Union." *Observatory of Religions and Secularism Report* (ORELA).

Salomon, G. 2000. *Technology and Education in the Information Age.* Tel Aviv: Zemora-Bitan.

Sela-Sheffy, R., and M. Shlesinger. 2008. "Strategies of Image-Making and Status Advancement of Translators and Interpreters as a Marginal Occupational Group." In *Beyond Descriptive Translation Studies: Investigations in Homage to Gideon Toury*, edited by G. Toury, A. Pymn, M. Shlesinger, and D. Simeoni, 79–90. Amsterdam and Philadelphia: John Benjamins.

Schejter, A.M., and N. Tirosh. 2016. *A Justice-Based Approach for New Media Policy: In the Paths of Righteousness*. New York: Springer.

Schwarz, O. 2009. "Good Young Nostalgia: Camera Phones and Technologies of Self among Israeli Youths." *Journal of Consumer Culture* 9 (3): 348–76.

Segev, E. 2010. *Google and the Digital Divide: The Bias of Online Knowledge*. Oxford: Elsevier.

Shamir, B. 1995. "Social Distance and Charisma: Theoretical Notes and an Exploratory Study." *Leadership Quarterly* 6 (1): 19–47.

Shaw, T. 1998. "Exploring the Role of Identification in the Privacy Decisions of Webmasters." *Proceedings of the International Conference on Information Systems* 38.

Shenhav-Keller, S. 2013. "Invented Exhibits: Visual Politics of the Past at the Museum of the Jewish Diaspora." In *Memory and Ethnicity: Ethnic Museums in Israel and the Diaspora*, edited by E. Trevisan Semi, D. Miccoli, and T. Parfitt, 21–43. Newcastle upon Tyne: Cambridge Scholars.

Shephard, K. 2003. "Questioning, Promoting and Evaluating the Use of Streaming Video to Support Student Learning." *British Journal of Educational Technology* 34 (3): 295–308.

Shifman, L. 2014. *Memes in Digital Culture*. Cambridge, MA: MIT Press.

Shils, E. 1975. *Center and Periphery: Essays in Macrosociology*. Chicago: University of Chicago Press.

Shner, M. 2012. *Born Virtual: The Free Spirit of Man in a Globalized World*. Tel Aviv: Mofet Institute. [Hebrew].

Shoemaker, P.J., and T. Vos. 2015. *Gatekeeping Theory*. London: Routledge.

Shouse, E., and T. Fraley. 2010. "Hater Jesus: Blasphemous Humor and Numinous Awe: (An Antidote for) Hatred in Jesus' Name?" *Journal of Media and Religion* 9 (4): 202–15.

Shoval, N. 2000. "Commodification and Theming of the Sacred: Changing Patterns of Tourist Consumption in the 'Holy Land.'" In *New Forms of Consumption: Consumers, Culture, and Commodification*, edited by M. Gottdiener, 251–63. Lanham, MD: Rowman and Littlefield Publishers.

Silberman-Keller, D. 2006. "Images of Time and Place in the Narrative of Nonformal Pedagogy." *Counterpoints* 249: 251–72.

Simon, B. 2015. "Christians of the Holy Land." *60 Minutes*, CBS Interactive Inc: http://www.cbsnews.com/news/christians-of-the-holy-land/.

Singer, J.B. "Out of Bounds." In *Boundaries of Journalism*, edited by M. Carlson and S.C. Lewis, 21–36. New York: Routledge.

Smith, C., K. Longest, J. Hill, and K. Christoffersen. 2014. *Young Catholic America: Emerging Adults In, Out of, and Gone from the Church.* Oxford: Oxford University Press.

Smith, M.M. 2007. "Nonprofit Religious Organization Web Sites: Underutilized Avenue of Communicating with Group Members." *Journal of Media and Religion* 6 (4): 273–90.

Southern, R.W. 1995. *Scholastic Humanism and the Unification of Europe,* vol. 1. Oxford: Blackwell Publishers, 102–33.

Spainhour, S., and R. Eckstein. 2003. *Webmaster in a Nutshell,* 3rd edition. Sebastopol, CA: O'Reilly Media.

Sripanidkulchai, K., B. Maggs, and H. Zhang. 2003. "An Analysis of Live Streaming Workloads on the Internet." In *Proceedings of the 4th ACM SIGCOMM Conference on Internet Measurement,* 41–54. New York: ACM.

Stadler, N. 2015. "Appropriating Jerusalem through Sacred Places: Disputed Land and Female Rituals at the Tombs of Mary and Rachel." *Anthropological Quarterly* 88 (3): 725–58.

– 2020. *Voices of the Ritual: Devotion to Female Saints and Shrines in the Holy Land.* Oxford: Oxford University Press.

Stark, W. 1965. "The Routinization of Charisma: A Consideration of Catholicism." *Sociological Analysis* 26 (4): 203–11.

Stoll, C. 1995. *Silicon Snake Oil: Second Thoughts on the Information Highway.* New York: Anchor.

Stolz, J. 2010. "A Silent Battle: Theorizing the Effects of Competition between Churches and Secular Institutions." *Review of Religious Research* 51 (3): 253–76.

Stolz, J., J. Könemann, M.S. Purdie, T. Englberger, and M. Krüggeler. 2016. *(Un)Believing in Modern Society: Religion, Spirituality, and Religious-Secular Competition.* New York: Routledge.

Strauss, A.L., and J.M. Corbin. 1998. *Basics of Qualitative Research: Techniques and Procedures for Developing Grounded Theory.* Thousand Oaks, CA: Sage.

Sullivan, W.M. 2000. "Medicine under Threat: Professionalism and Professional Identity." *Canadian Medical Association Journal* 162 (5): 673.

Surowiecki, J. 2005. *The Wisdom of Crowds.* New York: Anchor.

Suryamani, E. 1989. *The Organization and the Semi-Professional: A Sociological Study of Nurses.* New Delhi: Jainsons Publications.

Susskind, R.E., and D. Susskind. 2015. *The Future of the Professions: How Technology Will Transform the Work of Human Experts.* New York: Oxford University Press.

Tambiah, S.J. 1984. "The Sources of Charismatic Leadership: Max Weber Revisited." In *The Buddhist Saints of the Forest and the Cult of Amulets,* edited by S.J. Tambiah, 321–34. Cambridge: Cambridge University Press.

Thomas, P.N., and P. Lee. 2012. *Global and Local Televangelism*. London: Palgrave Macmillan.

Thorburn, E.D. 2014. "Social Media, Subjectivity, and Surveillance: Moving on from Occupy, the Rise of Live Streaming Video." *Communication and Critical/Cultural Studies* 11 (1): 52–63.

Tonks, A.P. 2012. "Photos on Facebook: An Exploratory Study of their Role in the Social Lives and Drinking Experiences of New Zealand University Students." Master's thesis, Wellington, New Zealand: Massey University.

Trope, Y., and N. Liberman. 2010. "Construal Level Theory of Psychological Distance." *Psychological Review* 117 (2): 440–63.

Tsuria, R. 2016. "Jewish Q&A Online and the Regulation of Sexuality: Using Foucault to Read Technology." *Social Media + Society* 2 (3): 1–10.

Turner, B.S. 2011. *Religion and Modern Society: Citizenship, Secularization and the State*. Cambridge: Cambridge University Press.

Turner, V. 2017. *The Ritual Process: Structure and Anti-Structure*. New York: Routledge.

Upton, T.P. 2007. "Sacred Topography: Western Sermon Perceptions of Jerusalem, the Holy Sites, and Jews during the Crusades, 1095–1193." PhD diss., University of Colorado at Boulder.

Vaidhyanathan, S. 2018. *Antisocial Media: How Facebook Disconnects Us and Undermines Democracy*. Oxford: Oxford University Press.

Vallely, P. 2013. *Pope Francis: Untying the Knots*. London: Bloomsbury Press.

Van Zoonen, L., F. Vis, and S. Mihelj. 2010. "Performing Citizenship on YouTube: Activism, Satire and Online Debate around the Anti-Islam Video Fitna." *Critical Discourse Studies* 7 (4): 249–62.

Violi, P. 2012. "Trauma Site Museums and Politics of Memory: Tuol Sleng, Villa Grimaldi and the Bologna Ustica Museum." *Theory, Culture & Society* 29 (1): 36–75.

Wagner, R. 2012. *Godwired: Religion, Ritual and Virtual Reality*. London: Routledge.

– 2013. "You Are What You Install: Religious Authenticity and Identity in Mobile Apps." In *Digital Religion: Understanding Religious Practices in New Media Worlds*, edited by H. Campbell, 199–206. London: Routledge.

Wagner, R., and C. Accardo. 2015. "Buddhist Apps: Skillful Means or Dharma Dilution?" In *Buddhism, the Internet, and Digital Media: The Pixel in the Lotus*, edited by G.P. Grieve and D. Veidlinger, 134–54. New York: Routledge.

Währisch-Oblau, C. 2009. *The Missionary Self-Perception of Pentecostal/Charismatic Church Leaders from the Global South in Europe*. Boston: Brill.

Wallace, C.D., and P.A. Abbott. 1990. *The Sociology of the Caring Professions*. London: Falmer.

Waxman, C.I. 2010. "Beyond Distancing: Jewish Identity, Identification, and America's Young Jews." *Contemporary Jewry* 30: 227–32.

Weber, M. 1968. *Economy and Society Vol. 1.* New York: Bedminster Press.

– 1978. *Economy and Society: An Outline of Interpretive Sociology,* vol. 1. Berkeley: University of California Press.

Weimann, G. 2004. *Cyberterrorism: How Real Is the Threat?* (vol. 31, no. 20–119). Washington, DC: United States Institute of Peace.

West, J.H., P.C. Hall, C.L. Hanson, M.D. Barnes, C. Giraud-Carrier, and J. Barrett. 2012. "There's an App for That: Content Analysis of Paid Health and Fitness Apps." *Journal of Medical Internet Research* 14, 3: e72.

Westbrook, D.A. 2018. "The Art of PR War: Scientology, the Media, and Legitimation Strategies for the 21st Century." *Studies in Religion/Sciences Religieuses* 47 (3): 373–95.

Wilkin, R.L. 1992. *The Land Called Holy: Palestine in Christian History and Thought.* New Haven: Yale University Press.

Yan, B., and G. Chen. 2011. "AppJoy: Personalized Mobile Application Discovery." In *Proceedings of the 9th International Conference on Mobile Systems, Applications, and Services,* Bethesda, MD, 28 June to 1 July 2011 (New York: ACM: 2011), 113–26.

Young, G. 2013. "Reading and Praying Online: The Continuity of Religion Online and Online Religion in Internet Christianity." In *Religion Online,* edited by L.L. Dawson and D.E. Cowan, 101–14. London: Routledge.

Young, K. 2009. "Internet Addiction: Diagnosis and Treatment Considerations." *Journal of Contemporary Psychotherapy* 39, 4: 241–6.

Zaleski, J. 1997. *The Soul of Cyberspace: How New Technology is Changing Our Spiritual Lives.* New York: HarperCollins.

Zängle, M. 2014. "Trends in Papal Communication: A Content Analysis of Encyclicals, from Leo XIII to Pope Francis." *Historical Social Research/Historische Sozialforschung,* 329–64.

Zeiler, X. 2014. "The Global Mediatization of Hinduism through Digital Games." In *Playing with Religion in Digital Games,* edited by A.H. Campbell and G.P. Grieve, 66–87. Bloomington: Indiana University Press.

Zerubavel, E. 1997. *Social Mindscapes: An Invitation to Cognitive Sociology.* Cambridge, MA: Harvard University Press.

Zisser, Eyal. 1995. "The Maronites, Lebanon and the State of Israel: Early Contacts." *Middle Eastern Studies* 31 (4): 889–918.

Zychlinski, E., and A.S. York. 2009. "Third-Sector Organizations: Current Directions." In *Non-Formal Education in a Changing Reality,* edited by S. Romi and M. Schmida, 551–68. Jerusalem: Magnes Press.